Art in a Multipolar World

Art in a Multipolar World

Mi You

DOCUMENTA INSTITUT

HATJE CANTZ

Contents

Preface

This book is a quest for a new paradigm for thinking about artistic practices, art theory, and art institutional practices. It is born out of the recognition of a slow burning yet unmistakable process that leaves what some perceive as a golden era of globalization in tatters. However, I argue that the grand alignment of several assumptions across the globe—the acceptance of neoliberal globalization, of liberal democracy as the only possible political form of a state, of the expectation of the state to deliver progress (however it is measured), and of the experience of economic stability for those included in the economic body politic—may have been a historical contingency. In other words, the confluence of these assumptions and beliefs may be accidental in many parts of the world over the last three decades or so.

Several key terms from economic, political, and development theory that have gained currency over those decades are employed and problematized through an analysis of the exhibition of art from the so-called "Global South" in the Global North, as well as geographically specific analysis of that art's production. Firstly, I use multipolarity to refer to a world with more than two poles where political, economic, military, and cultural powers concentrate. Such a model carries and reproduces a realist undertone which makes it at best a placeholder for the complex and multifaceted world order as it exists today. Even though discussions of “de-globalization” have become commonplace in tandem with a multipolar outlook, “globalization” can still be measured by the trade of goods across borders, services, investment, and cultural exchange, and shows no major signs of slowing down. In traditional studies of global relations and political economics, neoliberalism traditionally denotes a paradigm of transfer of economic control from the government to the private sector, including the marketization of the allocation of resources, economic and political deregulation, reduction in public spending, a limitation in government control of industries, and free trade. In this book, I follow this definition, though my analysis is not confined to the periodization of neoliberalism given the engagement with numerous studies that have demonstrated the *longue durée* of many of these economic approaches before the advent of the term. Since the 1980s, globalization has more or less been guided by neoliberal policies both nationally and through international institutions such as the World Trade Organization (WTO) and The World Bank. And not coincidentally, this wave of globalization and its incumbent aesthetic imperatives structures the parallel globalization of a sector of art production and consumption, which is today typically enabled by global art fairs, biennales, discourses, and media. While the extent and features of all these areas are fuzzy, there is an acute sense of a paradigmatic shift.

For those of us involved in any way with the art sector, we can only work towards a productive relationship between art and politics—or rather between a nominally aesthetic realm of production and the realm of political activity that liberalism admits to the operations of the state—if we work to unravel the nature of this contingent alignment of global neoliberalism as it is expressed in art. For such a project, we would need to admit that the contemporary artworld has thrived on peak globalization as evidenced in the widely held assumption that critique can meaningfully act on the world rather than just reproduce it. The response can no longer be focused on the foibles of art or its autotelism (art for art's sake): no one really believes that art has the power to set political agendas, at least not from the institutions that reproduce the relations and functions of already existing institutions. In the face of geopolitical fallouts, the shattering of a liberal progressive social contract, rising claims to value pluralism, the survival of art's exceptionalism depends on realism. Will the artworld continue sleepwalking into the next existential crisis? What concessions can be made without cutting the ground from under one's feet? How to make space for subtlety, while keeping the scale of politics and economics closely in sight? We need to make space for cultural practices that differentiate the political means and ends while celebrating political debates that are not zero-sum (or that are purely representational). Concretely, we must encourage the capability of commanding divergent intellectual resources to moderate collisions of opinions in a way that allows for political change to not only be invoked but made material.

This book builds on reflections from the last four years, characterized by intense experiences of the breakdown of liberal orders and the fragmentation of the world into different "blocs," often magnified by the media. But the root of the post-globalization, multipolar world order lies deeper than the disintegration of previously hegemonic forms of order. These reflections are guided as much by analytical theoretical inquiries as by my practice as a researcher and curator from a non-Western country working in the West. Everybody knows that much of the cultural sector operates within a symbolic "economy": where actors trade some elements from their world only to confirm the biases of others, whether it be how colonialism and capitalism lead to subjugation, or how indigenous epistemologies resist that subjection. While I come from an embodied perspective, I also speak beyond my own lived experiences. I argue that it is urgent to address skewed intellectual appetites for complexities in the many contexts where I work. I am motivated by many peers in similar situations, who strive toward future art and cultural institutional practices carefully and confidently, and who are neither confrontational nor apologetic.

Chapter 1 offers an in-depth analysis of what came after the realignment of the dominant world order in the last three decades, tracking the neoliberal Washington consensus, globalization, and the conflation of liberal values, progress, and certain forms of state power. What I refer to as the "precept of art" in a multipolar context necessarily changes, which in turn shifts the baseline for critiques of capitalism and neoliberalism in the arts and the moral imperatives contained therein. Chapters 2 and 3 explore two case studies that present divergent discursive poles in the multipolar artworld, namely documenta fifteen (d15) and Chinese state art (policy) that oscillates between particularistic and universalist claims. Each case presents internal tensions, such as how the Global North imagines (and legislates) art and community practice in the Global South and what it should look like, or how a particularistic approach to art and culture can be co-opted by non-Western nations. Each case, however, also suggests moments of lowercase-u universality, in the sense of the interaction, communication, and competition of particular universals that transcend the notion of universality that is laden with moral baggage in the West.[1] Throughout the book, I try to stay at the descriptive level to document how the contestation of multipolarity is playing out in the artworld. While there is no viable path to return to an old—or arrive at a new—unipolarity, most people involved in the artworld seem to have picked a side. The crucial question that resounds throughout the book is, what is a "good," consensus-based multipolarity? In this light, and to conclude the book, Chapter 4 points to a horizon for thought and experiment that can help us navigate this era of multipolarity.

1 I cannot do justice to the philosophical debates on universalism. See the excellent work on the topic undertaken by scholars such as Souleymane Bachir Diagne, Omri Boehm, Sum Ge, Xudong Zhang, among others.

11

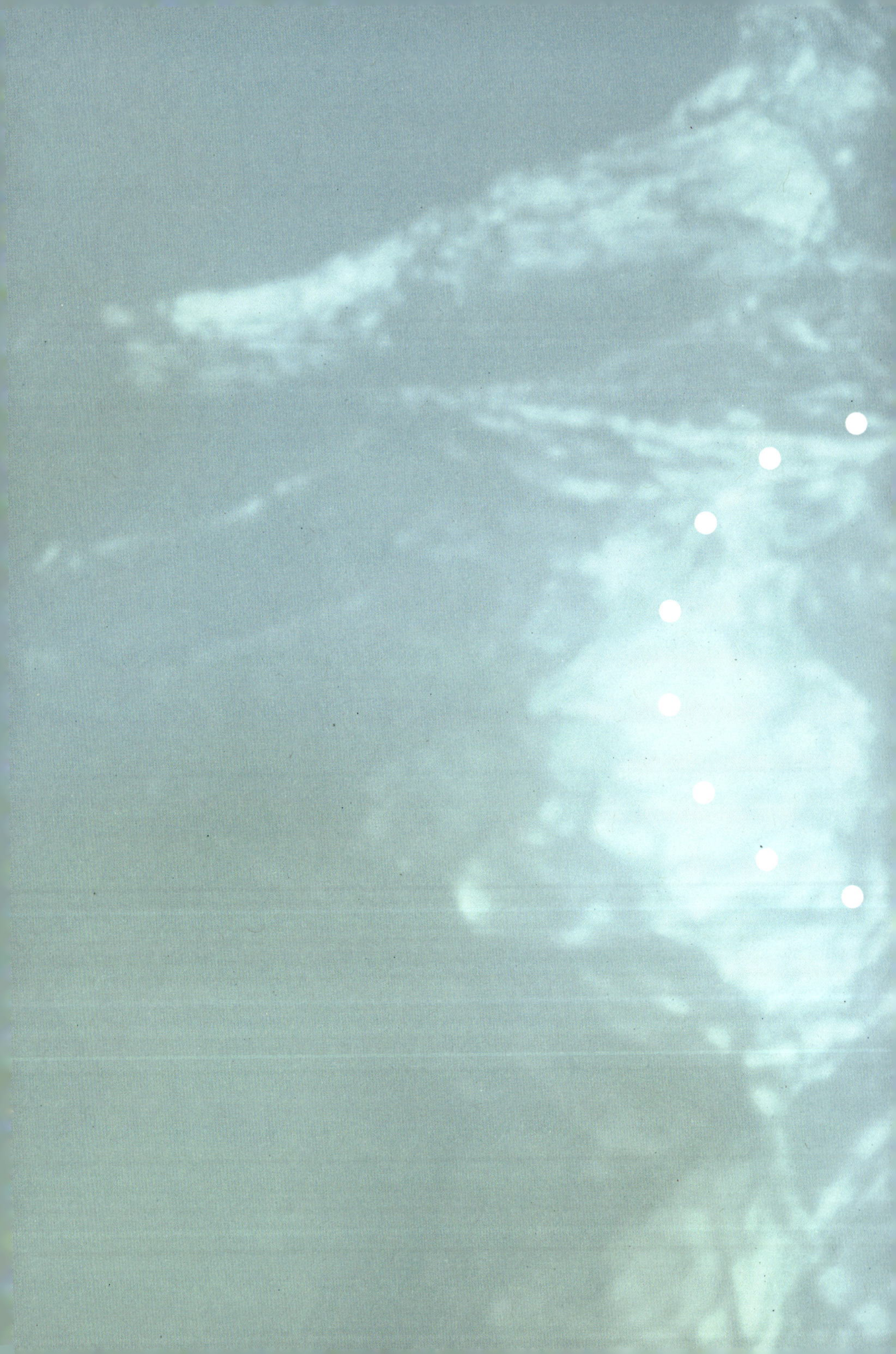

Chapter 1

Problem Analysis for the Artworld

Chapter 1

Problem Analysis for the Artworld

Over the last half-century, a number of assumptions have come to be accepted by much of the world in a grand alignment of neoliberal globalization: the notion of liberal democracy as the only functional political form of a state, the expectation of the state to deliver progress (by whichever measurements), and relative economic prosperity in the West. However, this alignment may have been a historical contingency in the West in the last three decades or so; it was neither necessary nor inevitable for one or another component to fall into this alignment. So was, it seems, the precept of global contemporary art, that is, a theoretical preconception of art that structures its epistemological perspective and method, which has been positioned by much (Western) art theory as both a subject of this alignment and a form for its discursive contestation.

Regarding the project of neoliberal globalization, nowadays the neoliberal Washington consensus is less accepted, at least in the West. It is no longer deregulation, trade liberalization, unfettered market growth that are taken as the only "rational" economic activity, but various other strategies have returned: industrialization, state intervention into ostensibly free markets, international trade policies, and friendshoring (the act of making economic agreements with international allies). Some may timestamp the dying breath of unbridled laissez-faire politics, finance, and trade to the 2008 financial crisis; others might instead point to the increase in trade protectionism ushered in by Donald Trump. We are stumbling into a world order variously theorized in terms of "plurilateralism," "heteropolarity," "multiplexity," or synthesizing all these, "deep pluralism," in which wealth and power, and cultural and political authority are diffusely distributed, rather than obviously centralized by traditional actors like the state in a unipolar world.[1] Perhaps we are seeing the popularity of a classical liberal perspective that would refute and claim that the function of the state is abstract and formal, serving to secure civic peace and not seeking ultimate truth, and thus should not be ascribed legalistic "rights."[2] Simultaneously, various non-liberal democratic states might argue that managed and planned economies have been delivering good, if not better, economic and social progress than their Western counterparts.

My theoretical project in this book is to work out the precept of art as it shifts and is formulated in relation to post-globalization multipolarity, the malleability of the role of the state, and the permeation of value pluralism in a post-liberal framework. These concepts stand in productive tension with neoliberalism, which allows one to grapple with neoliberal dynamics while they shift to become something else. This something else that neoliberalism is transforming into is not its opposite; it is something we do not yet have a name for. Therefore, it is useful to single out

1 See Amitav Acharya and Barry Buzan, *The Making of Global International Relations* (Cambridge, UK: Cambridge University Press, 2019); Feng Zhang and Barry Buzan, "The Relevance of Deep Pluralism for China's Foreign Policy," *The Chinese Journal of International Politics* 15, no. 3 (2022), pp. 246–71.

2 See John Gray, *Post-Liberalism: Studies in Political Thought,* 1st ed. (London and New York: Routledge, 1996).

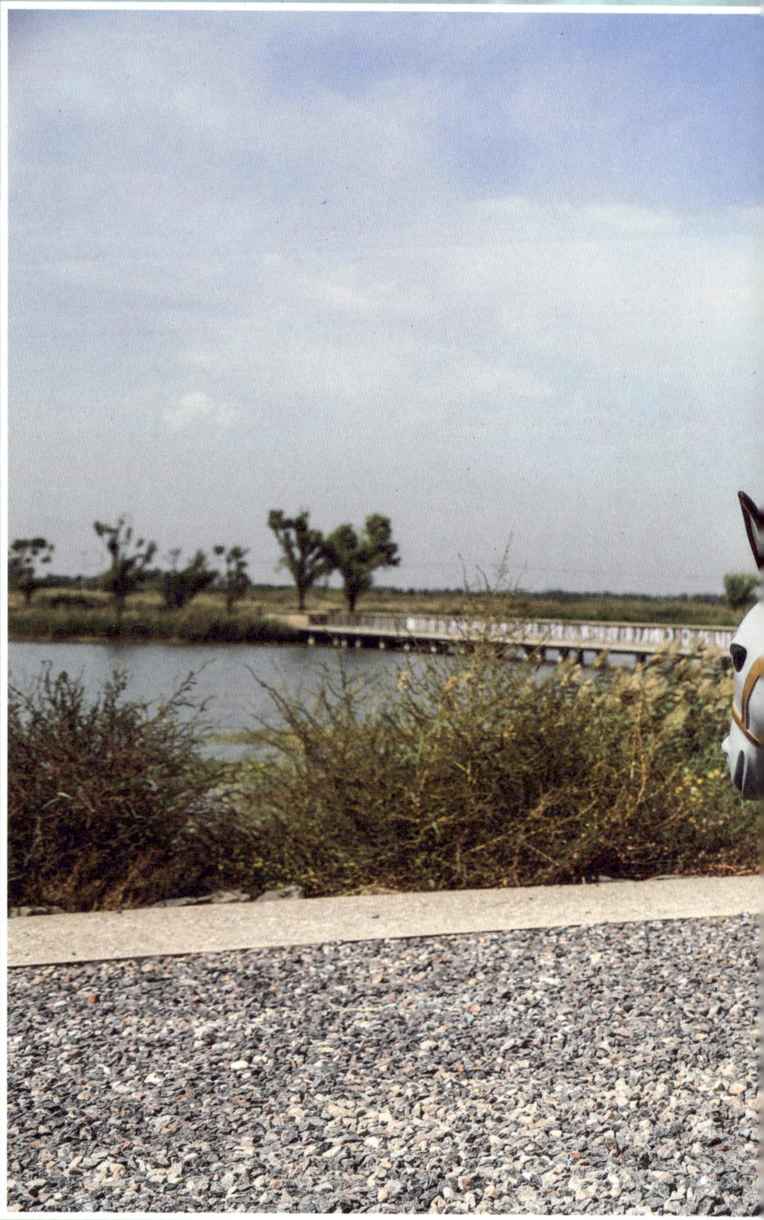

Slavs and Tatars
Molla Nasreddin the antimodern, 2012
Fiberglass, lacquer paint, steel, 180 × 180 × 80 cm
Installation view at Yinchuan Biennale, 2016

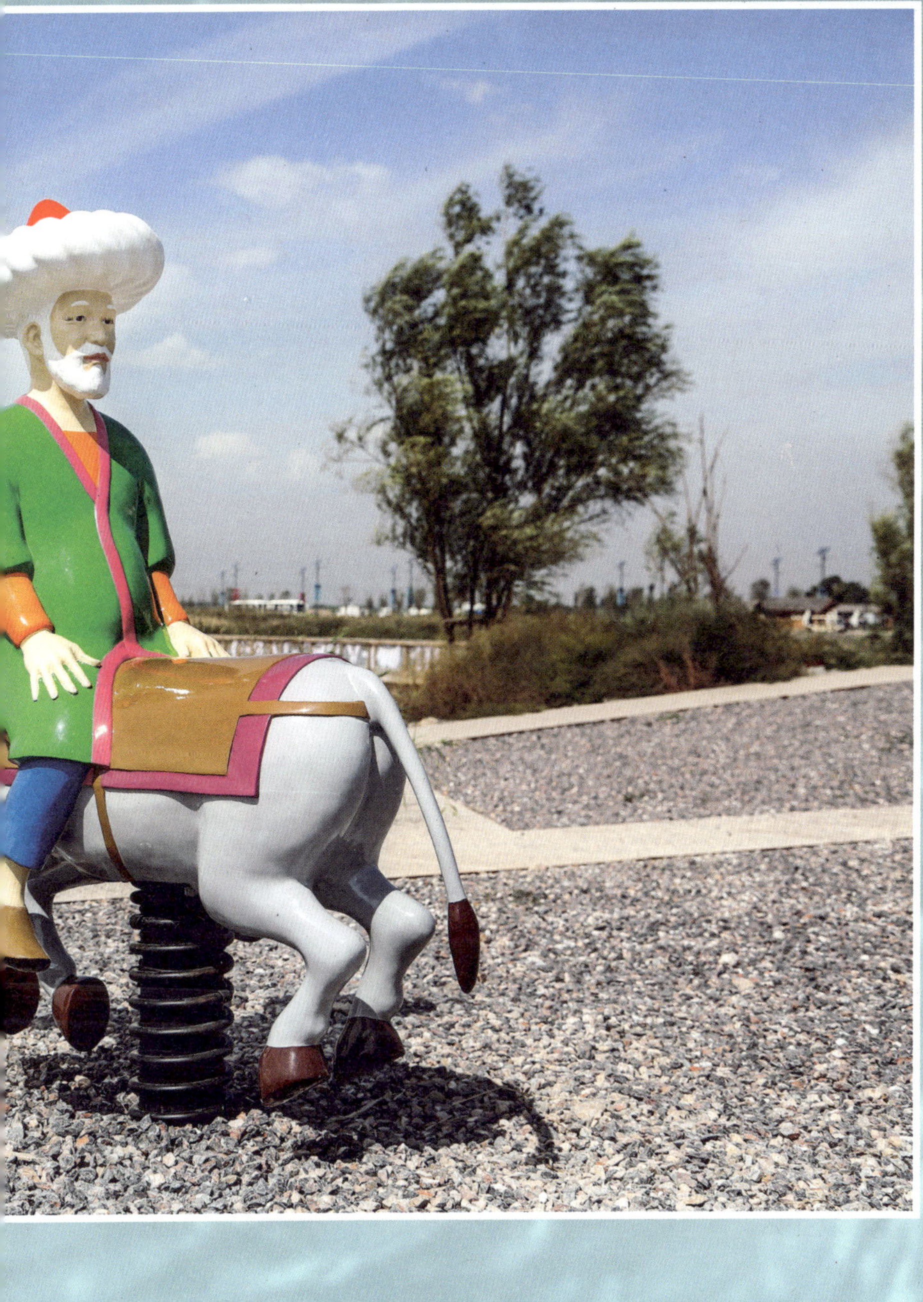

these concepts and use them to intercontextualize each other.

During the past three decades, the global artworld (from small galleries to large multinational institutions) has thrived from the infrastructures of peak globalization and has consequently internalized value-systems that are embedded in the alignment between liberal democracy, the progressive state, and neoliberal metrics of economic stability. The alignment produces auxiliary notions in the artworld that operate quite self-sufficiently, such as certain artistic forms of production or distribution as embodying liberal and/or progressive values in themselves, and the upholding of artistic "freedom" as a condition, rather than a product, of the system. The results are sanctimonious critique, where an academic or general audience decry anything from late capitalism to the pervasive political swing to the right across the world. While the critique fails to map onto actual state-society mechanisms, social structures, and political economic institutions, it often turns inwards towards institutions in the artworld itself, limiting analysis to a circular logic. Thus, after decades of institutional critique in the arts, there seems to be a strange telos that leaves us (critical practitioners) more or less in the same place where the critical project began: one that names rather than intervenes.[3] Perhaps this happens when one knows the answer and yet still looks for the problem. Meanwhile, the object of critique is transforming, starting from the very locus of neoliberal globalization. While this doesn't mean that neoliberalism (as a political and cultural

3 As demonstrated in numerous studies, the most recent "wave" of institutional critique has concentrated on the creation of alternative institutions following the understanding of art as a process of building what Gerald Raunig terms "instituent practices." Such practices have been variously theorized as "infrastructural critique," "para-institutional," "translocal organizations," "alter-institutional," and "para-institutional organizations." See Gerald Raunig, "Flatness Rules: Instituent Practices and Institutions of the Common," *Institutional Attitudes: Instituting Art in a Flat World*, ed. Pascal Gielen (Amsterdam: Valiz, 2013), pp. 67–179; Marina Vishmidt, "Only as Self-Relating Negativity: Infrastructure and Critique," *Journal of Science and Technology of the Arts* 13, no. 3 (March 2022), pp. 13–24; Tom Holert, *Knowledge Beside Itself: Contemporary Art's Epistemic Politics* (London: Sternberg Press, 2020); Binna Choi and Marion von Osten, "Trans-Local, Post-Disciplinary Organizational Practice: A Conversation between Binna Choi and Marion Von Osten," *Cluster: Dialectionary*, eds. Binna Choi, Maria Lind, Emily Pethick, and Nataša Petrešin-Bachelez (London: Sternberg Press, 2014), pp. 274–83; Sven Lütticken, "Social Media: Practices of (in)Visibility in Contemporary Art," *Afterall* 40 (Autumn/Winter 2015), pp. 4–19.

system of signification and planning) is going away any time soon, it does present epistemological implications for those traditionally posited in antagonistic relations with neoliberalism in the arts.

The world after globalization doesn't necessarily signal the total discarding of the alignment I introduced above, but rather its reconfiguration. Because Western art's foundational forms and epistemologies (as codified in the canon of art history and theory) are related to those means of governance, art's production will necessarily reconfigure as well. The condition of global multipolarity is already shifting the baselines for critiques of capitalism and neoliberalism in the arts and the moral imperatives bestowed on art in certain parts of the world. This book attempts to illustrate those shifts by way of examples, without attempting to produce a detailed map. Through this theorization, the book calls for refocusing critique in the artworld by reassessing the shibboleth of neoliberalism, the role of the state in relation to development and delivering progress, and other associated norms and values key to the logics and processes of globalization. We should also take care to not reproduce geopolitical assumptions in the most literal sense.

The Critique of Neoliberal Capitalism in Art Theory

What is missing in much art theoretical writing is system-oriented discussion about paradigm shifts to the neoliberal Washington consensus and its ramifications for contemporary art—its production, reception, and circulation.

Inspecting the critique of neoliberalism in much art theory, those changes are hardly felt. That said, this book is neither a denial of nor apology for neoliberalism. Nor is this a reiteration of how neoliberalism recasts the artworld in its own image at local levels, whether in the proliferation of "immaterial labor" or the championing of entrepreneurialism—the former denoting forms of work that produce information and the latter signaling the centrality of individuation to neoliberal subject-formation and valorization.[4] Stepping back, it is necessary to confront uncomfortable discrepancies in much art theoretical thinking. For example, how do critics of neoliberalism in the artworld stack their near constant invocation of neoliberalism as a "great evil" with similar arguments proffered by authoritarian, illiberal regimes, both economically and ideologically? What happens if it is no longer necessary to defend art against neoliberalism? What is one to make of the effusive praise of the "community" against art's role in the reproduction of individuation?

To inspect where art theory converges with scholarship on neoliberalism and to set the scene for a rigorous study on what the transformation of neoliberalism in post-globalization means for the arts, it is worthwhile to turn to historian Philip Mirowski's telegraphed summary of neoliberalism in the format of "Ten Commandments of Neoliberalism":

> (1) "Free" markets do not occur naturally. They must be actively constructed through political mobilization. (2) "The market" is an information processor, and the most efficient one possible—more efficient than

4 See Angela McRobbie, *Be Creative: Making a Living in the New Culture Industries* (Cambridge, UK: Polity Press, 2016); Ulrich Bröckling, *The Entrepreneurial Self: Fabricating a New Type of Subject* (London: SAGE Publications Ltd., 2016); Lin Zhang, *The Labor of Reinvention: Entrepreneurship in the New Chinese Digital Economy* (New York: Columbia University Press, 2023).

any government or any single human ever could be. "Open" is a truncated code-word for the sorts of ideal political epistemic structures wherein markets exhibit their superior efficacy. In these societies, "experts" need to be rendered subordinate to the superior wisdom of impersonal markets. (3) Market society is, and therefore should be, the natural and inexorable state of humankind. It is especially required in any instance of the communal use of knowledge in society. (4) The political goal of neoliberals is not to destroy the state, but rather to take control of it, and to redefine its structure and function, in order to create and maintain the market-friendly culture. (5) The most important virtue—more important than justice, or anything else—is freedom, defined "negatively" as "freedom to choose" or "openness," and most importantly, as the conflation of markets with political liberty. Democracy is subordinate to this mandate. (6) Capital has a natural right to flow freely across national boundaries, as does "data"—labor, not so much. (7) Inequality—of resources, income, wealth, and even political rights—is a good thing; it supercharges productivity, because people envy the rich and strive to emulate them. People who complain about inequality are either sore losers or old fogies, who need to get hip to the way things work nowadays. (8) Corporations can be treated as if they were legal persons, with all their attendant rights: for instance, enjoying the legal guarantee of "free speech." If they achieve a monopoly position in some market,

> that is merely evidence that they have been the best at what they do. (9) The market, engineered and promoted by neoliberal experts, can always provide solutions to problems seemingly caused by the market in the first place: there's always "an app for that." (10) There is no difference between what is and what should be: "free" markets both should be (normatively) and are (positively) the most efficient economic system, and the most just way of doing politics, and the most empirically true description of human behavior, and the most ethical and moral way to live—which in turn explains, and justifies, why their preferred versions of "free" markets should be, and as neoliberals usurp more and more power, increasingly are, universal.[5]

There is a lot to work through here. The most important insights for the sake of this book are those that point to the sometimes nebulous connection between neoliberalism and liberalism, which, in a post-globalization era, are even less evident than they were before. Though it is true that the neoliberal takeover of the state by financialized capital disrupts the organization of the classical liberal small state, authoritarian state capitalism (sometimes) also represses private business and the notion of the liberal small state. Furthermore, the undermining of progressive neoliberalism in the West turns our gaze to a more classical understanding of the state as a force of civic peace keeping, rather than truth-seeking. There are, in contrast, places with state-led "neoliberal" development such as in

5 This is an abridged version of "commandments of neoliberalism" in a forthcoming book by Philip Mirowski. See an extended version of the "commandments" in Philip Mirowski, *Never let a serious crisis go to waste: how neoliberalism survived the financial meltdown* (London: Verso, 2013).

China (more on the mixed terminologies in Chapter 3) that not only uphold a promise of economic and, to some extent social, progress, but also actively attempt to redefine what fundamental concepts like democracy and freedom mean through illiberal practice. In other words, non-liberal state policy is not incommensurable with neoliberal economic policy. Some of these connections are historically construed under the sweeping ideology of globalization, such as the conflation of markets with political liberty, or markets and democracy, and the slippage between normative and positive conceptions regarding the most efficient economic system and just political system. However, the underbelly of these conflations is freedom defined negatively (freedom from something), which should be balanced with positive freedom (freedom to do or be something).

In general, these nuances wither away in artistic critical production that concern neoliberalism. There is a growing body of artworks and art theory that critique neoliberal market fundamentalism, market solutionism, and the exceptionalism of big corporations, and for good reasons.[6] But why is art inclined to address some of our present woes more than others?

Many claims in the artworld are complicit in creating an interpretative, rather than an explanatory, framework for assessing its object of critique. An interpretative framework demands a working concept as well as a coherent narrative within the context of the phenomenon, even though they might only reveal certain dimensions of an issue with multiple causes. Hence, due to their unfalsifiability—i.e.,

6 Such as Zach Blas's work *Contra-Internet,* https://zachblas.info/works/contra-internet/; Simon Denny's exhibition *The Personal Effects of Kim Dotcom*, https://simondenny.net/the-personal-effects-of-kim-dotcom-2/ or https://simondenny.net/the-personal-effects-of-kim-dotcom/; Mark Lombardi's exhibition *Global Networks*, https://curatorsintl.org/exhibitions/8953-mark-lombardi-global-networks; and Femke Herregraven's work *Taxodus*, http://taxodus.net/.

the inability to formulate an alternative hypothesis to prove or disprove the validity of the claim, this framework presents the end, rather than the start of a discussion.

What constitutes the core of the explanatory framework is the comparison with similar cases, which propels one to identify why one explanation is better than another. Understood as such, symbolic capital—Pierre Bourdieu's sociological critique[7] in which artworkers have knowledge of and which purportedly all cultural workers strive for—is an interpretative framework. It stipulates the behavior of rational subjects acting within any given society, thus presupposing a model in which the behaviors of the actors are formal and the structure of the society are empirical. Its insufficiency as an explanatory framework lies in the generalized treatment of capital as an independent variable, rather than a dependent variable that constitutes a composite indicator among other dimensions of explanations. Is the best critique available one that merely investigates patterns of consumption? While art theory in a Marxian methodology seeks to establish a lucid framework of understanding the production of value in art as it relates to the production of value under the present capitalist mode of production, it often ends up eschewing the framework of the labor theory of value and affirming the exceptionality of art,[8] or more elegantly, but also more speculatively, finding the realignment of art and reproductive labor.[9] The Marxian model requires an understanding that the structure of the society is formal—i.e., with a fixed mode of production—while the actors are lively, empirical

7 Pierre Bourdieu, *Distinction: A Social Critique of the Judgement of Taste*, trans. Richard Nice (Cambridge, MA: Harvard University Press, 1984).

8 See Dave Beech, *Art and Value: Art's Economic Exceptionalism in Classical, Neoclassical and Marxist Economics* (Leiden, The Netherlands: Brill, 2015); Sven Lütticken, "The Coming Exception: Art and the Crisis of Value," *New Left Review*, no. 99 (May–June 2016), pp. 111–36.

9 Kerstin Stakemeier and Marina Vishmidt, *Reproducing Autonomy: Work, Money, Crisis and Contemporary Art* (Berlin: Mute, 2016).

human beings in that they may both be rational and driven by emotion and tradition.[10] An empirical critique of a formal model is ineffectual, just as a formal critique of an empirical model does not yield many insights. Rarely do we see art theory poised to establish a model that combines empirical and formal understandings of the social, political, or economic structures *and* of the actors in those structures.

Another ubiquitous argument in contemporary art theory concerns the similarity between modalities of speculation employed in art and financial capital,[11] though in many instances the distinction between a traditional neoliberal logic of financialization and the general notion of speculative markets which are not specific to neoliberalism are glossed over. While the neoliberal logic reflects itself in the might of financial capital over productive capital via the figure of the shareholder, this does not conversely imply that all speculative markets are automatically neoliberal or that speculation is the central, novel feature of neoliberalism any more than it is simply an extension of capitalist abstraction. The ways in which speculative pricing is employed in the art sector can be explained in terms of the immanent dynamic of art production itself and its fragile relation to questions of value without a need to overstate the "foreign influence" of external financializing forces. Empirically, as Olav Velthuis notes, the relationship between the art market and speculation is rather conflicted with many galleries and collectors actively trying to keep speculators out of the art circuit. Similarly, the actual average time that

10 Dingxin Zhao, *Politics of Legitimacy: The State-Society Relations in Contemporary China* (Taiwan: National Taiwan University Press, 2017).

11 The most rigorous study is Marina Vishmidt, *Speculation as a Mode of Production* (Leiden, The Netherlands: Brill, 2018). Vishmidt's project calls for speculation to be wrested back from financialized capital.

a collector keeps a work before selling it (which is longer than one would expect) suggests that artworks are not as liquid as commonly thought.[12]

This does not refute, however, that contemporary art can aesthetically and philosophically reflect the logics and functions of financial capitalism, which often lead to cynical, careerist art(ists)—though this is not exclusive to contemporary art. As Theodor W. Adorno writes: "Yet it is precisely as artifacts, as products of social labor, that they [artworks] also communicate with the empirical experience that they reject and from which they draw their content (*Inhalt*). Art negates the categorial determinations stamped on the empirical world and yet harbors what is empirically existing in its own substance."[13] Rather than that cynicism being the result of an "ontological" takeover of the artworld by neoliberalism, it is more likely that art as an autonomous field, including its market(s), appropriates and integrates neoliberal fragments in accordance with its own logic. Art is neither the harbinger nor the victim of neoliberalism, but simply its "fellow traveler." Speculation in art as a form of thinking beyond established frames does not neatly map onto financial speculation as a means of pushing the established frames of capital into the future in order to extract/produce value. Likewise pinpointing the perpetual crisis of art and its relation to the social sphere solely on the "nefarious influence" of neoliberalism amounts to little more than muddying the waters. Does this not universalize the "enemy" in ways that leads to a poorer, instrumentalizing notion of art or, conversely, an aestheticization of finance

12 Various studies put the holding time of a work before resale in the range of twenty-five to forty years. See Olav Velthuis and Erica Coslor, "The Financialization of Art," *Handbook of the Sociology of Finance*, eds. Karin Knorr Cetina and Alex Preda (Oxford: Oxford University Press, 2012), pp. 471–87; Clare McAndrew, Suhail Malik, and Gerald Nestler, "Plotting the Art Market: An Interview with Clare McAndrew," *Finance and Society* 2, no. 2 (2016), pp. 151–67, https://doi.org/10.2218/finsoc.v2i2.1728. The Art Basel and UBS research on resale period also noted the reluctance to sell works by the majority of collectors surveyed. See Clare McAndrew, *The Art Market 2018: An Art Basel and UBS Report* (Basel: Art Basel, 2018).

13 Theodor W. Adorno, *Aesthetic Theory*, eds. Gretel Adorno and Rolf Tiedeman (New York: Continuum, 2002).

as the purest form of art? All the while, this normalizes a form of critique that misses its target from the start.

One red thread in this book is how the alignment between the role of the state as a political form, the aspiration for progress, and associated norms and values is being put on trial by art in the geopolitical sea change of post-globalization. It is a constituent moment when art becomes politics. The critique of art in this context often feels misguided, since it only needs to prove its validity in a frame set up and accepted by most people in the global art circle, whereas what is really needed is a clear-headed critique of politics. I will return to this in Chapter 3.

Peak Neoliberal Globalization and Peak Global Art Discourses

The apodictic tone in critiques of neoliberalism in the artworld shows its failure to grasp the transformation of neoliberalism, and much less what to do with the forces causing this shift.

The neoliberal practice that upholds economic freedom above all other freedoms is undermined by the polycrises of the world. For one example, as political scientist Dieter Plehwe points out, managing climate change is unthinkable without infringing on fossil fuel sector property rights.[14] A similar conflict emerges between the "freedom" of economic transactions and the rule of law as protection from discriminatory government policy. Industrial policies such as the CHIPS Act and the Inflation Reduction Act in the US, as well as the more modest European equivalents,

14 Dieter Plehwe, "Dieter Plehwe in the Past, Present, and Future of Neoliberalism," *The Syllabus*, https://www.the-syllabus.com/ts-spotlight/post-neoliberal-moment/conversation/dieter-plehwe.

effectively undo the formerly prevalent doctrine that states should not direct capitalist development, much less engage in direct economic planning. Much of this is driven by geopolitical sea change. "The big question about post-neoliberalism," remarks political scientist Dani Rodrik, "is whether it's going to be driven by our [US] domestic concerns or by geopolitical competition with China."[15]

At the same time, neoliberalism is mutating into what Reijer Hendrikse calls "neo-illiberalism," by which he means more sovereigntist, nationalist, and authoritarian.[16] If the implementation of neoliberalism has historically been achieved through illiberal means (see the sections on NIEO and WTO in Chapter 4), the so-called "progressive" neoliberal moment may have indeed been the outlier to liberal rule, and liberalism's true face is now being exposed.

Most of the theories and projects of globalization, whether they come from sophisticated Marxist and poststructuralist critical accounts or from liberal-international spokespersons like in the recent Director general of the WTO Ngozi Okonjo-Iweala's manifesto for "reimagining—not abandoning—globalization,"[17] not only suppose that globalization and post-globalized world are dialectically and closely connected, but also structure their critique of Western ordered globalization with a lofty imagination of post-globalization as a "better" or true globality without hegemony. Less cheerful analysts point toward an era of "centrifugal multipolarity"[18] where "global growth might produce not harmony and convergence but conflict and contradiction."[19]

15 Dani Rodrik, "Dani Rodrik on choosing the right policy priorities," *The Syllabus*, May 9, 2023, https://www.the-syllabus.com/ts-spotlight/post-neoliberal-moment/conversation/dani-rodrik.

16 Reijer Hendrikse, "The Rise of Neo-Illiberalism," *Krisis* 41, no. 1 (June 15, 2021), pp. 65–93.

17 Ngozi Okonjo-Iweala, "Why the World Still Needs Trade: The Case for Reimagining—Not Abandoning—Globalization," *Foreign Affairs* 102, no. 4 (2023), pp. 94–103.

18 Adam Tooze, *Shutdown: How Covid Shook the World's Economy* (London: Penguin UK, 2021).

19 Adam Tooze, "Putin's Challenge to Western Hegemony—the 2022 Edition," *Chartbook* (blog), January 12, 2022, https://adamtooze.substack.com/p/chartbook-68-putins-challenge-to.

Much ink has been spilt on international relations (IR) that rearticulate multipolarity under present geopolitical contentions. As Feng Zhang and Barry Buzan put it:

> Some assumed globalization to be the main trend and so emphasized the relative disempowerment of states and the rise of non-state actors of various kinds. Others emphasized the diffusion of wealth and power and the relative decline of the West. Most saw a more complex, multifaceted type of world order, rather than a simple realist "polarity" vision of a system of states jockeying for wealth and power. A reversion to the old realist ideas of multipolarity or bipolarity could not capture the main architecture of what was happening in this layered and complex diffusion of power.[20]

Thus, Zhang and Buzan propose "deep pluralism" as a working concept, which captures how wealth and power, and cultural and political authority are diffusely distributed. These criteria sharply contrast with the preceding decades of Western domination and globalization, in which wealth and power, as well as cultural and political authority, were relatively concentrated. As we will see later, the notion of deep pluralism is useful in empirically describing the phenomena of artworlds in a multipolar world. It will, moreover, offer normative insights as to how to navigate this multipolar world based not on contestation but consensus among various actors, artists included.

20 Feng Zhang and Barry Buzan, "The Relevance of Deep Pluralism for China's Foreign Policy," *Chinese Journal of International Politics* 15, no. 3 (2022), pp. 246–71.

Art and cultural theory tend to produce theories of globalization that are commensurable from one context to another. In other words, the critique of globalization often reinforces the very idea of globalization. The advent of global art, coming of age as the effect of globalization in the shadow of Western hegemony, is not only polycentric as a practice, but also demands a polyphonic discourse, a global art history.[21] A global art history vacillates between the fact that it is and is not a unified enterprise throughout the world.[22] In Marxist analyses of space, for example, globalization and capitalism are argued to *produce* spatial and epistemological difference.[23] In postcolonial theory and decolonial thinking, on the other hand, the world becomes multipolar, multinarrative, and multiepistemological by re-articulating global designs from local histories.[24] Schematically, the universalizing process of economic globalization and the proliferation of differences seem to share one explanatory axis that not only rests upon but affirms the irreversibility of globalization. This pluralism under unipolar globalization can play into local power games, as in the multiculturalism that has been experienced in the West for decades. But it is a stratified version of pluralism, premised on a society in which political, ideological, and economic power coincide ontologically.

Diving beneath the epistemological contours of the theorization of neoliberalization discussed here, Zhivka Valiavicharska recognizes a disjuncture between discourse about art and critical discourse about globalization, especially the role art has played as "an agent and an instrument

21 Hans Belting, "From World Art to Global Art. View on a New Panorama," *What's next?*, reader (2013), http://whtsnxt.net/011.

22 James Elkins, *Is Art History Global?* (New York and London: Routledge, 2007); Marc James Léger, "Art and Art History after Globalisation," *Third Text* 26, no. 5 (2012), pp. 515–27.

23 Henri Lefebvre, *The Production of Space,* vol. 1 (Oxford, UK: Wiley-Blackwell, 1992); David Harvey, "Globalization and the 'Spatial Fix,'" *Geographische Revue* 2 (2001), pp. 23–30.

24 Walter, D. Mignolo, "Local Histories/Global Designs: Coloniality, Subaltern Knowledges, and Border Thinking," *Princeton Studies in Culture/Power/History* (Princeton, NJ: Princeton University Press, 2000).

of social transformation projects with neoliberal agendas,"[25] in concrete instances of "how contemporary art production, art display, and the production of various historical knowledges of art participate in, say, the neoliberal reforms taking place in postsocialist Russia, or the formation of a transnational business class in Hong Kong, or how cultural policy projects have employed the arts towards an eastward expansion of the European Union."[26] This is a clear formulation of "art equals politics," and the gap in empirical research points to the lack of self-understanding of its operation in the arts at the time of neoliberal globalization. We could return to figures such as Peter Ludwig, who functioned as a self-appointed cultural ambassador of the liberal West/Germany by establishing ties to the Soviet Union and China through donations of Western modernist paintings to national art museums in both countries.[27] The availability and viability of data points make it evident that it is easier to identify the covert operations of cultural politics when the world is opening up, than when it is closing down. If we are to establish a correlation, though not a causal one, between the neoliberalization of a society and certain kinds of artistic expressions, how do these expressions fare now under regimes of ostensible de-globalization? Do they signal the need for a dependency theory of the artworld, i.e., that the periphery world will forever serve the needs of the center, as emerging 1970s theory from Latin America argued? Or, given the rising economic and political standing of many non-Western countries, how can they serve as acute reminders of dispersed synchronicities and tenuous

25 James Elkins, Zhivka Valiavicharska, and Alice Kim, *Art and Globalization* (Philadelphia: Penn State University Press, 2015), p. 91.
26 Elkins, Valiavicharska, and Kim, p. 91.
27 See Heinz Bude, *Peter Ludwig. Im Glanz der Bilder* (Cologne: Bastei Lübbe, 1996).

interrelations between aesthetics, social transformation, and ideology?

New Left and New Right Art

My usage of "deep pluralism" allows me to derive a triad of analytical lenses—political, ideological, and economic—to assess any phenomena in cultural production. While art history research traditionally reinforces ideology, art and culture need to have a sober understanding of what politics it emerges from and how it claims to—and in reality does—effectuate politics, as well as what economics is at stake. On politics, we may differentiate actual and academic, institutionalized forms of politics, class struggles, or pragmatic politics which involve collaboration with power. Each of these come with certain ideological underpinnings, be it liberal left, progressive, New Left, or realist. Economics involves the broader sense of political economy and economic policy, a subtle understanding of complexity in value chains which connects to the funding and markets of art and culture. These lenses may overlap but cannot be replaced by one another. Applied together, they allow nuanced assessments to emerge, such as when we examine why certain "apolitical" art practices are seen as political to Western funders, what happens when one's leftist ideology as expressed via culture is embraced by a state, and how the Western leftist political playbook holds elsewhere if one adds the layer of economic globalization. These cases of multipolarity—and not the literal version of it—will be fleshed out throughout the book.

A multipolar, deeply pluralist understanding of the world promises nothing less than inconsistencies and contradictions in the traditional political spectrum from left to right. To give an example, the liberal thinker Qin Hui points out that while Leftists in Western welfare states should oppose globalization, Leftists in China should welcome it, but simultaneously push for political reform, so that it can benefit the Chinese working class and the disadvantaged.[28] The role of the state in relation to politics and society is paramount, which will be examined closely in Chapter 3. But liberals are far from unitary. It takes hard work to establish sophisticated liberalism(s) from the perspective of an individual, a version of which, as an instance, should fully digest the historical experiences of Western liberalism while pointing out the possibility of separating—or the attempt to do so—liberalism from state form. The lumping together of diverse components—individual freedom, private ownership, market logics, democracy, the civic sphere—into one doctrine often does liberalism a disservice. Recently, from the Chinese pro-democracy and pro-market liberal camp, there are several intellectuals that have come out to idolize Donald Trump. Underlying this Trumpian turn is the complex combination of both a "neoliberal affinity" and a sense of "civilizational vindicativism" predicated on scientific racism that makes the liberals receptive to Trump's alt-right, anti-immigrant, and Islamophobic ideologies.[29] All of this poses infrastructural and ideological conundrums to political commentators and cultural producers alike who try to universalize the functioning of ideological systems and processes for divergent

28 Qin Hui, "Dilemmas of Twenty-First Century Globalization: Explanations and Solutions, with a Critique of Thomas Piketty's Twenty-First Century Capitalism," *Reading the China Dream*, November 15, 2018, https://www.readingthechinadream.com/qin-hui-dilemmas.html.

29 See, for example, Yao Lin, "Beaconism and the Trumpian Metamorphosis of Chinese Liberal Intellectuals," *Journal of Contemporary China* 30, no. 127 (2020), pp. 85–101.

contexts. The situation of the Chinese New Left is no less convoluted. What remains of their position when there is no longer the need to defend the state against neoliberalism? Ironically, would the state itself become a meta-aesthetic rendering of "New Left art," overshadowing Boris Groys's theorization of *Gesamtkunstwerk Stalin*?[30] One can certainly contrast this with contemporary Maoists singing red songs in choirs and wearing red scarfs.

In this context, I contend that the supposed alignment of artistic form and political ideology can only be stretched to its limit by looking through the broken mirror of post-globalization. In the better days of unipolar globalization, there was nothing incoherent or unfashionable, and indeed even perhaps political to borrow left, even "far left" aesthetics from a patently left country and appropriate it in the West. However, incongruence and naivety emerge as soon as we shift contexts, starting with what such New Left aesthetics mean for the home context where the New Left is oppressed, taken over by the state, or there is an oscillation in between these positions. To instantiate a "New Left art," artists from former socialist countries, such as the art collective *Chto Delat* founded in Saint Petersburg, began to sport socialist aesthetics in Western, broadly leftist, art circles. But this position was inevitably rendered unviable after Russia's full-scale invasion of Ukraine in February 2022. For now it serves little for a New Left position to distinguish itself from a broad liberal anti-war alliance, not to mention the preponderance of anti-war art in galleries across the West. The critique of neoliberal global hegemony—taken

30 Boris Groys, *The Total Art of Stalinism* (NJ: Princeton University Press, 1992).

together with the wavering of internationalism, which was traditionally connected with identity issues for post-Soviet progressive intellectuals—becomes more problematic during the polarizing war in Ukraine. Shock from the war as well as public conjuncture shifted most of them to a rather one-dimensional critique of "Russian fascism" and/or to the appeals "to decolonize Russia." Such one-dimensionality stems also from the fact that there is a severe lack of interest in non-Western knowledge in the West that could be useful in asking burning questions like how did the rise of the New Right happen, and what are its aesthetic strategies? Very few intellectuals try to keep some degree of complexity in their critical position like the last *steirischer herbst* edition, titled *A War in the Distance,* which points to nuances in Western subjectivity, namely the geopolitical repression of wars out of Europe with proxy politics and the rise of military teletechnologies.[31]

Moving away from a New Left position, we enter the nebulous camps of, broadly speaking, progressivism and contemporary liberalism, where identity, cultural difference, and generally depoliticized notions of decolonial, local, and ancestorial traditions are championed (at the expense of genuine anti-colonial politics). The more globalization progresses, the more the same ready-made agendas are reproduced, such as working situatedly on local issues/traditions. This is a fair point of critique by global art discourse, albeit mostly at the level of business model, i.e., who gets to do what and under what conditions, like the international artist parachuted into a biennale context

31 See Ekaterina Degot, and David Riff, eds., *steirischer herbst '22: A War in the Distance. Ukraine and the Return of History* (Berlin: Hatje Cantz, 2023).

to work on local issues, who are generally divorced from meaningful local action. Again, is the consumption pattern of art spectators and producers all we have to engage with? We add more lurid details in our naval gazing, gain more piecemeal learnings from affable personalities (for example, "lessons I learn from my grandmother"), but fall short on theoretical lenses that help define an agenda of art appropriate to our changing political context because of the focus on embodied experience. For those of us coming from a nationalist, non-Western context, the penchant for the local is a worrying development. Most of us have experienced the better days of the two lefts and are witnessing a course correction. Do we want to see a premature de-intellectualization, after the pre-mature de-industrialization of the Global South? Clearly, the crucial difference is whether the "local" approach is open to differences and whether it has a cohesive and inclusive political vision beyond the immediate community one belongs to, and in striving for a post-modern, post-individual community, how can we avoid lapsing back into a pre-modern, pre-individual community? This will be discussed further in the next chapter on documenta fifteen (d15).

And finally, on the New Right. In the West, many populist parties recognize what Antonio Gramsci identified as the cultural hegemony, or "metapolitics," of art and culture, and consequently support art because of its power to change perspectives and shape discourses. Thus, we can identify an emerging "New Right art," which describes artistic positions that explicitly or implicitly aestheticize anti-liberal or anti-modern narratives and blur the established opposition between left-liberal, supposedly progressive, (post-)modernist, and right-authoritarian conservative anti-modernists positions. The belief that contemporary Western art is aligned with a left-liberal perspective is no longer tenable, if it ever was.

Right-wing ideologies and artistic practice are especially entangled in places where the Western liberal tradition is being politically and philosophically challenged. Social, economic, and political grievances interface not only with more prominent right-wing populisms but also with seemingly obscure ideologies like neo-traditionalism, esoteric proponents of a conservative revolution, and neoreactionaries of the so-called Dark Enlightenment (NRx), which promote right-wing accelerationism and libertarian post-humanism. In the post-socialist Eastern European and Russian context, it is especially astounding to witness how proponents of this anti-modern aesthetics indiscriminately connect formerly progressive art movements such as non-conformism since the 1960s, late Conceptualism in the 1980s, and Actionism in the 1990s. The results are perplexing entanglements of contemporary art: a quasi "universalist" discourse that propagates the reintroduction of anything from traditionalist art and folklore into contemporary art institutions, the adoption of formerly leftist postmodern artistic methods with right-wing politics, and the ambiguous fascination of artists with techno-apocalyptic, crypto-fascist, and occult aesthetics, even as they proclaim themselves to be neither left nor right.[32]

32 Studies on the New Right are useful for analyzing this phenomenon, especially by investigating how they adopt anti-capitalist, anti-statist (mostly in relation to liberal democratic states), but also anti-liberal rhetoric, much of which can be seen as altered versions of traditionally leftist arguments, as discussed in Tamir Bar-On, *Where Have All the Fascists Gone?* (New York and London: Routledge, 2007); how they adopt Gramscian counter-hegemonic tools for anti-liberal struggle, as analyzed in Karl Ekeman, "On Gramscianism of the Right," *Praxis* 13, no. 13 (November 11, 2018), https://blogs.law.columbia.edu/praxis1313/karl-ekeman-on-gramscianism-of-the-right/; how they put a focus on metapolitical cultural strategies of ideological struggles between left-liberal and New Right narratives in the "culture war" as investigated in Daniel Rueda, "Alain De Benoist, Ethnopluralism and the Cultural Turn in Racism," *Patterns of Prejudice* 55, no. 3 (May 27, 2021), pp. 213–35. See also Tamir Bar-On, "Understanding Political Conversion and Mimetic Rivalry," *Totalitarian Movements and Political Religions* 10, no. 3–4 (September 1, 2009), pp. 241–64. On how museums, in this context, can be seen as a soft combat and geopolitical assemblage of the affective biopolitics that "enroll" visitors, see Jacob C. Miller and Sharon Wilson, "Museum as Geopolitical Entity: Toward Soft Combat," *Geography Compass* 16, no. 6 (May 6, 2022).

Building on Deng Xiaoping's political wisdom that "we must be vigilant against the right, but mainly against the left" in the wake of post-Mao reform, sociologist Dingxin Zhao incisively points out a principle in politics: a political party is more likely to be bound by a politically correct discourse that is consistent with the party's original ideological orientation. Thus, a rightist party must guard against the right, a liberal party against liberalism, a religious party against fundamentalism, and a party with a strong nationalist orientation against nationalism.[33] Within a given society, this not only gives descriptive clarity to the contours of new political alliances, but also prescribes what form of address could be effective. Negotiations, diplomacy, and compromises in the hope of discursive peacekeeping give way to polarized political debates and public opinion. All things considered, commanding divergent intellectual resources to moderate the collisions of opinions and channeling the center-right to deal with the extreme right may be the most pragmatic move. What about seeing politics as a form for practical reasoning, rather than any sort of demonstrative reasoning resting upon fixed ideologies? What about even more counterintuitive maneuvers such as the recent proposal to marshal right-wing parties to advance the political integration of Europe?[34]

Post-liberal Art in a Deeply Pluralist World

Those who find themselves in the middle of the geopolitical tectonic shifts tend to embrace a degree of mixed allegiances to various political ideologies. This is due as much

33 Dingxin, *Politics of Legitimacy*.
34 Lorenzo Marsili and Fabrizio Tassinari, "Are we heading towards a far-right European Union?" *Al Jazeera Opinions*, July 19, 2023.

to survival as it is to an engagement with political theory. Western scholars have proposed "post-liberalism" as an alternative approach beyond the binaries between "liberal" and "illiberal" or "democratic" and "authoritarian" that are reproduced by governments. Admittedly, there is a conservative clamor for marketing its use.

In the post-liberal transition, the essential contestability of social science concepts—i.e., their ability to be inherently liable to rival interpretations—rapidly increases.[35] Practices and discourses of ordering may be simultaneously perceived and experienced to conform to liberal as well as non-liberal conceptions of social and political order.[36] This is due to the fact that national paths of development, policy making, and the social ordering of younger nations are rarely being determined by free and collective decision making as envisaged in liberal political and economic theory.[37] After the so-called "end of history," the sweeping force of third wave democracy leaves some countries as low-level democracies and others in tatters. The consequence is a slow-burn crisis of liberalism in general.[38] Instead of adhering to the abstract, doctrinal and ideological claims pertaining to liberalism on any side, some scholars argue that the only acceptable way through this contestability is via a form of pluralist "practical reasoning"—that is, a cooperative, dialogical, and practice-based approach focused on sensitivity to the local practices.[39] These approaches could be labeled as decolonial or post-liberal. In particular, the post-liberal approach focuses on the co-production of non-Western, non-liberal

35 Gray, *Post-Liberalism*.
36 Philipp Lottholz, *Post-Liberal Statebuilding in Central Asia: Imaginaries, Discourses and Practices of Social Ordering* (Bristol: Policy Press, 2022).
37 Philipp Lottholz, "Political Change in Post-socialist Eurasia: Towards a Post-Liberal Research Agenda," *openDemocracy*, February 27, 2019, https://www.opendemocracy.net/en/odr/political-change-in-post-socialist-eurasia/.
38 See Zhao, 2018.
39 Bent Flyvbjerg, Todd Landman, and Sanford Schram, eds., *Real Social Science: Applied Phronesis*. (Cambridge, UK: Cambridge University Press, 2012); Nurbek Bekmurzaev, Philipp Lottholz, and Joshua Meyer, "Navigating the safety implications of doing research and being researched in Kyrgyzstan: cooperation, networks and framing," *Central Asian Survey* 37, no. 1 (2018), pp. 100–18; and Philipp Lottholz, *Post-liberal Statebuilding*.

regimes via Western foreign policies and international regulatory frameworks, capturing the global networked character of authoritarian regimes, as well as the inbuilt authoritarian and nationalist tendencies of capitalism in its global historical constitution.[40] They presuppose analytical heterodoxy rather than theoretical orthodoxy and essential contestability of notions such as "contemporary art," "civil society," or "autonomy" in social sciences and humanities.

Guided by this, art can do better than reproducing the rhetorical and moral geographies of current affairs. That art and culture becomes political tools of a state or actors aligned with the state is nothing new.[41] However, it is more convenient to critique the dubious role that state politics play through art if one can steer clear of one's own position and identify an external counterpart, be it an entity one deems bad—such as neoliberalism whose very complexity we've been trying to pin down—or a historically delineated moment such as CIA- or Soviet-sponsored art and culture during the Cold War. The moral equation argues that denouncing something as bad makes one's own position good. There is no way around understanding the actual situation of these non-Western, non-liberal places than via practical reasoning to work out what "liberal values" in art, "civil society," or "artistic autonomy" mean—without the certainty of how they should look like and function in a society.

One case is the Diriyah Biennale in Saudi Arabia. Clearly part of the state's soft power exercise to cleanse its image and enter the geopolitical arena, the biennale made

40 Philipp Lottholz, "Political Change in Post-socialist Eurasia."

41 Most famously the research on the CIA's involvement in the circulation of post-war Euro-US art, and emerging scholarship on Soviet-sponsored art and culture networks. See Rossen Djagalov, *From Internationalism to Postcolonialism: Literature and Cinema between the Second and the Third Worlds* (Cambridge, UK: Cambridge University Press, 2020); Masha Salazkina, *World Socialist Cinema: Alliances, Affinities, and Solidarities in the Global Cold War* (Oakland, CA: University of California Press, 2023).

many Western art professionals raise their eyebrows.[42] Similarly, the governmental Arts and Cultural Development Foundation of Uzbekistan has created the Aral Culture Summit not only to "art wash" the region but also to attract international investment for the region.[43] The Summit will present not only speculative art projects exploring the narrative and affective potentials of the Aral Sea, but also feature projects that bridge culture, education and the development sector.[44] Both countries attract disparaging remarks on their politics by Western critics. Both countries are undergoing liberalization and neoliberalization. Hence such initiatives present an intellectual challenge as to whether it enforces an authoritarian illiberal regime or its liberalization. For the art practitioners involved, should we dismiss the opportunity to work with bright, genuinely interested cultural workers and students who are aspiring to become social actors just because their country is not democratic enough? Does this imply a wholesale agreement with the politics of Western countries where those same practitioners participate?

A typical argument is that the government instrumentalizes art and culture to accrue symbolic capital. Stephanie Bailey offers a balanced and thoughtful account of the Diriyah Biennale that is neither blind exaltation nor quiet apology. It is worth quoting her at length:

> It's hard to tell what silence means sometimes. It doesn't necessarily mean submission, nor does it signal outright refusal. Most of the time, it just reflects

42 Andrew England, "'Bridges with everyone': how Saudi Arabia and UAE are positioning themselves for power," *Financial Times*, August 23, 2023, https://www.ft.com/content/3889c33d-4830-407c-a3f6-f9e3cfaaa35f.

43 In its Uzbek part, Aral is situated in the autonomous region of Karakalpakstan which makes up 40 percent of Uzbekistan's territory and where there was a large protest movement in 2022. See Darina Solod, "A Guide to the Violent Unrest in Uzbekistan's Karakalpakstan Region," *Open Democracy*, August 4, 2022, https://www.opendemocracy.net/en/odr/protests-karakalpakstan-uzbekistan-former-soviet/.

44 documenta Institut has been engaged in setting up a sci-fi workshop *The Future that Will Have Been* for Karakalpak youths in August 2023. See more in *Workshop report: The Future that Will Have Been*, https://www.documenta-institut.de/en/artikel/workshop-bericht-the-future-that-will-have-been.

> the reality when your life is bound by a different set of rules—whether cultural or political—than those in a Western liberal democracy. Maybe the effort to deal with parachuters projecting their geopolitical macro-narratives, rather than offering their allyship through a nuanced understanding of context, is exhausting—there are ways of entering into such discussions sensitively, after all, especially when taking into account the real liabilities that Western observers often ignore when projecting their expectations on native informants for the sake of a good story. Perhaps it is this long view that foreign critics lack when they expect to see a reflection of their own liberal values echoed back to them at events like this, or expect those on the ground to cross extant political lines, at the expense of their safety, in the interest of confirming existing biases.[45]

It seems that not only is the community of practitioners discredited for anything they have done and will achieve in such a context, but that the viability of art to have a function in a society, *au fond*, is denied.

Taking the long view, the least useful thing for cultural workers is the toxic cynicism of naval-gazing art critique. These are students, artists, cultural managers working in public and private sectors eager to learn what art can do for society and are willing to expand the space of imagination and action. And crucially, in both countries, art emerges to be an actor in civil society. One does not have

45 Stephanie Bailey, "Diriyah Biennale, between the lines," *Spike Art Magazine*, March 22, 2022, https://www.spikeartmagazine.com/articles/diriyah-biennale-between-the-lines.

to go far to exercise inductive reasoning for the "authoritarian exit" thesis that the theorist of post-liberalism John Gray made on post-totalitarian regimes, which would allow them to prop up civil society on the way to liberty and prosperity.[46] One hopes that these encounters will cultivate sophisticated liberalism(s), that may indeed overlap with but also distinguish itself from both Western and non-Western precedents.

Another case that shows the shifting baselines is China. Amidst the surging scholarship on the Belt and Road Initiative, the cultural and artistic ramifications of BRI have only slowly gained academic interest.[47] Granted, there are few cultural diplomatic considerations from the Chinese government in this largely economic and geopolitical project, if one deems the kitschy, government-sponsored Silk Road-themed gala performances are too poor to be taken into consideration, an easy culprit for exoticization and (self-)orientalization.[48] On the other hand, there is a layer of critical contemporary artists who venture into the Western regions of China, avowing to excavate and preserve local histories and epistemologies in what could be generalized as a postcolonial mode. While many working in critical contemporary art may have a categorical disdain for "propaganda art" such as Socialist Realist paintings or the themed galas gazing in the same regions, I propose a thought experiment: if China had adopted critical contemporary art in its cultural mission in the BRI, then what would critics say?[49] As much as it appears unthinkable from today's perspective, China intelligently deployed critical contemporary art

46 Of course, there can also be foreign infiltration via NGOs.
47 See, for example, the *New Silk Roads* initiative based in the University of Leiden: https://newsilkroads.info/
48 Jonathan Holslag, "The EU's 'global gateway'—an answer to China, or a dead-end?" *EU Observer*, December 1, 2021, https://euobserver.com/opinion/153678.
49 See 3.1 for a case study by Emily Verla Bovino.

in the early 2000s by supporting international exhibitions with Chinese contemporary art—an exercise of soft power that willingly assimilates critical positions. This would mark a much more insidious kind of cultural diplomacy, one that actively engages with contemporary art with its inherent progressive values and critical virtues.

Ultimately, there seems to be no coherent code of conduct when foreign liberals find state-sponsored responses to some of their political claims, but not others. What is inconvenient for them to acknowledge is that many actors in art and, more broadly, in knowledge production in the postcolonial contexts do not want to or cannot fully detach their activity from the state, as the proponents of radical decoloniality suggest, even if this state is authoritarian. For example, as postcolonial academic Alima Bissenova acknowledges, for theoreticians of decoloniality "any collaboration with state is unacceptable." However, "we, well understanding all the shortcomings of the post-colonial state, nevertheless are an inseparable part of it through the universities, grants, involvement in the activities of other state-sponsored and state-controlled institutions. Many post-colonial actors come to the scene through the state and state-initiated projects."[50] Meanwhile, China has reached a level of confidence and autonomy from economic dependency that moves beyond mere historical recrimination. Art scholars have formulated geo-specific epistemes such as "*bentu*" (native land) or calls for a "post-West" society, as in Shiming Gao's writings accompanying the Third Guangzhou Triennial titled *Farewell to Post-Colonialism*.[51]

50 Alima Bissenova, ed., *Kasakhstan: Labirinty sovremennogo postcolonialnogo discursa* (Kazakhstan: The labyrinths of the contemporary postcolonial discourse) (Almaty: Tselinny publishing, 2023), p. 35.

51 Gao Shiming, "The Dismantling and Re-Construction of Bentu ('This Land' or 'Native Land'): Contemporary Chinese Art in the Post-Colonial Context," *A New Thoughtfulness in Contemporary China: Critical Voices in Art and Aesthetics*, eds. Jörg Huber and Chuan Zhao (Bielefeld: transcript Verlag, 2011), pp. 103-20.

Due to the hidden desire of the West for controlling the meanings of postcoloniality much of these discourses do not circulate in global art discourse. Down the road, we will need to reckon with fundamental proposals about humanism that come from non-Western illiberal regimes.[52]

It might be too hasty to declare that non-liberal countries are blanketly transforming their policies to emphasize specific cultural values or to enshrine a telos between an economically and politically multipolar world with that of art produced in those countries. As we have seen, not all illiberal countries are consciously cultivating contemporary art as a form of soft power. What we do see is deep pluralism at play in the state interaction with art. At the level of the state, there is an uneven distribution of power—sometimes rising political power not matched with cultural power, sometimes building cultural power to increase economic power. We also witness deep pluralism in terms of tolerance and recognition of other cultures with different political forms at the level of the state. But is this pluralism consensual? Or in other words, do the main players in global society not only tolerate the material, cultural, ideological, and actor-type differences of deep pluralism, but also respect and even value them as expressions of diversity?[53] The effect of critique on these cultural programs in Western media, even though they might miss the mark, is sometimes escalatory. While they have all the right to do so, it fulfills a moral end exempted from political consequences, for those who stop short of understanding, let along living, the complex realities of the respective contexts. We shall not forget "No

52 Take, for example, the Islamic Biennale in Saudi Arabia or the exhibition *Ancient Sculptures: India Egypt Assyria Greece Rome* at the Chhatrapati Shivaji Maharaj Vastu Sangrahalaya museum in Mumbai. See Neil MacGregor, "An ambitious Mumbai museum project sets Indian history in a world context," *Financial Times*, December 30, 2023, https://www.ft.com/content/e14aea71-f668-46c8-aad5-4860ca17cdb0

53 Zhang and Buzan, pp. 246–71.

scientific law can determine a moral end save by deserting the principle of the interdependence of means and end."[54] Could art move up the scale of complexity and offer a way of thinking through deep pluralism, rather than just being its complacent end product? Doing so would require rigorously updating Raymond Williams's "homologous structures" or "mediation," established between the superstructure (New Right art, nation-building art, and their dynamic variations), the base (multipolarity in the economic sphere), and more expansive rationales that present us with mixed allegiances. Could the uneasy overlaps of certain state forms and contemporary art be seen as a form of experimentation to develop more nuanced understandings of publics? Could art serve as a force of practical reason amidst multiple moving targets? Could this art accord itself a renewed role of cultural diplomacy precisely when all parties are too beholden to their own unipolar interests? Could art do it without becoming bad copies of state functions? And more tantalizingly, if this art does not resemble the form of art as we know it today, how might it appear? Would it be an aesthetics of the state, covert diplomacy, pop culture, or a conjunction between tech and art?

The Museum of Contemporary Art in Antwerp (M HKA) is trying to connect pluralism at the level of states, power, and their value systems at large to a level of tangible social interaction. Riffing off the "multivectoralism"—Kazakhstan's much touted geopolitical strategy—as a model for institutional vision, they want to develop a framework based on a pragmatic, non-ideological foundation,

54 Leon Trotsky, John Dewey, and George Novack, *Their Morals and Ours: Marxist Versus Liberal Views on Morality* (New York: Merit Publishers, 1966).

that can nonetheless be embedded with a political and ethical consciousness.[55] Concretely, we can study how this is translated into their program and research: in what way is it possible to show art from or about aspects of a "enemy nation" like Russia?[56] This commitment to a functionalist institutional mission of connecting the spaces to the degree it is possible, and to intermediary and reflexive positions is both valuable and vulnerable. Of course, this is a voice from a big Western institution, and all these questions could be raised in a more paradoxical and self-reflexive critical manner. But in times of war and shrinking communication, such a moderate, alter-globalist position is itself a result of complicated work. It is perhaps not surprising that away from the Western centers, discussions are more vivid.

The Tselinny Centre of Contemporary Culture in Almaty, founded in 2018, has been a key player in promoting education, critical thinking, and curatorial practices of this kind. In the wake of the January 2022 protests, it hosted a series of talks with artists, journalists, and social scientists to think through the events. Recently, they have been organizing seminars and publications dedicated to the theories and practices of decolonization from a Central Asian perspective. They recognize that, on the one hand, Kazakhstan is a post-Soviet independent state able to represent itself in the international arena, and on the other hand, that it is dependent on global markets, regional military alliances, and ideological structures, both from the former metropole and new metropolitan centers in Europe and North America. In the words of Bissenova, "We find ourselves in

55 Nav Haq, "Preface," in *Eurasia. An Atlas,* eds. Nav Haq and Joanna Zielińska (Antwerp: Antwerp Museum van Hedendaagse Kunst Antwerpen and Jap Sam Books, 2023).

56 For many years, M HKA has had a "Eurasian" program for collecting and exhibiting art from REEE region (Russia, Eastern Europe and Eurasia), of which there has been a rather strong Russian presence. Bart De Baere, director of M HKA, has long professional and personal connections with actors of contemporary art in Russia and, in particular, he curated the 6th Moscow Biennale (2015) *How to Gather? Acting in a Center in a City in the Heart of the Island of Eurasia*, where the ideas of Eurasianism were discussed. Until the Russian invasion of Ukraine, M HKA ran a joint program with the Russian V-A-C Foundation in supporting Russian contemporary art. However, after 2022, M HKA, as many others, faced the urgency to revise its alignment with Russian artists according to the changed situation. In 2023, De Baere issued complex reservations on the current situation by claiming to "learn from Ukraine," take collective responsibility, and act against "reductive blaming" of all Russians. According to him, "conscious ways of acting might gradually open up a space again for works from the Russian cultural sphere not favored by the Kremlin"—for "Russia revisited." See Bart De Baere, "Whatever the Future Will Be, It Is Made Now," *Afterall*, (March 14, 2023), https://www.afterall.org/articles/whatever-the-future-will-be-it-is-made-now-2/.

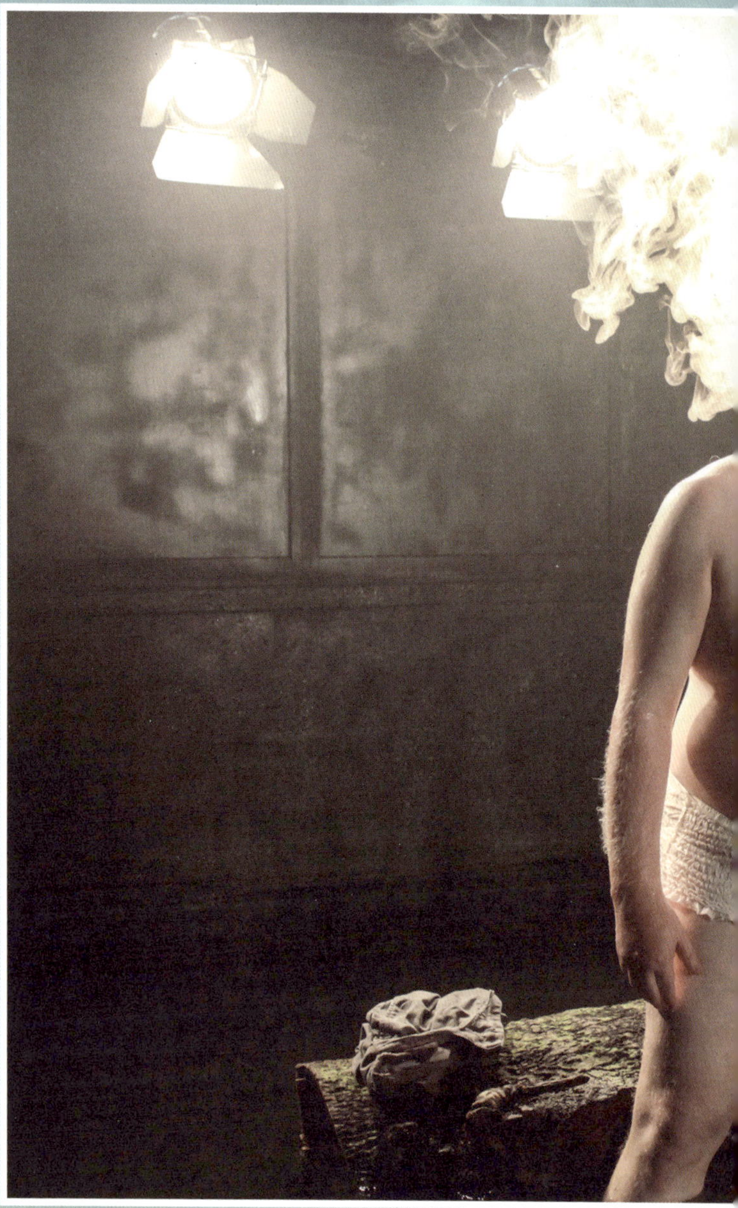

Ho Tzu Nyen
The Cloud of Unknowing, 2011
Single-channel HD projection (16:9 format, color, and 13-channel sound, 28 min), smoke machines, floodlights, show control system

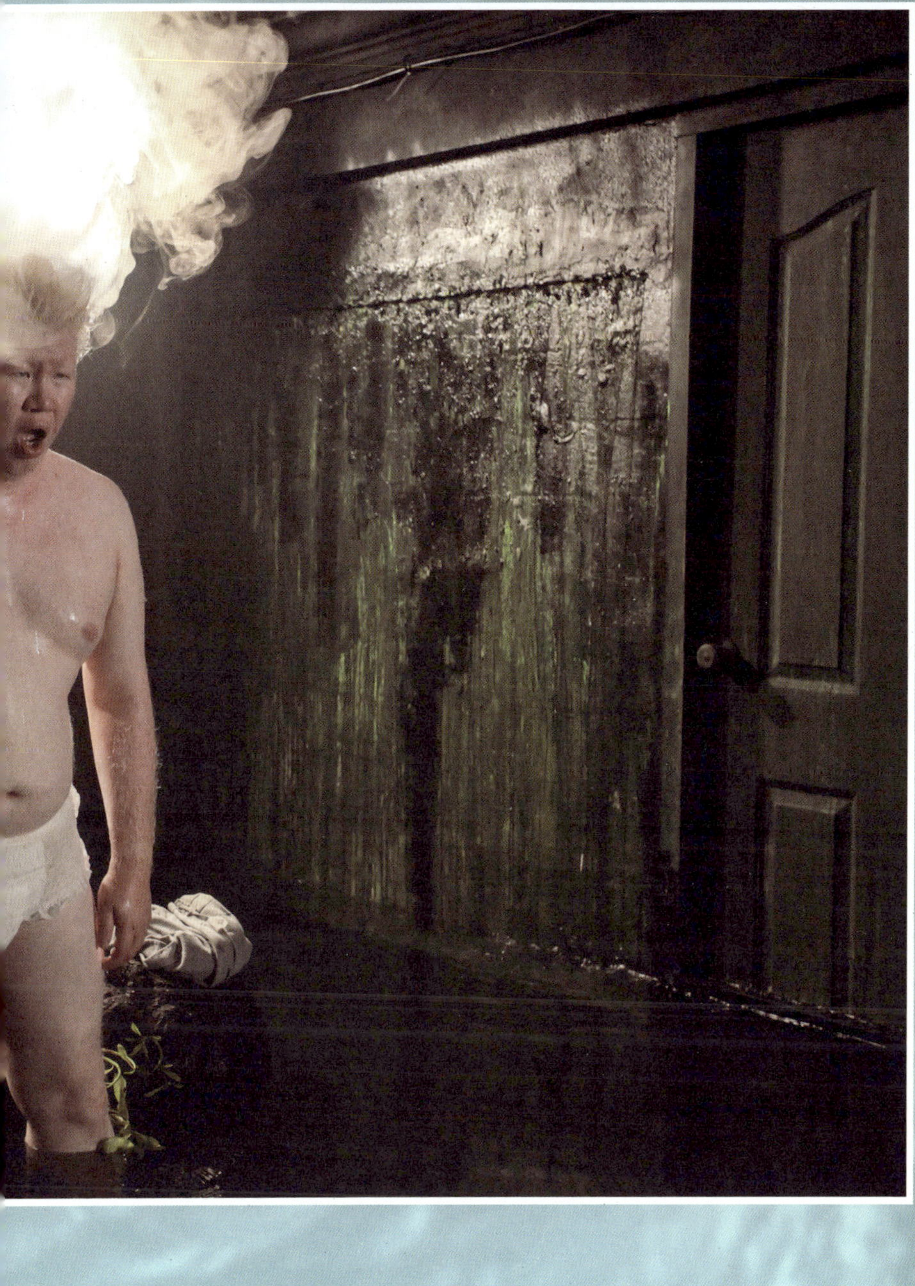

a situation of 'double coloniality' in relation to Russia and the Soviet past, when the old structures of coloniality are still alive, and in relation to the West—our already new culture and intellectual dependence on some external standards of modernity, formed in another 'context'—not ours. That is, without yet digesting, reflecting and overcoming our previous coloniality, we are already in another kind of new 'hybrid coloniality,' despite political independence."[57] Add to this economic (but not yet ideological) pressure from China, citizens of Kazakhstan are in an "inter-imperial post-colonial zone."[58] Hence the desire to declare oneself and formulate one's own position is widespread.

Since the Russian invasion of Ukraine, this need has become even stronger. In summer 2023, as part of seminars organized by Tselinny, practitioners from diverse social backgrounds engaged in vivid debates through a wide spectrum of positions ranging from the call to erase all Soviet architecture to considering the Russian language as one's own heritage that one must work through. As Madina Tlostanova puts it, there is a danger in the competition of trauma, as in a claim like "my injury is more important than yours and I should get more social capital, reparations, support." She calls for us to listen to each other, and for the understanding of one's own privileges and how they affect one's theories and practices.[59] This is a call for art practitioners and critics to leave their comfort zone of critique, positionality, and value precepts. The following chapters offer case studies that try to exemplify and extend this thinking.

57 Bissenova, *Kasakhstan*, p. 30. Translation by Nikolay Smirnov.
58 Bissenova, *Kasakhstan*, p. 13.
59 Madina Tlostanova, "Id'et sorevnovaniye travm. A nuzhno nauchit'sya slushat' drug druga" (There is a competition of injuries. But we need to learn to listen to each other), Teatr Soprotivleniya (Theater of Resistance), August 13, 2023, https://syg.ma/@resistancetheatre/madina-tlostanova-idiet-sorievnovaniie-travm-a-nuzhno-nauchitsia-slushat-drugh-drugha/.

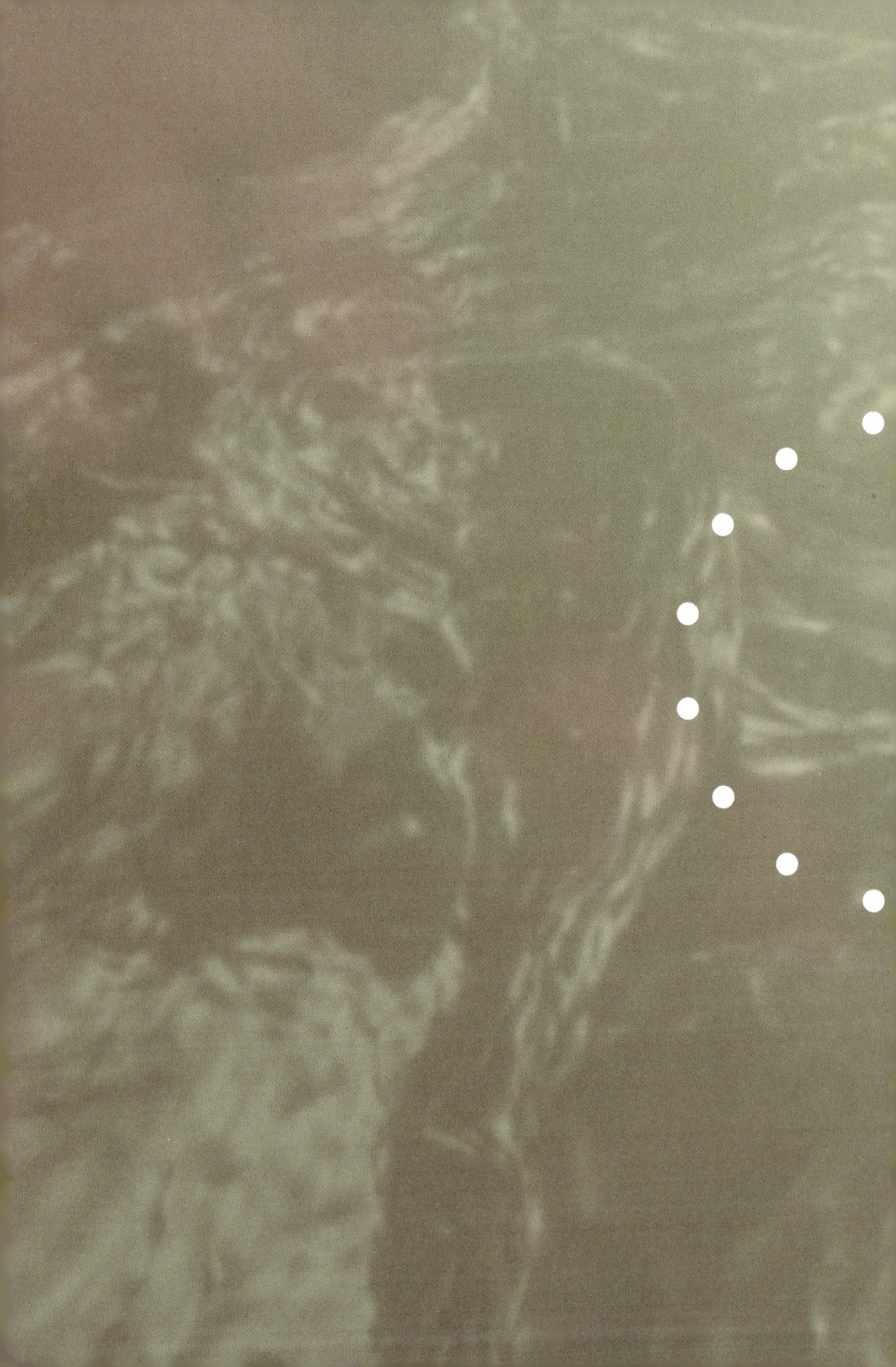

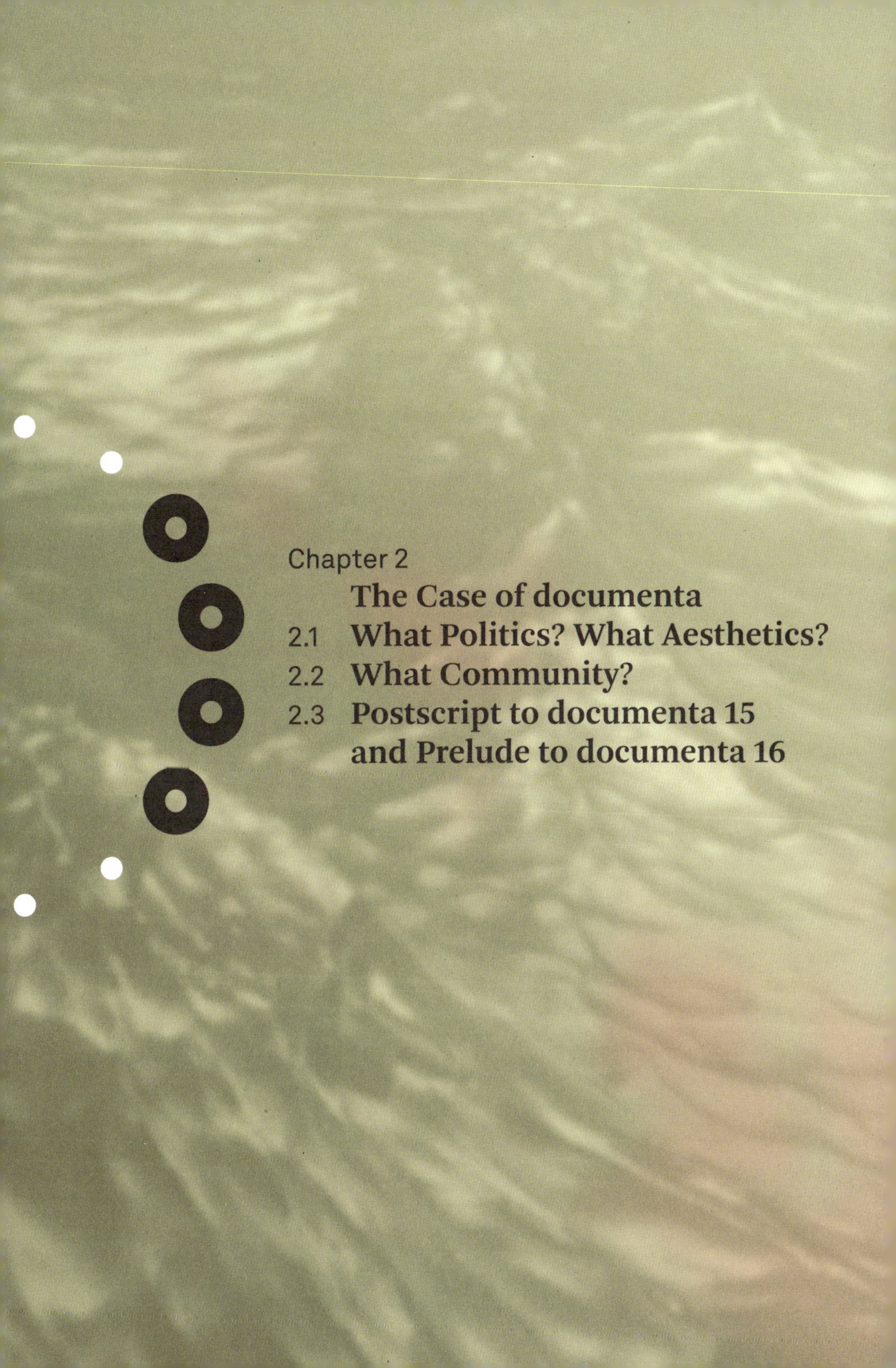

Chapter 2

The Case of documenta

Chapter 2

The Case of documenta

documenta takes place every five years in Kassel, Germany, and is one of the largest, longest running, and best-known contemporary art festivals in the Western World. According to the exhibition's five-year economic plan from 2019–2023, the budget for documenta fifteen (d15) was €42.2 million.[1] d15 (2022) welcomed over 730,000 visitors over one hundred days. The Jakarta-based artist collective ruangrupa (established in 2000) were appointed artistic directors and proposed "*lumbung*" (a term for a type of collectively managed rice barn) as a theme for the curatorial approach. The concept mobilized the term for curatorial practice to signal that modalities of collaboration, redistribution, and collective governance are key to conceptual processes and material realization of a collective that produces art and social gatherings. In the spirit of the lumbung, ruangrupa invited other artists and art collectives, primarily from the Global South, to organize the various parts of the exhibition. Initially, ruangrupa invited seventy-two artists and art collectives, which in turn invited an additional 1,500 artists, activists, and writers from their extended ecosystems to participate in the exhibition and related public programming. The announcement and unfolding of d15 was met with both celebration and contention as the global art community

1 This amount is made up of the following: admission fees €12.5 million; third-party funds and other income €4.7 million; the shareholders—the city of Kassel and the state of Hesse—€10.75 million each; and the German Federal Cultural Foundation €3.5 million. On top of that, a buffer of €5–6 million is set aside for contingencies.

and art theorists widely welcomed the curatorial format for its non-hierarchical, decentralized, and non-universalistic approach.[2] Against the backdrop of global inequalities (which are often discursively rather than materially attended to in global art projects), d15 continues the conflictual aesthetics of "biennials of resistance"[3] and seemingly enacted what David Graeber refers to as "fragments" of dispersed social, political, and economic experimentation.[4] These fragments exhibit, in part, struggles of survival and resistance where communities learn to live together in an increasingly precarious global economic system that revolves around subjection based upon national origin, ethnicity, gender, and skin color.

Following the revealing of the Yogyakarta-based collective Taring Padi's colossal work *People's Justice* (2002), in which figures evoking classical anti-Semitic stereotypes set off alarms, a cascade of events unfolded. These included: charges made by Global South artists who experienced racial and transphobic harassments in Kassel; rallies of solidarity with ruangrupa by a number of artists in documenta and beyond; and withdrawals and distancing from other documenta participants, along with the resignation of the CEO of documenta. The public, the news media, politicians, and some art critics both in Germany and across the world reacted to what happened during the exhibition. This controversy set forth a context in which such critics debated the exhibition's form, characterizing it as "DIY Chaos,"[5] "inclusive—to a fault,"[6] "without appropriate contextualization and reflection,"[7] a product of European

2 See, for example, Eyal Weizman, "In Kassel," *London Review of Books* 44, no. 15, August 4, 2022, https://www.lrb.co.uk/the-paper/v44/n15/eyal-weizman/in-kassel; Sabine Schormann, "Statement by Dr. Sabine Schormann on the deinstallment of the banner 'People's justice' by Taring Padi," documenta fifteen, June 21, 2022, https://documenta-fifteen.de/en/news/statement-by-dr-sabine-schormann-on-the-deinstallment-of-the-banner-peoples-justice-by-taring-padi/; Abhijan Toto, "Abhijan Toto and Pujita Guha for the Forest Curriculum on documenta 15," *Artforum* 61, no. 1 (September 2022), https://www.artforum.com/events/abhijan-toto-and-pujita-guha-for-the-forest-curriculum-on-documenta-15-250197/.

3 Oliver Marchart, *Conflictual Aesthetics: Artistic Activism and the Public Sphere* (London: Sternberg Press, 2019).

4 David Graeber, *Fragments of an Anarchist Anthropology* (Chicago: Prickly Paradigm Press, 2004).

5 Nadine Khalil, "The DIY Chaos of Documenta 15," *Frieze*, July 7, 2022, https://www.frieze.com/article/diy-chaos-documenta-15-2022-review.

6 Terry Smith, "DOCUMENTA 15, 2022: Collectivism and Controversy," *Artlink*, April 11, 2022, https://www.artlink.com.au/articles/4983/documenta-15-2022-collectivism-and-controversy/.

7 Jörg Heiser, "'Contested Histories': On Documenta 15," *e-flux Criticism*, June 29, 2022, https://www.e-flux.com/criticism/477463/contested-histories-on-documenta-15.

funding,[8] or even a kind of "cultural 9/11."[9] These debates, whose flames were stoked by the media frenzy, came about in a context of near-constant accusations of racism, wokeism, anti-Semitism, among others, and engendered conversations about decolonial politics, identity politics,[10] colonialism's heritage,[11] the obfuscation of the German colonial context,[12] and the role of economic, social, and cultural inequalities between artists, curators, and institutional actors and inequalities between Europe and the home countries of many of the artists.[13] As a result, critics put the future of documenta as an institution into question.[14] Just as debates over d15 calmed, documenta sixteen was already on fire. This time triggered by anti-Semitism charges levied at a member in the finding committee of documenta sixteen.

It is within the context of these contradictory reactions that I begin my inquiry. Specifically, I evaluate the infrastructures and ideologies in place that facilitated the form of d15 and continue to facilitate contemporary art practices in the Global South—a contentious term in itself. While the emergence of the term aimed to replace previous problematic terms such as "Third World" and "non-Western," the term Global South nonetheless, as Walter Mignolo writes, reinforces the premises of an unequal world order.[15] Most public debates on d15 have generally accepted the position that it exhibited art practices "from" the Global South in the Global North, however, the relation of the South to the North is far more nuanced and in need of investigation, especially in light of the public reaction to the exhibition.

8 Mohammad Salemy, "Antisemitism Is the Least of Documenta Fifteen's Problems: Let's Be Fucking Honest," *Arts of the Working Class*, June 24, 2022, https://artsoftheworkingclass.org/text/antisemitism-is-the-least-of-documenta-fifteens-problems.

9 Ingo Niermann. "Documenta 9/11?" Accessed April 18, 2023, https://ingoniermann.ch/documenta911/. It seems that the text was deleted by the author at some point, but its traces can be found here: https://momus.ca/reviewing-the-reviews-documenta-15/.

10 Daniel Ben-Ami, "Identity Politics Is Breathing New Life into Anti-Semitism," *Spiked*, July 3, 2022, https://www.spiked-online.com/2022/07/03/identity-politics-is-breathing-new-life-into-anti-semitism/

11 Eyal Weizman, "In Kassel"; Speech by Ade Darmawan (ruangrupa) in the Committee on Culture and Media, German Bundestag, July 6, 2022, documenta fifteen, July 9, 2022, https://documenta-fifteen.de/en/news/speech-by-ade-darmawan-ruangrupa-in-the-committee-on-culture-and-media-german-bundestag-july-6-2022/.

12 Hito Steyerl, "Context Is Everything, Except When It Comes to Germany," &&&, June 4, 2022, https://tripleampersand.org/context-everything-except-comes-germany/.

13 Collective letter, "We Are Angry, We Are Sad, We Are Tired, We Are United: Letter from lumbung Community—Notes—e-Flux," *e-flux Notes*, September 10, 2022, https://www.e-flux.com/notes/489580/we-are-angry-we-are-sad-we-are-tired-we-are-united-letter-from-lumbung-community; Kabir Jhala, "'Germany Has Cancelled Us': As Embattled Documenta 15 Closes, Its Curators Ruangrupa Reflect on the Exhibition—and What They Would Have Done Differently," *The Art Newspaper*, September 22, 2022, https://www.theartnewspaper.com/2022/09/22/documenta-15-closes-curators-ruangrupa-exhibition-kassel; Siddhartha Mitter, "Documenta Was a Whole Vibe. Then a Scandal Killed the Buzz," *The New York Times*, June 24, 2022, https://www.nytimes.com/2022/06/24/arts/design/documenta-review.html.

The first two sections in this chapter were written during the fermenting debates over d15, focusing on its organizational form and political intentions to investigate those nuances between the North and the South. As such, they capture the urgency for art practitioners to shape a discourse when public opinion was in freefall. In section 2.1, I reproduce an essay I originally published in *e-flux Journal* titled "What Politics? What Aesthetics?: Reflections on documenta fifteen," in which I analyze the cultural context in which the concepts of d15 were formed, the politics of showcasing art from the Global South in the Global North, and the political economy of NGO-funded art initiatives that have a developmentalist agenda. In section 2.2, I include my contribution to the publication of the highly mediated symposium *Kontroverse documenta fifteen. Hintergründe, Einordnungen und Analysen* (Controversial documenta fifteen. Background, classification and analysis) in Hamburg for the German audience, where I trace the discussions of the notion of "community" in peasant societies in Southeast and East Asia and point out what is at stake in invoking the "community" in "community art" in the Global South. Both texts look to the possibility of expressing and activating an internationalist and emancipatory politics in the arts sector in the Global North. The last text, section 2.3, is a postscript to the chapter, addressing debates on the future of documenta as the process of documenta sixteen has been under renewed public scrutiny.

The anti-Semitism debates appear to tear at what remains of the veneer of art globalization because they reveal

14 Rahel Aima and Catherine G. Wagley, "Reviewing the Reviews: Documenta 15," *Momus*, December 10, 2022, https://momus.ca/reviewing-the-reviews-documenta-15/.
15 Walter D. Mignolo, "The Global South and the World Dis/Order," *Journal of Anthropological Research* 67, no. 2 (July 2011), pp. 165–88, https://doi.org/10.3998/jar.0521004.0067.202.

fundamental divergences in perspectives (unlike the presented unipolar liberalism) and break apart previously held assumptions of a rather universal "cosmopolitanism." However, to only learn this from what transpired at Kassel is not enough. In what follows, I unpack components that are taken for granted in the liberal alignment discussed in Chapter 1, such as the individual, community, civil society, and notions of progress, and map them onto the partially disjointed realities across the Global North and South that cause some of the fundamental misreadings of d15. Along the way, I take note of practical reasonings (by which I mean pragmatic forms of inquiry that do not trade on preset value judgements) of institution-building from the Global South that tease out ways to (paradoxically) come to the defense of documenta—not in its former image as a bastion of art in a globalized world, but as an institutional force to be reckoned with in a post-globalization world.

59

2.1

What Politics? What Aesthetics?

Whether d15 should be defended is not the question. The question is how it can be defended in a way that also allows for a constructive critique of the exhibition.

A local group had already levied accusations of anti-Semitism on Palestinian participants in d15 four months before the exhibition opened, which quickly escalated to become a national news story, and was later made real by the actual exhibition. This cast dark clouds over what is arguably the world's largest contemporary art exhibition and culminated with documenta's decision in June to remove a banner made by the Indonesian collective Taring Padi depicting the political violence of the Suharto regime, in which the public noticed anti-Semitic caricatures. Prior to this, a cascade of events had been fermenting for months. These include a January blog post[1] by a small Kassel-based organization decrying members of the Palestinian collective The Question of Funding as anti-Semitic; a cancelled series of public debates on anti-Semitism and racism in May; various instances of inadequate crisis management by documenta; and before the opening, the exhibition space of the Palestinian collective was vandalized with a cryptic death threat. All the while, pressure was building up at the top levels of German politics, where the Green cultural

1 "Documenta fifteen: Antizionismus und Antisemitismus im lumbung," *bga-kassel* (blog), January 7, 2022, https://bgakasselblog.wordpress.com/2022/01/07/documenta-fifteen-antizionismus-und-antisemitismus-im-lumbung/.

minister was involved in mitigating the scandal since the first allegation.

Before the conflicts had grown to a fever pitch, under the theme of "lumbung," a metaphor for sharing, commons, solidarity, gift giving, and mutual aid, the exhibition venues were transformed into buzzing showcases of art and activism, collaborative community-building processes, and various archival projects that are revisited and kept alive. The accompanying programming, from talks to DJ sets, from shared meals to cleansing rituals, extended the gesture of hospitality to the audience and lent the event a festive atmosphere. The media was split between homing in on perceived instances of anti-Semitism (such as the German weekly *Der Spiegel*'s overstatement of "Antisemita 15"[2]) and cheerleading for the "good vibes" provided by ruangrupa's inclusive exhibition concept.

It is regrettable that the potential for anti-Semitic content was not mitigated—and could not be—as multiple parties kept talking over each other. While some[3] referred to the specific German historical burden of preventing hate speech, others[4] pointed to the perpetuation of racial prejudice, counter-charging the initial allegations of anti-Semitism as racist and made in bad faith—which, of course, they were. But it is even more regrettable to see that in this febrile and frequent hostility in the media, when faced with political headwinds, art practitioners, curators, managers, and the public all turned on one another. No one came away from the turmoil unscathed. That is, except for those on the far-right clamoring for the defunding of this event in the

2 Sascha Lobo, "Willkommen auf der Antisemita 15," *Der Spiegel*, June 6, 2022, https://www.spiegel.de/netzwelt/netzpolitik/sascha-lobo-ueber-den-documenta-skandal-willkommen-bei-der-antisemita-a-424a0c6f-ec04-4158-92be-9ab8f03f17ad.

3 See, for example, "Zentralrat der Juden: Bei Documenta nicht berücksichtigt—Kritik an Roth," *Monopol*, April 28, 2022, https://www.monopol-magazin.de/zentralrat-der-juden-bei-documenta-nicht-beruecksichtigt-kritik-roth.

4 See, for example, Elke Buhr's commentary in the beginning of the allegation, "Antisemitismus-Polemik gegen die Documenta geht nach hinten los," *Monopol*, January 13, 2022, https://www.monopol-magazin.de/antisemitismus-polemik-gegen-die-documenta-geht-nach-hinten-los.

future, who have seen massive dividends for their positions. It is perhaps not altogether surprising that international leftist art critics have broadly aligned with curators and artists against what is considered a German bureaucratic managerial machine that enforces what it purports to be benevolent censorship. The media's simplistic deployment of the term "Global South" to homogenize disparate realities and serve as a placeholder in a political morality play—in which the West is always already cast as the baddie—are rightly subject to critique.[5] It is easier, evidently, to take an antiestablishment view than to consider the difficulties of building an institution that can endure calamities of public opinion and have societal impact. Many from the "Global South" intimately know how important it is to build and maintain institutions. Navigating between and working with various governmental actors, representatives of the private sector, foreign funding bodies, and diverse community actors is difficult but extends a much-needed lifeline to initiatives in the "Global South." When so much is at stake in what is both a crisis of the institution and of the hitherto hegemonic "Global North," could the South champion decolonization by putting its know-how into a spirited defense of institutions? Could this be done, if only to acknowledge that it is possible to build something—something institutional—together, despite considerable geopolitical and ideological differences? How could this be done with defiance, to rise above being cast as the permanently victimized junior partner? Admittedly, this is a counterintuitive, perhaps even an unfashionable and untimely ask.

5 Florian Cramer made a detailed map of the German media and the political factions behind the documenta debates in his contribution to the symposium "(un)Common Grounds: Reflecting on documenta fifteen" hosted by the gallery Framer Framed, Amsterdam, on September 23, 2022. See "Symposium: (un)Common Grounds," *framerframed.nl*, https://framerframed.nl/en/projecten/uncommon-grounds-reflecting-on-documenta-fifteen/.

The cognitive dissonance between perceptions of reality from the North and South runs deep. One might therefore be forgiven for assuming that the antiestablishment thrust of d15 issues from an anti-Western, counter-hegemonic framework, as cultural commentators in Germany have noted with an air of haughty disapproval.

Upon first seeing the exhibits at d15, I immediately thought that the World Social Forum must have been the curatorial reference for this documenta. An umbrella for the alter-globalization movement with the bold claim that "Another World Is Possible," the annual World Social Forum, founded in 2001, hosted diverse groups of activists from worker, peasant, transgender, Indigenous, and peace movements, deliberately accompanied by an art and culture program, which was visited by 150,000 people at the Forum's peak in the mid-2000s. Where else would one expect to see (a bit of a throwback to) so many artistic and cultural manifestations of grassroots activism and organized causes across the world? But when invited by the World Social Forum to present their work in 2004, ruangrupa declined the offer by saying: It's too political for us.

A constructive critique might take the transnationalization of political alignments and the instrumentalization of the arts in the Global South today as its starting point, rather than an end to conversation.

The Socioeconomic Context

ruangrupa is a collective that was established in 2000, two years after the collapse of Indonesia's Suharto regime and the concomitant New Order that reigned from 1966 to 1998 and deliberately stymied mass participation in the political process. Originally a small group of artists who wanted to open a meeting space to engage with diverse artistic practices, ruangrupa has deftly navigated between foreign funding bodies, local government agencies, and the private sector to support their activities which include video festivals, public art projects, publishing, and art education. They received a large sum of money from the Ford Foundation around 2018, which led to a schism in the collective. Those who remained in the collective used the money to build a space and cultural infrastructure in Jakarta. Clearly, foreign donors not only carry the danger of the "NGO-ization" of the art sector in the Global South,[6] but also risk presenting artists and art organizations in increasingly interchangeable ways, whereby an art collective is asked to solve a social issue.[7] ruangrupa's approach to institutions could be described as "tactical," combining activism and populism while trying to find their own place in the food chain of sponsors.[8] One could argue that this dilemma informs a practice that transcends the critique of the instrumentalization of art, a critique rehearsed ad nauseam in Western art discourse, and focuses instead on the embeddedness of art in society. But when asked to curate documenta, ruangrupa had to ask themselves how to carve out a place for this approach in the "hegemonic center" of the artworld.

The curatorial premise for the exhibition, "lumbung," refers to Indonesian rice barns where surplus crops are stored,

6 Hanan Toukan interprets the depoliticizing effects of the "NGO-ization" of society as resulting from the professionalization of activism and a shift from a grassroots "political society" to a professionalized elite "civil society." See Hanan Toukan, "On Being The Other in Post-Civil War Lebanon: Aid and the Politics of Art in Processes of Contemporary Cultural Production," *Arab Studies Journal* 18, no. 1 (Spring 2010), pp. 118–61. See also Minna Valjakka, "Arts and Ecosystems: Building Towards Regeneration of 'Cultural Resilience' in Indonesia," *Forces of Art: Perspectives from a Changing World*, eds. Carin Kuoni, Jordi Baltà Portolés, Nora N. Khan and Serubiri Moses (Amsterdam: Valiz, 2021).

7 See, for example, Justin Malachowski's study on documenta fifteen member El Warcha: "Staging Arts in the Historic City: Development Funding, Social Media Images, and Tunisia's Contemporary Public Art Scene," *Journal of City and Society*, vol. 34, issue 2–3, pp. 147–225, 2022.

8 David Teh, "Who Cares a Lot? Ruangrupa as Curatorship," *Afterall*, no. 30 (Summer 2012), https://www.afterall.org/articles/who-cares-a-lot-ruangrupa-as-curatorship/.

which are then redistributed in times of need. The term is held up as a paradigm of collective practice and serves as a model for ruangrupa's modus operandi of resource allocation and sharing among the participating artists and surrounding society. However, the use of the concept is not devoid of self-exoticization, and the image of community life and self-governance is not as simple, or simply good, as it seems. lumbung also symbolizes the perennial issue of food insecurity, with Indonesians caught between the aspiration for self-sufficiency and international marketization and development. The moral order of sharing and exchange through lumbung coexisted with centralized management of decentralized lumbungs in historical empires such as Ubud. Later, the imperative for self-sufficiency was as much on the political agenda of Suharto's government as in now-president Jokowi's development of a national food reserve called "Lumbung Pangan Nasional."[9] The latter emerged to manage the disastrous realities caused by global food conglomerates and development agencies. But there is more to the curatorial use of lumbung than an uncomfortable terminological affinity with the populists in power. Marxian cultural theorists will rightly recognize the incorporation of a residual practice (communal culture based on surplus) into a dominant system of practices and values (as rhetoric serving neoliberal statecraft).[10]

There is nothing natural, spontaneous, or, for lack of a better word, innocent about public and community art in Indonesia. The brief episode of Keimin Bunka Shidoso

9 Lula Lasminingrat and Efriza Efriza, "The Development of National Food Estate: The Indonesian Food Crisis Anticipation Strategy," *Jurnal Pertahanan & Bela Negara* 10, no. 3 (2020), pp. 229–48. See also an analysis on the deployment of lumbung, both historical and in policy speak, in Graeme MacRae and Thomas Reuter, "Lumbung Nation," *Indonesia and the Malay World* 48, no. 142 (December 2020), pp. 338–58.

10 See, for example, Raymond Williams, "Base and Superstructure in Marxist Cultural Theory," *New Left Review*, no. 82 (November/December 1973), https://newleftreview.org/issues/i82/articles/raymond-williams-base-and-superstructure-in-marxist-cultural-theory.

(KBS, literally "Institute for People's Education and Cultural Guidance" and popularly known as "cultural center") formed part of the propaganda machine during the Japanese occupation of Indonesia from 1942 to 1945 and has left a legacy in modern art history. The Japanese pursued three propaganda objectives that left an imprint on Javanese art. Locals were encouraged to engage in artistic practices that emanated from everyday life, to foster public involvement, and to exhibit in places easily accessible to the public. In this vein, Takashi Kono, graphic designer and supervisor of the Fine Art department of KBS, contended that art "should not be above but right in the middle of society."[11] Now, as ever, one needs to articulate what collectivity means and be clear-headed about co-optation.

Other Indonesian traditions of collectivism harkening back to the pre-independence 1930s include *gotong-royong* (mutual cooperation) and *sanggar*, a collective space where members share their learning experiences under the auspices of a mentor.[12] The group Seniman Indonesia Muda (SIM, founded in 1946) played a prominent role in popularizing sanggar, becoming a "national model" for artist collectives in Indonesia. The key difference between sanggar and more conventional masterclasses and workshops in the Western tradition is the centrality of political discussion, if not of indoctrination,[13] that helped to promote the anti-colonial agenda, both in its nationalist and leftist iterations. In this sense, the sanggar model is closer in form to the Artists' Union of the USSR, which arose at approximately the same time.

11 See, for example, Antariksa, "Cross-Cultural Counterparts: The Role of Keimin Bunka Shidosho in Indonesian Art, 1942–1945," in *Tsuyoshi Ozawa: The Return of Painter F*, eds. Keiko Toyoda and Fumi Toyoda (Tokyo: Shiseido, 2015), English translation available from Nusantara archive, https://www.heath.tw/nml-article/cross-cultural-counterparts-the-role-of-keimin-bunka-shidosho-in-indonesian-art-1942-1945/?lang=en.

12 Agung Hujatnika and Almira Belinda Zainsjah, "Artist Collectives in Post-1998 Indonesia: Resurgence, or a Turn (?)," International Conference on Aesthetics and the Sciences of Art (AESCIART), published in *Art Creation, Mediation, and Reception in the 21st Century Indonesia* (Bandung: Bandung Institute of Technology, 2020), pp. 256–63.

13 Claire Holt, *Art in Indonesia: Continuities and Change* (Ithaca, NY: Cornell University Press, 1967).

Another key feature of sanggar is the collective production of art. During the authoritarian era of the New Order, the formation of art collectives was prevalent, but they were strongly depoliticized, even as they exalted their commitment to a modern understanding of nationhood. The sanggar system of training was replaced by professionalizing art academies and eventually transformed into a mere space to study or produce paintings together.[14] Since 1998, new "alternative" models of collective production have proliferated, growing out of the *reformasi* mindset and its liberal and individualistic tendencies that resonated with an era that was neoliberal in its economic outlook and postmodern in its aesthetic sensibilities. Reminiscences of the sanggar or New Order hierarchical academic models can be seen in cases where a senior artist (usually the founder) acts as a "mentor" to educate or guide young artists.

ruangrupa's self-management, although aiming to overcome vertical authority in favor of horizontal structures, has fallen victim to the siren song of hierarchical organization.[15] The group owes something to the representational logic of the New Order, practicing a hotchpotch of activism and populism.[16] At the same time, however, the instrumentalization of art and its collective coproduction conjure the original sanggar spirit. Like lumbung, sanggar constitutes a peculiar hybrid of artistic autonomy and social responsibility that emerges from specific historic and political conditions. The conceptual duality of these notions means that the artistic activities can be both antagonistic and ameliorative.[17]

14 Hujatnika and Zainsjah, "Artist Collectives in Post-1998 Indonesia."
15 Valjakka, "Arts and Ecosystems."
16 Teh, "Who Cares a Lot?"
17 Elly Kent, "The History of Conscious Collectivity Behind Ruangrupa," *ArtReview Asia*, July 6, 2022, https://artreview.com/the-history-of-conscious-collectivity-behind-ruangrupa/.

What Politics? What Aesthetics?

If the roots and operations of collectives in the Global South merit more attention, the ways in which they become projections of politics for the consumption of audiences in the Global North also require further investigation. The transformation of community-based, collective, and participatory art from a formal principle to a method for the merging of art and politics remains in need of sustained inquiry. As Claire Bishop described in a talk reflecting on her 2012 book *Artificial Hells: Participatory Art and the Politics of Spectatorship*, the kind of participatory art she set out to criticize abandoned politics for representation. In other words, faced with a perceived political gridlock in the late 1990s and early 2000s, artists transposed political discourses and practices onto the field of art and its adjacent institutions. On the other hand, later artistic practices and social movements tended to pick up elements of participatory, community-based, but also relational art in support of political activism (Occupy Wall Street, Black Lives Matter, Gilets Jaunes, environmental activism, the Estallido Social protests in Chile, etc.).[18] Bishop's reflections outline the different modalities of collective and community-based art in the West, channeling Walter Benjamin's oft-cited distinction between the "aestheticization of politics" and the "politicization of aesthetics."[19]

From a perspective from the Global South, perhaps the best one could have hoped for from this documenta was an energizing "anti-aesthetics of anti-politics" that would celebrate the efficacy of art and the positive sense of

18 See Florian Malzacher, conversation with Claire Bishop, et. al., "XIV: Audience as Allies, Witnesses, and Enemies (Claire Bishop, Tania Bruguera, Ann Liv Young & Florian Malzacher)," *Art of Assembly* (podcast), March 28, 2022, https://art-of-assembly.net/podcast/xiv-audience-as-allies-witnesses-and-enemies-claire-bishop-tania-bruguera-ann-liv-young-florian-malzacher/.

19 Walter Benjamin, "The Work of Art in the Age of Mechanical Reproduction," *Illuminations*, ed. Hannah Arendt, trans. Harry Zohn (New York: Schocken Books, 1969).

"anti-politics."[20] The World Social Forum has vanished into relative insignificance mostly because of global socioeconomic transformations and the lack of adequate institutional fora to articulate protest. What remains of the original impetus can be observed at documenta, an institution that has historically reflected on the social function of art, but has also functioned as a conduit for art-driven internationalist politics (paving the way for the "First Transnational," as Peter Osborne wryly termed it).[21]

When institutions in the Global North showcase contemporary art from the Global South, sometimes mediated by curators from the Global South, there is a tendency to abide too readily to the idea that the separation of art and (everyday) culture is completely irrelevant to artistic discourses in the Global South.[22] Projecting the solution to the problem of art's social function on an absolute "other" creates a convenient shortcut to bypass the issue. Typically, institutional programs take the form of proposing either an immanent synthesis, in which art is defined either in utilitarian terms within a given society, or as a transcendental medium, if not to say a spiritual force that possesses agency within everyday life (see the over-exhibition of rituals at documenta). Regardless of the form that is emphasized in individual cases, such artworks are presented as fully incommensurable within the logic of autonomous art associated with the Global North, thereby foreclosing any political or even aesthetic critique based on distinctions between art and nonart. At the same time, art from the Global South is not necessarily framed as an

20 The positive sense of "anti-politics" was manifested by Václav Havel, as "one of the ways of seeking and achieving meaningful lives, of protecting them and serving them" beyond the technology of power and manipulation. Quoted in Michael Welton, "Václav Havel and the Power of the Powerless," *Counterpunch*, February 26, 2016, https://www.counterpunch.org/2016/02/26/vaclav-havel-and-the-power-of-the-powerless/.

21 Peter Osborne, *Anywhere or Not at All: Philosophy of Contemporary Art* (London and New York: Verso, 2013).

22 See Juliane Rebentisch, "Autonomie? Autonomie! Ästhetische Erfahrung heute," *Ästhetische Erfahrung: Gegenstände, Konzepte, Geschichtlichkeit*, ed. Sonderforschungsbereich 626 (Berlin: FU Berlin, 2006); See also *Antinomies of Art and Culture: Modernity, Postmodernity, Contemporaneity*, eds. Terry Smith, Okwui Enwezor, and Nancy Condee (Durham, NC: Duke University Press, 2009).

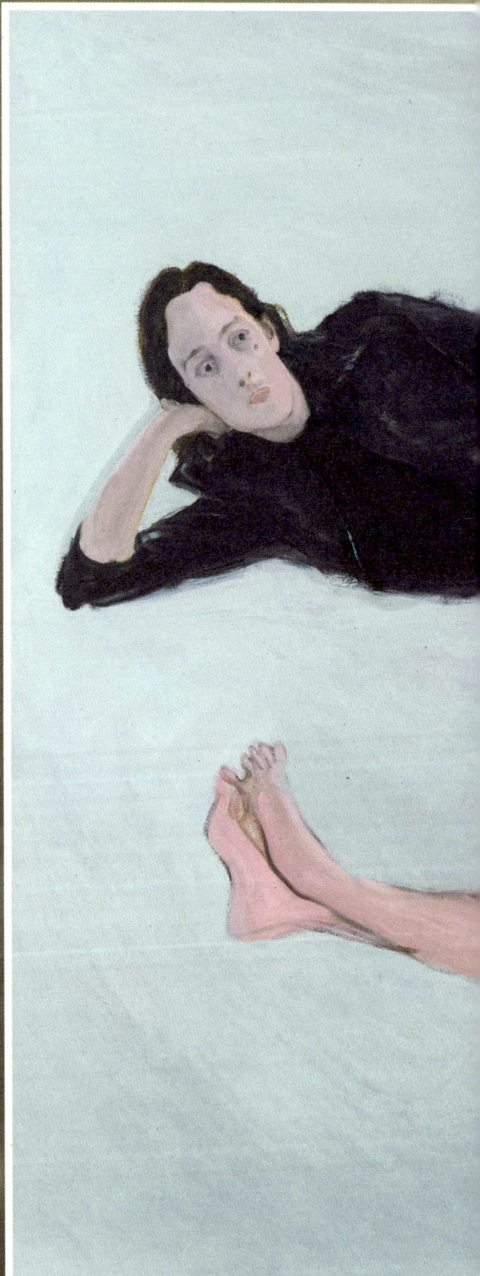

Xinyi Cheng
Midday Troubles, 2021
Oil on linen, 160 × 200 cm

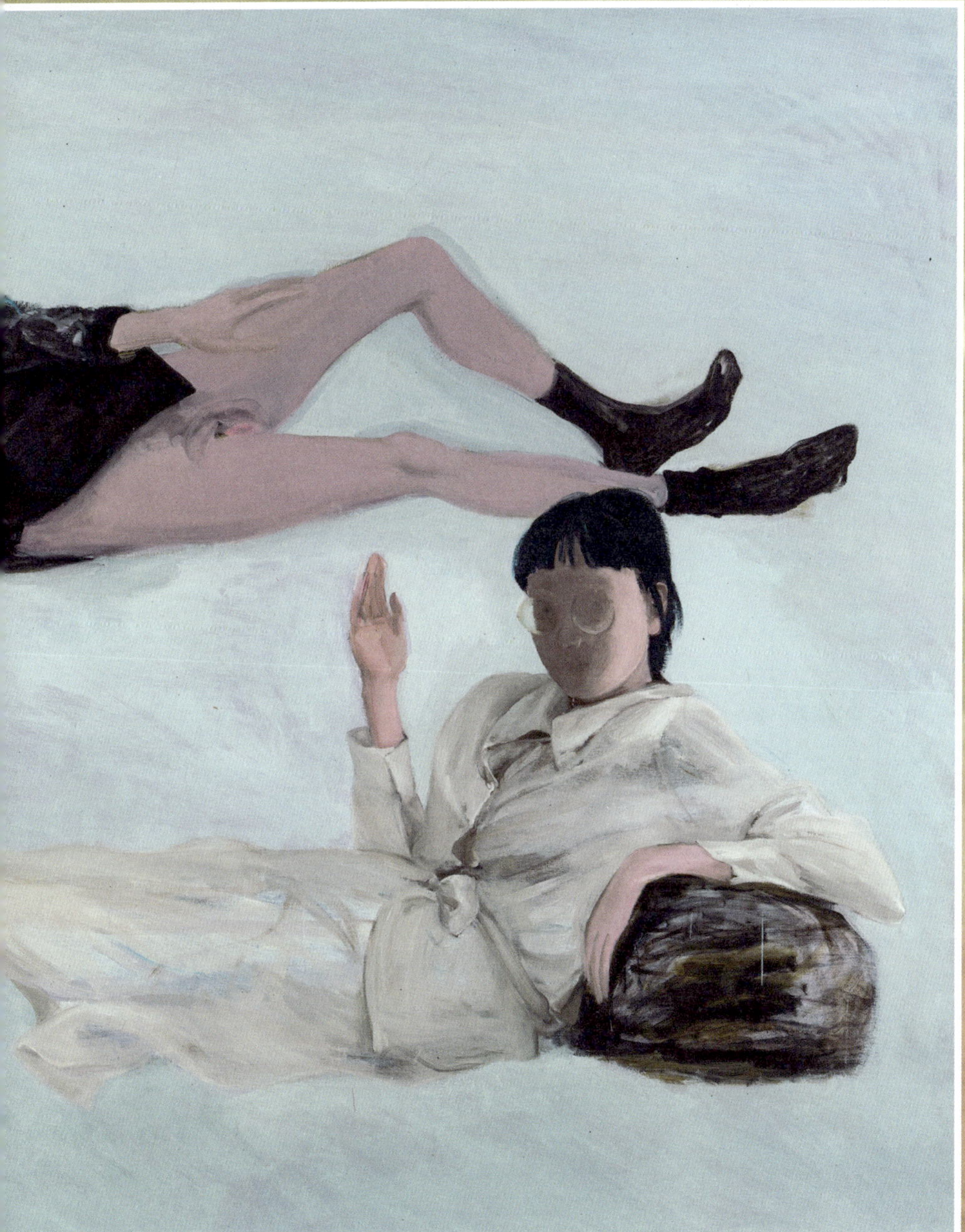

intentional and radical counterpoint to depoliticized global art, but rather as integrated social practice, with individual artists and collectives supposedly representing the tenets of "their culture."

Arguably, the greatest opportunity inherent in this documenta was to go beyond such sterile oppositions and to encourage the practice, and not just the display, of different ways of doing and making art and culture. Toward these ends, ruangrupa incorporated the thriving ecosystem of local—often small—social and art initiatives into its "*ekosistem*" and offered space for them to work, network, and create programs along with the invited artists and groups. Dynamo Windrad, a local Kassel football club with strong leftist leanings, has long been offering political education alongside its sports activities, working with migrant children for example. In this spirit, d15 hosted a "Fussballalla" event to coincide with the UEFA European Football Championship in 2021, collaborating with Dynamo to put together a program for the exhibition. However, it was hard to break through the wall of scandal and outrage surrounding the latest edition of documenta to offer something meaningful to the crowds usually drawn to Dynamo games. By all means, the football club has already cultivated a well-functioning ecosystem that is both social and artistic; d15 aspired to achieve something similar (with added artistic elements) but was not geared towards long-term commitment. As part of d15, artists could be led to draw inspiration from Dynamo's negotiation with political parties for funding, not just piggyback on its successes and subsume it into the art machine. In return, Dynamo stood to benefit from entering exchanges with other initiatives present in Kassel. Neither happened nearly enough. At d15, even those initiated by those coming from the Global South, interactions were in short supply.

Those intent on learning from non-Western operational models would be well advised to immerse themselves in the context in which they originated. One example of artists operating beyond the art machine is Jatiwangi art Factory based in rural West Java, which has reanimated a local clay roof tile factory, successfully keeping it afloat for more than twenty years. In addition, it established a practice of making music with clay tiles. With local and international support, the collective has opened a terracotta museum and art biennial, integrated the music program into local school curricula, and hosted spectacular live performances. Jatiwangi's presentation at documenta was a clever mix of artistic installations, interactive projects, and performance, where the audience was invited to join in the celebration of grassroots DIY creativity. However, from a curatorial point of view, one might object that if the stated point of the exhibition was to deliver more than moments of collective elation, then the curators should have provided an account of how Jatiwangi art Factory juggles small-scale grassroots creativity and large-scale municipal government and international NGOs. Here, things may not be all that joyful after all. Does a public oath to protect Jatiwangi culture and cultivate clay sworn by local political leaders and repeated by thousands of villagers and students really lend itself to being a paragon of emancipatory politics?[23] And if that's the price to pay for collective self-empowerment, are there any lessons from this experiment that practitioners elsewhere might heed?

For starters, practitioners in Germany, or anywhere else in the more developed parts of the world, should learn not to take their cultural funding for granted. Indeed, given the multiple crises engulfing Western societies today, even in Germany art funding may not be sustainable at current levels in the long run. Demonstrating one's own social relevance and tapping into alternative funding sources, whether political, developmental, private, or otherwise, are surely skills that will come in handy. As will be learning to anticipate the compromises that different types of funding entail. Add to that a healthy distance from the more excessive outgrowths of the puritanical morality that, over the last decade or so, has made significant inroads into the artworld.[24] Emancipatory politics could be possible even under compromised funding conditions if one is articulate about one's own politics and contradictions. The critique is a means to an end—a horizon of progressive politics, not an end in itself.

Money and What to Do With It

There is a recognizable ecosystemic turn in organizational and curatorial practices today. Ecosystems strive to structurally integrate different "stakeholders" including artists, audiences, and their wider communities, administrators, and curators, as well as infrastructures. Writings

23 See a portrait of the collective published on documenta's YouTube channel, which was also on display in the exhibition: Jatiwangi art Factory, "Introducing the lumbung members: Jatiwangi art Factory," YouTube video, 33:43 min., uploaded by documenta fifteen, April 23, 2021, https://www.youtube.com/watch?v=S9SRLhyYmzs.

24 Ghalya Saadawi has made a comprehensive exposition on the "critical virtue" of art with which art reproduces itself while economically and ideologically lubricating capitalism. See Ghalya Saadawi, "Vapid Virtues, Real Stakes," *Between the Material and the Possible*, ed. Bassam El Baroni (London: Sternberg Press, 2022). See also Victoria Ivanova's analysis of art as a new container for the liberal subject of human rights: "Two Lives, One Order," *The Draft* (blog), June 2014, https://barddraft.wordpress.com/wp-content/uploads/2015/01/ivanova.pdf. An interesting critique of this was also made by Strike MoMA, arguing that social movements in the art sector cannot aspire to "purity." They wrote: "No one is pure in a colonized world. We all live by our contradictions. Working at MoMA and disgusted with MoMA? Being an artist and hating the art system? Teaching at a university and wanting to tear it all down? Studying freedom in college while you go deeper into debt? Struggling to pay rent but displacing someone else? A Ford Fellow who protests the Ford Foundation? Oppressed but also contributing to the oppression of others? This is the entangled dystopia of our present. We can see contradictions as impediments and be consumed by frustration, ambivalence, and despair, or we can acknowledge and heighten them. Quiet forms of subversion, deep conversations, mobilizations, large and small: each act we take further undermines the principles that sustain MoMA." Strike MoMA, "Strike MoMA: Framework and Terms for Struggle," *Decolonial Hacker*, April 8, 2021, https://decolonialhacker.org/article/framework-and-terms-for-struggle-strike-moma.

on ecosystems thinking have proliferated since the 1960s, most notably in the wake of "systems ecology" championed by, among others, the biologist Eugene Odum. Key elements in this development were the rise of eco-energetics (the analysis of functional attributes like flows of matter and energy), efforts at resource conservation, comprehensive recycling systems, and a broader awareness of the dynamics of ecosystems. In the 1980s and '90s, ecosystem studies shifted from a descriptive to a more prescriptive regime, especially as far as resilience, sustainability, and a new ethics of preservation were concerned in spheres such as business and technological innovations. This is not surprising, given the cybernetic undertones of the term "ecosystem" and the techno-social managerial imaginaries inherent in it. In arts and culture, one finds David Moss's "ecosystem-based arts research" and recent calls to conceive of museums as ecosystems, for example the Taipei Biennial in 2018, *Post-Nature—A Museum as an Ecosystem*.[25]

By enumerating the different actors within the field of art, ecosystem thinking is supposed to help adjust and improve the system. Concretely, however, it is often aimed at a more or less comfortable form of artistic survival in places lacking the appropriate infrastructure. ruangrupa cofounder Ade Darmawan explains the role of self-organized art collectives in this way: "In the absence of formal art infrastructure, they work to improve the local system. They attempt an ideal system ... Artistic strategies are developed in accordance with the ecosystem in which the initiative of artists lives."[26]

25 Ian David Moss, "An Ecosystem-Based Approach to Arts Research," *Fractured Atlas* (blog), October 17, 2011, https://blog.fracturedatlas.org/an-ecosystem-based-approach-to-arts-research-e95cbc0946fe; and "Post-Nature: A Museum as an Ecosystem," *Taipei Biennial*, website, https://www.taipeibiennial.org/2018/?lang=en

26 Quoted in Nuraini Juliastuti, "Ruangrupa: A Conversation on Horizontal Organisation," *Afterall*, no. 30 (Summer 2012), https://www.afterall.org/articles/ruangrupa-a-conversation-on-horizontal-organisation/.

On a slightly bigger scale, the art organization Koalisi Seni (Indonesian Art Coalition) is working directly within legal and administrative spheres to promote (and ratify) the goal of a "healthy" or "balanced" art ecosystem.[27] Policy papers from cultural politicians and legislative texts in Indonesia teem with "ecosystem" terminology. For example, Law No. 5/2017 on the Advancement of Culture discusses the role of cultural ecosystems (*ekosistem Kebudayaan*) at length.[28] The current left-leaning cultural minister has injected terms such as "participation," "empowerment," and "social entrepreneurship" into his policy dispensations, all the while diminishing the room to maneuver for artistic initiatives and cultural organizations.

Talk of ecosystems can be an exercise in shrewd political PR as much as it can point to a conceptual edifice built on sheer material necessity. All too often, the use of the term by the curators at d15 mistook one for the other. Several endogenous initiatives and ecosystems on display in Kassel came into being in places where infrastructural development was lagging, making it necessary to assemble the resources needed for cultural production under conditions of scarcity. But now, bolstered by generous funding from d15, such initiatives are faced with the unnerving question of what to do with this money.

d15's experiments and reconfigurations did not occur in a vacuum. They blossomed, admittedly on a smaller scale, under such monikers as "infrastructural critique," "para-institutions,"[29] "translocal organizations,"[30] "alter-institutional and para-institutional organizations,"[31] and

27 Valjakka, "Arts and Ecosystems."
28 Indonesia, *Undang-Undang Nomor 5 tahun 2017 tentang pemajuan kebudayaan* (Law of the Republic of Indonesia Number 5 of 2017, Regarding Advancement of Culture), http://kebudayaan.kemdikbud.go.id/wp-content/uploads/2017/12/Undang-Undang-No-5-Tahun-2017-tentang-Pemajuan-Kebudayaan.pdf.
29 Marina Vishmidt, "Between Not Everything and Not Nothing: Cuts Towards Infrastructural Critique," *Former West: Art and the Contemporary After 1989*, ed. Maria Hlavajova and Simon Sheikh (Cambridge, MA: MIT Press, 2017); and Vishmidt, "Only as Self-Relating Negativity: Infrastructure and Critique," *Journal of Science and Technology of the Arts* 13, no. 3 (2017), pp. 13–24. See also Tom Holert, *Knowledge Beside Itself: Contemporary Art's Epistemic Politics* (London: Sternberg Press, 2020).
30 Coined by Marion von Osten. See "Trans-Local, Post-Disciplinary Organizational Practice: A Conversation between Binna Choi and Marion von Osten," *Cluster: Dialectionary*, eds. Binna Choi, et. al. (London: Sternberg Press, 2014).
31 Sven Lütticken, "Social Media: Practices of (In) Visibility in Contemporary Art," *Afterall*, no. 40 (Autumn/Winter 2015), https://www.afterall.org/articles/social-media-practices-of-invisibility-in-contemporary-art/.

“instituent practices.”[32] Yet the flourishing of these concepts raises an intriguing question: Does the organizational become an end in itself, a kind of institutional self-actualization of the artists, curators, and community organizers? Are we entering an era in which artistic curatorial practices are merged into organizational development, or even something like entrepreneurship?[33]

That institutional funding irrigated, as it were, the ecosystems of many local initiatives around the world might indicate that ruangrupa managed to reconfigure the biennial format from the “back end.” d15 relied on a governance structure of “mini *majelis*” (meaning gathering or meeting in Indonesian): based on their affinities, five collectives or individual artists from the documenta artist list were grouped together to share ideas, skills, programmatic outlooks, and a common space. They were also expected to oversee the management of their financial resources. In addition to the seed funding (or honorarium) of €20,000 and the €50,000 to €60,000 production budget allocated to each participating collective or individual artist, there was a €20,000 allowance for each group or artist that went into the collective pool of each mini *majelis*. The five collectives were to decide jointly on how to spend the €100,000. In reality, spending the money was subject to certain rules imposed by the institution. Most importantly, it needed to be spent within the documenta framework, which meant that artists ended up inviting their friends and colleagues to organize “something” at documenta. By spreading the money too thin, what was heralded as collective

32 Gerald Raunig, “Flatness Rules: Instituent Practices and Institutions of the Common,” *Institutional Attitudes: Instituting Art in a Flat World*, ed. Pascal Gielen (Amsterdam: Valiz, 2013); and Tal Beery, “Instituent Practices: Art After (Public) Institutions,” *Temporary Art Review*, January 2, 2018, https://temporaryartreview.com/instituent-practices-art-after-public-institutions/.

33 Timon Beyes and Ditte Vilstrup Holm, “How Art Becomes Organization: Reimagining Aesthetics, Sites and Politics of Entrepreneurship,” *Organization Studies* 43, no. 2 (February 2022), pp. 227–45.

self-empowerment was reduced to an assemblage of small gestures. The contacts between the invited artists, their peers, and the audience often did not amount to anything resembling a learning experience worthy of the name. The back-end of a biennial is still the back-end of *a* biennial, and those in the Global South should know that the resources of this back-end run downstream.[34] While attempts to rethink the economy of biennials and to reconfigure their organizational structure are not only welcome but overdue, at the end of the day, redistributing downstream from a fixed-use pot will not affect, let alone threaten, the status quo in the artworld.

Given that the value chain in the artworld is predictably short, it only takes two or three levels of downstream redistribution to reach the much-vaunted "communities." The exhibition's lumbung shop, rather than generating revenues upstream, embodied everything that is problematic about value chains in the artworld. Handcrafted goods from small communities in the Global South, created in association or coordination with artists, were sold at documenta and beyond its duration. This is the well-worn value-adding mechanism of eco-minded artisanal consumer goods, with the veneer of art. The artworld's fetishization of handicraft has invited objections as early as the Arts and Crafts movement in nineteenth-century England, and yet there was little engagement with diverse and complex value chains at this documenta. To be sure, certain participating artists displayed nuanced understandings of economics, but the lack of explicit curatorial framing detracted from many

34 "Upstream" and "downstream" are terms used in supply-chain studies and business contexts that are applicable to the artworld if one traces the flow of funding and the availability of venues and avenues, together with value-adding mechanisms in the arts. Some artists have comprehensive understandings of this and have been trying to push artists "upstream." See Gary Zhexi Zhang, "The Artist of the Future," *ArtReview* (April 2020), https://artreview.com/back-to-the-drawing-board/.

critical propositions, or even better, critical viabilities, of such nuanced projects.

INLAND, an art and agriculture initiative based in Spain, advises the EU on the use of art for rural development policies while facilitating the movements of shepherds and nomadic peoples.[35] It is also reconstructing an abandoned village for collective artistic and agricultural production in northern Spain. Over the years, the group has set up a Shepherds School and a multidisciplinary syllabus shedding light on the relationship between art, farmers' know-how, and agro-ecology. Their presentation at d15 was a balance of art, documents, ethnographic objects, and a pavilion selling cheese. To highlight how INLAND's practice aligns with larger public and private interests, my colleague Vienne Chan and I have designed a Social and Environmental Investment Plan to create sustainable funding for the Shepherds School. This is a creative development based on the cogent analysis of Social Impact Bonds (SIBs) made by Emily Rosamond.[36] Identifying specific points through which INLAND's projects develop these supporting structures, we align them with existing lines of public funding and examine how private investment can reinforce governmental efforts beyond financial contributions and the logic of investment.[37] At the same time, INLAND, together with artist Hito Steyerl, has been working on a "Cheesecoin" to model a noncapitalist economy that has its supply tied to annual cheese production, and hence to ecological well-being. The coin, endowed with a gift-like or even talismanic character, is supposed to circulate in the community.

35 INLAND's proximity to power means their position is, of course, much more privileged than that of many other like-minded initiatives.

36 Emily Rosamond, "Shared Stakes, Distributed Investment: Socially Engaged Art and the Financialization of Social Impact," *Finance and Society* 2, no. 2 (2016), pp. 111–26.

37 Mi You, "Another Currency, Another Speculation: Reflections on Art and Economies Projects at Documenta Fifteen," *On-Curating* 58 (2023), https://www.on-curating.org/issue-58-reader/another-currency-another-speculation-reflections-on-art-and-economies-projects-at-documenta-fifteen.html.

At documenta, Steyerl produced a video with her signature tongue-in-cheek narrative that framed Cheesecoin as a fictive currency fueling the struggle against a reality TV show encroaching on INLAND.

The intention of INLAND to go beyond art cannot evade the pull of the artworld, which collapses serious endeavors to change society into speculative narratives. Still, the actual practice of INLAND exceeds the attention economy of the artworld, and some of the initiatives do carry out situated and long-term social and cultural work beyond the exhibition format accorded to them by documenta. If the political battles of the artworld were the only battles that they—and all of us involved in art—were waging, then some complacency in curatorship and in viewership could be allowed. Instead, we might very well flex the wrong muscles for too long, until we realize politics is happening somewhere else.

81

2.2

What Community?

At the time of writing in early 2023, the debates on anti-Semitism at d15 show no sign of resolving. Despite continued efforts to start a concrete conversation on anti-Semitism and postcolonialism, commentators in the media keep returning to a pattern of assumptions. To demand a productive and dignified conversation, accountability, and the acceptance of mistakes, a kind of "We do this, you do this" confession, could be a realistic approach to mitigation. Correspondingly, such self-reflection would need to delve deep into one's own biases; a big and uneasy expectation, especially since the schism between international art and culture media and German media plays into a narrative by the former that Germany is "bad." German intellectuals need to reckon with the question: Why would ruangrupa and the exhibiting artists be incentivized to mediate such an exhibition in Germany when they are celebrated elsewhere, both in the Global North and South?

This section builds on the analysis from Chapter 2.1, and focuses on the vastly different, if not antagonistic, understandings and models of "community." I contend that most participants in the d15 debates prefer not to see these basic conceptual differences, some out of conviction and others out of obliviousness, but mostly through the mirror of mutual projections, exoticization, and self-exoticization. This vagueness usually achieves a kind of win-win situation, or the social surplus of the artworld that glosses over conceptually murky notions and celebrates them as political and progressive. However, this self-congratulation falls apart at a certain limit, and this is exactly what happened at d15. Meanwhile, the real "alterity" of some community practices from the Global South stays unrecognized in art venues in the Global North, and it would be inconvenient to make a real case for them (e.g., my analysis of Jatiwangi art Factory in the previous section). These real discrepancies in understanding what a community is and can be lead to scandals like the one at d15.

Questions and Speculations

First, the problems in the current debates and mitigation efforts must be stated. There was a paradox of perspectives on the side of the defense of documenta when the banner by Taring Padi was displayed. *People's Justice* was created in 2002 shortly after the end of the Suharto regime and depicts scenes of violence inflicted by the Suharto regime by employing familiar imageries from an activist, anti-imperialist art tradition that extended beyond the Indonesian context into a critique of global capitalism. Stereotypes of "capitalist globalists," that are well within the tradition of such works, can be read in conjunction with similar historical Western depictions, both in National Socialist propaganda but also contemporaneous socialist propaganda. A figure labeled "Mossad," in a line with other figures that bear labels in reference to various secret services, directly depicts the contemporary state of Israel as part of an oppressive and hegemonic global military power. Together with these depictions, one figure reminiscent of historical anti-Semitic tropes and one connecting contemporary Israel to the oppression of the Global South, incited the critique that the banner reproduced or normalized an anti-Semitic world view. On the one hand, statements by d15, ruangrupa, and Taring Padi themselves defaulted to the Western idea of freedom of expression as a right above politics as a potential defense, and on the other hand, they appealed to unpacking the particular visual references (in its particularist way) by situating it in its specific cultural-historical context. This applies both to the self-statements and to the perspectives from the public debate. Could both perspectives be brought into dialogue with each other, rather than appearing as excuses for non-confrontation, to make a concerted effort of mitigation?

And, what do we mean by "we"? Too often charges and comments are made on the assumption that there is an "Indonesian," or a "German," or "Western" perspective, or—as things spiraled—a Global South perspective on the Global North. This is naturally unproductive. At no time should we identify a whole nation, population, or region as the unit of study. When thinking about Indonesia, the foreign critic must take account for the history of the region in colonial and post-Independence times, the coup and its global ramifications (the so-called "Jakarta method"), but also the neoliberalization of the country along with contemporary populism and religious fundamentalism. On the German side, the different political factions, all motivated differently to participate in the debate, highlighted the need to specify where the allegation and critique was coming from, the history and the sociopolitical leanings of the authors, in order to have a balanced discussion. To this end, Florian Cramer made a detailed map of the German media and the political factions behind d15 debates in the symposium "(un)Common Grounds: Reflecting on documenta fifteen" hosted by Framer Framed in 2022. Could a clear articulation on the part of the participating artists—not only in terms of their own politics, but also on how their politics can be embedded in larger political narratives—help to create a differentiated view of the politics d15 stands by?

Some members of the public seemed to project what they imagined to be radical, leftist politics onto d15, categorically relating d15 to anti-Israel, anti-imperialist, and anti-capitalist positions. I commented earlier that this was a mischaracterization. Here, I would like to expand on the question of "community," which was univocally uttered at d15 and seemed so central to its political claims. It is crucial to develop more precise definitions of "community" where it appeared in d15—in working with local communities through art, in the structure of self-governance, in the image conjured as the historical reference for the curatorial concept and method, and as the moral core for claiming autonomy against state machines or the activities of transnational activism. To do so, I argue we first must think about how community operates in the context from which ruangrupa emerged.

1 Deni Junaedi, "Benturan Estetis antara Liberalisme, Sosialisme, dan Islam" (Aesthetic Clash between Liberalism, Socialism and Islam), *Proceeding of JICM (Jakarta International Conference of Muslim Intellectuals)* (Jakarta: University of Indonesia, 2013), p. 32.

To what extent did the emphasis on the "lumbung community" and the superimposition of ruangrupa's own practice on the various practices and politics of artists present at documenta serve to level these politics and allow for crucial (but possibly productive) differences and conflicts to remain unnoticed? Within the Indonesian art scene, the practices of ruangrupa and Taring Padi are only tangentially related—with ruangrupa's practice focusing, among other things, on urban education programs like the Gudskul in Jakarta as well as international networks like the Arts Collaboratory. Taring Padi's work, on the other hand, centers around grassroots, often rural, political agitation and (in their own words) "political propaganda"—as can be seen in their extensive work with Indonesian farmers in land struggles. It has been argued that even though Indonesia has transitioned to neoliberal capitalism, a notion of popular art reminiscent of the role of art in socialist society is still evident in Taring Padi's work. Taring Padi has some concerns about a government that prioritizes economic interests, which results in art only becoming a cultural product and as a tool to obtain revenues in the form of foreign exchange, leading to alienation or misunderstandings of art between artists and society in general.[1] These politics may or may not be in harmony with the rest of the exhibition, which exalts "community" in a broader sense.

Given this difference in approaches, both the dynamics of ruangrupa publicly "answering" for Taring Padi's work and the media associating ruangrupa's own alleged affiliations with the global movement for Boycott, Divestment, and

2 See for example Juliane Rebentisch, "Autonomie? Autonomie! Ästhetische Erfahrung heute," *Ästhetische Erfahrung: Gegenstände, Konzepte, Geschichtlichkeit*, ed. Sonderforschungsbereich 626 (Berlin: FU Berlin, 2006); Terry Smith et. al., *Antinomies of Art and Culture: Modernity, Postmodernity, Contemporaneity* (Durham, NC: Duke University Press, 2009).

Sanctions against the state of Israel with the work of Taring Padi betray a strange conflation of all positions present at d15. This might be partly due to common Western constructions (both from critics and proponents) of a uniform Global South and its politics, including the perspective on the ongoing conflict between Israel and Palestine—but we must ask whether the curation and mediation strategies of d15 might have inadvertently enabled such a reading of all artistic statements—as if they were coming from a singular, homogenous voice.

Earlier, I problematized the tendency of Global North curators and thinkers to abide by the idea that the separation of art and (everyday) culture is completely irrelevant to artistic discourses in the Global South.[2] Art of the Global South is defined either in utilitarian terms within a given society, or as a transcendental medium possessing spiritual power, incommensurable within the logic of autonomous art associated with the Global North. At the same time, art from the Global South, when it is exhibited in the North, is not necessarily framed as an intentional and radical counterpoint to depoliticized global art, but rather as integrated social practice, with individual artists and collectives supposedly representing the tenets of "their culture." I have touched on how this alterity in the conception of Global South art is reinforced from both sides in the structural image of ecosystems and organization. Yet given the different paths to a "community" and differently resourced "ecosystems," can we assume the organizational work needed for art to become a utopian, “instituent practice”[3] implies the same organizational methods and aims worldwide?

Most of the theories produced in the Global North that address the rise of community-based art, assume that a move away from self-interested individuals to a community is necessarily good. But the jump from ostensibly individualized (coded capitalist) and for the “community” (coded communalist or collectivist) does not specify *what* is being done. Could there be an honest acknowledgment of the gap between doing something for the “community” and doing something politically for the community? The meanings of community vary vastly and imply concepts anywhere from Karl Marx and Fredrich Engels’s “motley feudal ties that bound man to his ‘natural superiors’” in “feudal, patriarchal, idyllic relations,” to the ideal future community rebuilt in the civic sphere.[4] In other words, there are pre-individual and post-individual communities and many gradients in between. But how to account for the different paths toward emancipatory community politics, while being aware of the local context?

Digging Deeper Into “Community”

This section investigates the complex intellectual genealogy of “community” in Southeast Asia. The larger political context is the transition of academic fields such as anthropology from the early twentieth century to the postwar period, whereby a generation of American anthropologists who wanted to see a peaceful world with its cultural differences gave way to a generation producing works better

3 Gerald Raunig, “Flatness Rules: Instituent Practices and Institutions of the Common,” *Institutional Attitudes: Instituting Art in a Flat World*, ed. Pascal Gielen (Amsterdam: Valiz, 2013).

4 Karl Marx and Friedrich Engels, “Manifesto of the Communist Party,” *Marx & Engels Collected Works*, vol. 6 (London: Lawrence & Wishart, 2010), pp. 486–87.

suited to Cold War purposes. This is epitomized by the anthropologist Margaret Mead, who acted as "a public moralist"[5] defending the differences between and harmonies among all cultures throughout her career but found herself no longer able to influence US policy towards the Third World after the Second World War.[6]

In the 1950s, a group of American social scientists spearheaded by Walt Rostow outlined the pathway to modernization for Third World countries that entailed developing the largely peasant-based societies into industrial societies, which in turn dictates the behaviors and modes of social organizations, such as mass consumption.[7] Mead argued for the holistic development, rather than making piecemeal changes. One cannot simply substitute subsistence farming with waged labor, or feudal rule with democratic voting procedures, she argued, without making calculated adjustments elsewhere in the culture.[8]

Amidst the Cold War and the US failure in Vietnam, scholarship on the peasant society in Southeast Asia surged. In 1963, the development-theory-minded Clifford Geertz published the influential *Agricultural Involution: The Processes of Ecological Change in Indonesia*, in which he put forward the concept of involution: change occurring inwardly rather than through the development of modern institutional forms external to the Java peasantry, becoming a buffer from the outside influences that would have modernized the nation. Instead, their "backward and obstructive values"[9] led them toward "shared poverty."[10] His critics pointed to empirical evidence that showed outside influences such

5 Thomas Meaney, "The Swaddling Thesis," *London Review of Books* 36, no. 5 (March 6, 2014), https://www.lrb.co.uk/the-paper/v36/n05/thomas-meaney/the-swaddling-thesis.

6 Peter Mandler, *Return from the Natives: How Margaret Mead Won the Second World War and Lost the Cold War* (New Haven: Yale University Press, 2013).

7 Walt Whitman Rostow, *The Stages of Economic Growth: A Non-Communist Manifesto*, 3rd edition (Cambridge, UK: Cambridge University Press, 1990).

8 Meaney, "The Swaddling Thesis"; Mandler, *Return from the Natives*.

9 Meaney, "The Swaddling Thesis."

10 Clifford Geertz, *Agricultural Involution: The Processes of Ecological Change in Indonesia* (Oakland, CA: University of California Press, 1963), p. 97. Geertz borrowed the concept of involution from Alexander Goldenweiser, who developed it to describe cultural patterns of internal complexitites in primitive societies. See, for example, Alexander Goldenweiser, "Loose Ends of Theory on the Individual, Pattern, and Involution in Primitive Society," *Journal of American Folklore* 43, no. 170 (1930), pp. 22-41, doi:10.2307/534973.

11 Yew-Foong Hui, "The (Un)Changing World of Peasants: Two Perspectives," *Journal of Social Issues in Southeast Asia* 24, no. 1 (April 2009), pp. 18–31.

12 Benjamin White, "'Agricultural Involution' and its Critics: Twenty Years After," *Bulletin of Concerned Asian Scholars* 15, no. 2 (1983), pp. 18–31; Clifford Geertz, "Culture and Social Change: The Indonesia Case," *Man* 19, no. 4 (December 1984), pp. 511–32.

13 Meaney, "The Swaddling Thesis"; Mandler, *Return from the Natives*.

14 James C. Scott, *The Moral Economy of the Peasant: Rebellion and Subsistence Southeast Asia* (New Haven: Yale University Press, 1976).

as the cultivation of cash crops did not seamlessly co-exist with the traditional subsistence economy.[11] Benjamin White replied that involution could be identified in the field of culture rather than agriculture, in the superstructure, rather than the base. Later, Geertz defended himself against White (and the rest of the critical chorus) by pushing against economism, even though he ceded that the involution applied to Indonesia as the "moral substance of a sort of existence," which effectively echoed White's point.[12] As Yew-Foong Hui notes, Geertz did argue that involution permeated not only the productive sphere, but rural family life, social stratification, political organization, religious practice, as well as the folk culture value system. Geertz's theory proved useful in Vietnam when the official US policy was that insurrections in South Vietnam resulted from an insurgency led by disciplined North Vietnamese cadres bent on stirring up the primordial feelings of an otherwise passive peasantry to resist modernizing reforms.[13]

But, against whom or what is the peasantry supposed to rebel against? In continental Southeast Asia, James C. Scott considers the moral calculus of the peasants as a form of rational consideration. The serf can tolerate the expropriation of the lord insofar as the serf is protected in bad years.[14] Scott's theory was refuted by Samuel Popkin, who in *The Rational Peasant* (1979) cast peasants as capable of risk-taking and being rational players in a market logic, which Scott aimed to transcend. Yew-Foong Hui rightly problematized how the two discourses were pitted against each other as if there were two poles of

15 Qin Hui, *Chuantong Shilu* (Ten Treatises on Tradition) (Shanghai: Fudan University Press, 2004).

16 Karl Marx, "The British Rule in India," in *Marx & Engels Collected Works*, vol. 12 (London: Lawrence & Wishart, 2010), pp. 131–32.

"moral peasants" and "rational peasants." Chinese historian Qin Hui takes this further and asks: If these two types of peasants are incompatible, can their incompatibility lead to their "inverse compatibility"? That is, if peasant society lacks rationality (specifically, "individual rationality"), does this imply "moral autonomy for small communities"? Conversely, if the peasant lacks a sense of attachment to the community or clan, does this necessarily mean that he is a "penny capitalist," with a developed personality or a rationalist individualist?[15]

Recognizing the historical function of self-governance in small communities in many parts of the world, Qin focuses on the Chinese peasantry, which cannot be essentialized into the "moral peasant" or the "rational peasant": the small community is underdeveloped, but this does not mean the development of individuality. On the contrary, the underdevelopment of the "small community" is the result of the expansion of the "big community": i.e., the state with its exercise of bureaucratic top-down control and legalist administrative measures that suppressed patriarchal law and clan power in most of the historical periods.

The moral dimension that Scott points to seems to present a conundrum for those from a simplistic class-based perspective: are the lords then not class enemies, the "bad guys?" Here, reading classical Marxist theory offers the insight that the peasantry should overcome the subordination of the individual to larger outdated "small semi-barbarian, semi-civilized ... idyllic village-communities."[16] This Marxist view (though Marx himself would begin to change

Tuo Wang
Tungus, 2021
Single channel 4K video

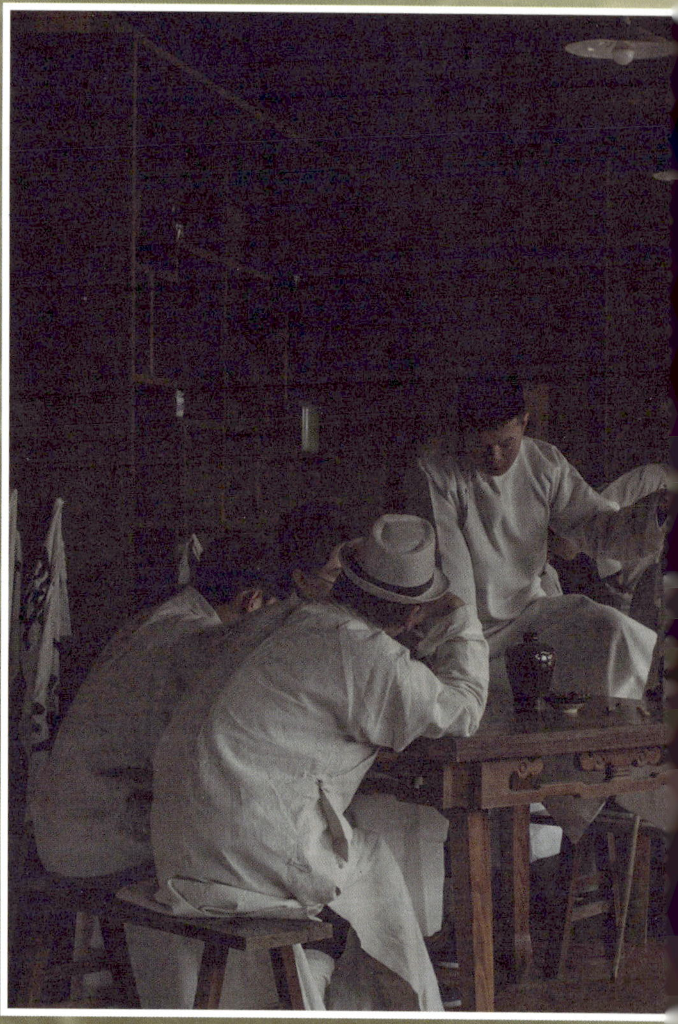

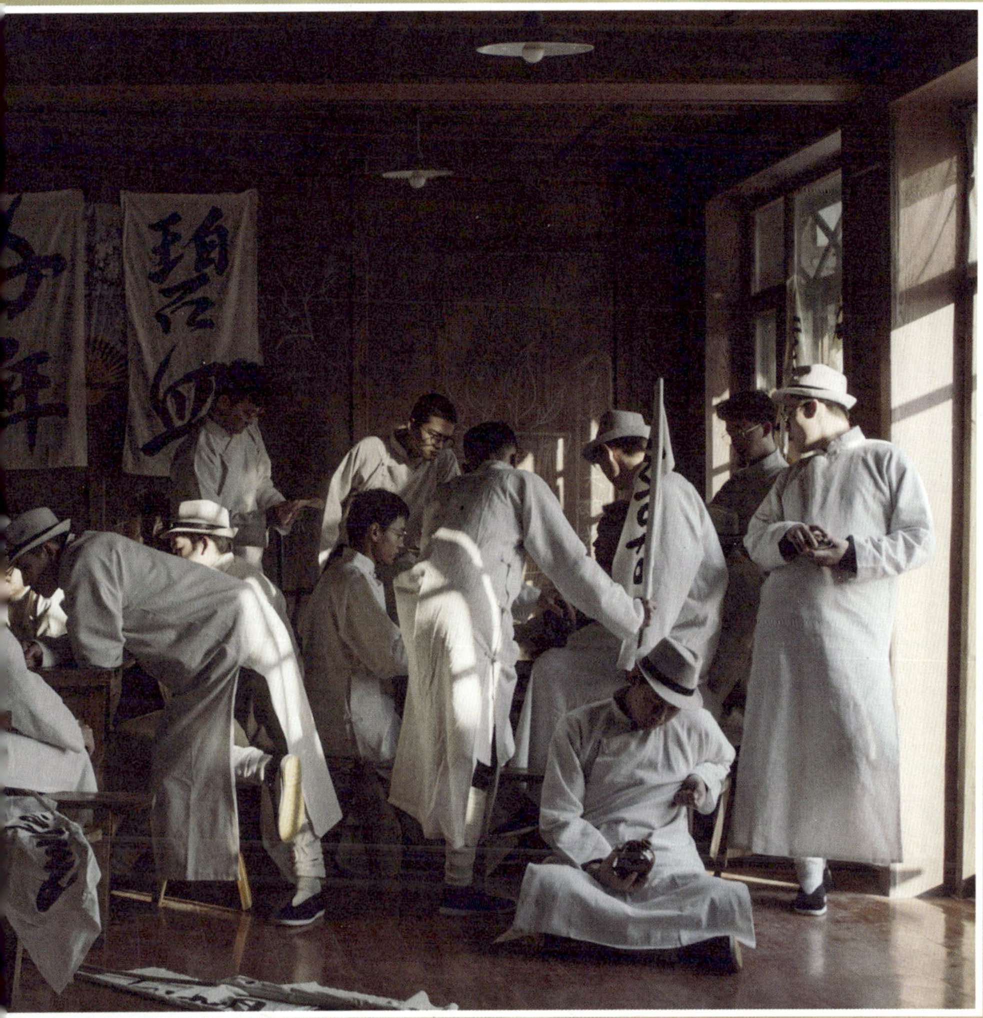

17 Ranajit Guha, *Elementary Aspects of Peasant Insurgency in Colonial India* (New York: Oxford University Press, 1983); Partha Chatterjee, *The Nation and Its Fragments: Colonial and Postcolonial Histories* (Princeton, NJ: Princeton University Press, 2020); Vivek Chibber, *Postcolonial Theory and the Specter of Capital* (London and New York: Verso, 2013).

18 Qin Hui and Jin Yan, *Tianyuanshi yu kuangxiangqu: guanzhong moshi yu qianjindai shehui de zairenshi* (Idyllic and rhapsody: The Guanzhong model and the re-understanding of the pre-modern society) (Beijing: Central Compilation & Translation Press, 1996); Qin, *Chuantong Shilu.*

his view after the Paris Commune), while bourgeoisie and industrial revolution destroy existing social relations to create something better (*aufheben*) in attacks on capital and capitalists at the cost of blood and violence, landlords are fundamental parts of the "community" and cannot be equated with the industrial capitalist class that arises in its place. But, as we know from postcolonial theory and its critique,[17] abolishing the land tenure system and the "class" of landlords does not necessarily lead to the emancipation of the peasantry. Instead, their subjugation to the community remains unresolved in the new hybrid social systems, and can be projected to the capitalist class when the "motley feudal ties" Marx spoke of are not fully destroyed but replaced by another kind of reactionary community orientation, now including the (post)industrial worker instead of the serf.

This is pertinent for laying bare the historical pattern that the dissolution of the small "unprogressive" community does not necessarily give rise to a social form based on the primacy of civil rights. Instead, it could tip over to an identification with a larger and even more repressive community. It could be seen in political transitions from the Roman to Byzantine Empire or in Marx's analysis of the parcel peasantry identification with the reactionary regime of Napoleon III. Identification with the larger community could take various forms, from kinship worship to renouncing one's own family for the sake of a larger cause like the Cultural Revolution in China, or how fascist regimes of Germany, Italy, and Japan claimed to fight for the cause of peasants.[18]

19 Jacques Rancière, "Aesthetic Separation, Aesthetic Community: Scenes from the Aesthetic Regime of Art," *Art and Research. A Journal of Ideas, Contexts and Methods* 2, no. 1 (Summer 2008), pp. 1–15; Chantal Mouffe, *The Return of the Political* (London and New York: Verso, 1993).

All these are complexities and impediments to be taken seriously on the way to establishing a political community, itself a product of modernity, with its inherent understandings of individual rights, civil society, and the rule of law. We shouldn't throw the baby out with the bathwater. Even when there is epistemological violence embedded in universalist notions such as human rights, it is not a birthright in many parts of the world. Increasingly, we have a post-individual, postmodern, and postcolonial notion of community at the foundations of progressive neoliberalism that champions the emancipation of communities together with the elements of pre-modern, pre-individual understanding as a part of a community's identity. This leads to highly syncretic community models, combining often contradictory elements in their own ideology for the thirst for "alternatives."

To be sure, it's not that we are not interested in this post-individual "community" in the West or see it without contradictions. The postmodernist and postcolonial optics imply that various geocultural models of community cannot be fully transferred to other contexts: If contemporary Indian communities "organically" combine capitalist relations with some feudal remnants and projections, then the contemporary Western understanding of community develops Enlightenment traditions more in common to Jacques Rancière's aesthetic community or traditions of Greek democracy as in Chantal Mouffe's "agonistic pluralism" of political community.[19] After the Covid pandemic, Judith Butler suggested a phenomenological understanding of community based on recognizing that "we pass the air we breathe to one another" instead of having bounded egos.[20] If psychoanalysis is anything to go by, we should drill to the core of the ego. In a sober critique, Eli Zaretsky points out that Butler's intersubjectivity pertains to selves, the psychical representation as in "self-image," and not ego, the seat of reason.[21] Importantly, a healthy, democratic group life relies on strong, delimited egos capable of resisting group pressure. Reading post-dramatic theater as an emblem of performing politics within the walls of theater's own disciplinary tradition, Keti Chukhrov intimates that liberal democracy is the democracy of individuals free from society, united in a quasi-community similarly free "from" society, and not a freedom "for" society.[22] An ideal kind of community is built on individuals not reverting to their subordination to a tyrannic community. Marxist legacy splits here, since starting from the critique of pre-individual, "self-barbarian" feudal communities, it leads both to their historical totalitarian/modernized versions as well as to the post-individualistic emancipatory critique of any repressive community. In fact, we observe in many parts of the West, a desire to enshrine the small community in both right-wing and anarchic and non-authoritarian leftist circles.

In the context of Indonesia, this essay put forward the potential for rigorous engagements with similar questions from the perspective of social sciences as a starting point for a constructive dialogue. Beneath the gleaming surface of many Asian societies is the lingering question of how

20 Judith Butler, *What World Is This? A Pandemic Phenomenology* (New York: Columbia University Press, 2022), p. 12.
21 Eli Zaretsky, "Injured Egos," *New Left Review* (blog), November 29, 2022, https://newleftreview.org/sidecar/posts/injured-egos.
22 Keti Chukhrov, "The Postdramatic Theater's Misadventures in the Age of Contemporary Art," *e-flux Journal*, no. 120 (September 2021), https://www.e-flux.com/journal/120/415768/the-postdramatic-theater-s-misadventures-in-the-age-of-contemporary-art/.

23 See, for example, the work of John Sidel, a student of Benedict Anderson.

24 Melani Budianta, "Decentralizing Engagements: Women and the Democratization Process in Indonesia," *Signs* 31, no. 4 (Summer 2006), p. 918.

25 Melani Budianta, "Discourse of cultural identity in Indonesia during the 1997–1998 monetary crisis," *Inter-Asia Cultural Studies* 1, no. 1 (April 2000), pp. 109–28.

26 Tania Murray Li, "Commons, co-ops, and corporations: assembling Indonesia's twenty-first century land reform," *The Journal of Peasant Studies* 48, no. 3 (April 2021), pp. 613–39.

peasant societies transform in modernity in ways that go beyond the "imagined community."[23] Certain aspects explicated above from other Asian cultural contexts may hold true, such as the identification of a traditional community projected onto a "modern" nation, seen in the fatherly figure of Suharto, whose New Order also implied "gender ideology, in which women ... meant to serve the interest of the state and the male citizens."[24] The post-Suharto era witnessed the resurfacing of a plethora of group identities, of ethnic, religious, ideological, and interest groups as a correction of Suharto's suppression.[25] What about the fatherly construct of regional heads after political decentralization? How are the mechanisms of subordination and identification there? Articulations on the identification mechanism in those communities that are sub-national but perhaps nevertheless exhibit features of the "big community" would be insightful. After all, identities of community survived both European and Japanese colonization as well as political centralization in the nation-building period. Furthermore, it is important to emphasize that customary communities (those based on traditional ethical order), can be made compatible with the continued operation of neoliberal capitalism. Nostalgic summoning of the "community" can serve to mask things done underhandedly. Divergent agendas can be made to align, appearing to create win-win solutions while keeping intractable problems at bay. For example, Joko Widodo, after becoming Indonesian president, proposed cooperatives as the primary vehicle of a "just economy" with a neoliberal twist.[26]

All of this begs for clarity for how it relates to the conflicts that emerged at d15. However, conversations between clear-minded commentators with good intentions and ruangrupa members to locate the meaning of the community seem to always default to a certain idealized image of the community that I have shown to be indebted to an essentialist, Western perspective. ruangrupa point to how mutual aid in communities have helped weather times of crises such as during the 1997 Asian Financial Crisis, and smooth out the differences between communities in diverse sociopolitical contexts, like those between rural Java and urban Germany. Just like the purportedly unifying signifier of the Global South and its perceived subsumption to postcolonialism does more harm than service to the current debates and a future horizon of decolonial politics in and outside of the art field, the empty signifier of the "community" likewise invites multiple projections of often contradictory understandings of community. Both the "traditional," moral, and resilient take and the "modern," rationalist take on community have been (over-)represented in anthropology in—one must say—not so innocent ways. Rather than (only) dismantling master narratives, a more pressing problem would be to formulate a cogent definition of the community on which d15 and so much related political thinking is focused on, but unable to actualize.

2.3

Postscript to documenta 15 and Prelude to documenta 16

It is increasingly clear that documenta has become a locus of multipolar art in a multipolar world. This section serves as a postscript to d15 and a prelude to documenta sixteen to reflect on how they are concomitant to multipolar value pluralism.

A chronicle of events: on November 9, 2023, an essay in the German daily newspaper *Süddeutsche Zeitung* accused the Indian writer and documenta sixteen finding committee member Ranjit Hoskoté of anti-Semitism, based on his signature on a 2019 BDS petition against a far-right event on "Zionism and Hindutva," cohosted by the Consulate General of Israel in Mumbai. This was followed by the prompt resignation of Hoskoté in a letter in which he detailed how a holocaust survivor in his own family applied her knowledge to heal the horrors of partition in post-war India. Meanwhile, the Israeli artist and finding committee member Bracha L. Ettinger resigned, citing personal reasons and the impossibility to delay the artist selection process amidst the ongoing war on Gaza. Soon after this, the four remaining members resigned due to concerns that documenta can no longer host open-ended and responsible discourse given the current political climate in Germany, where historical responsibilities run the risk of being misused to suppress undesired

1 Ranjit Hoskoté, "Documenta Resignation Letter," *e-flux Notes*, November 13, 2023, https://www.e-flux.com/notes/575318/documenta-resignation-letter; Simon Njami et al., "Documenta Resignation Letter, *e-flux Notes,* November 16, 2023, https://www.e-flux.com/notes/575919/documenta-resignation-letter.

speech and discussion. Hardly a few days had gone by before another open letter came out, on November 23, 2023, from Manuel Borja-Villel and Vasıf Kortun. The two were invited to submit proposals for documenta sixteen, decided to form a joint proposal, which, after being discussed by the finding committee, was rejected due to an administrative formality. All resignations were published on *e-flux Notes*.[1]
From the moment Hoskoté's association with the global movement BDS surfaced, it became clear that one cannot both protect documenta in Germany against the political and public demands to defund it and save its international reputation. Neither documenta nor the state and federal cultural ministers could risk having the committee continue. It was a hard choice, not least because choosing to estrange Hoskoté in Germany meant, in the same breath, discrediting a person who is against the right-wing, ethno-nationalist government in India. In recent years, many filmmakers, authors, and artists came out in protest against Narendra Modi's government. Some in Hoskoté's milieu were evicted or imprisoned, sending chills down the spines of many in the intellectual sphere there. How could they digest the outcry in Germany now? Meanwhile, in Germany, watch dogs eagerly want to prove the association of Global South intellectuals with "anti-Semitism." Even after acknowledging that any BDS affiliation is intolerable in Germany, which both Hoskoté and documenta promptly did, there was barely any sense of understanding, let alone remorse in the German media for the lesson not learnt from Hoskoté's resignation letter.

Following these events, one should not be surprised that international art and culture, once again, produced the image of a "German problem" which does not distinguish differentiated positions of the German public sphere, politicians of all levels, and the organization of documenta. The international art media went down an escalatory path in reaction to the resignation letters in op-eds and on social media. Amidst all this, the question that no one seems to want to ask remains: have we ruled out other alternatives of crisis management at documenta? And for the art community, is all-out declaration of political misalignment and administrative mistreatment the only solution?

One of the members of the selection committee told me anonymously: "My first instinct was to talk to the Culture Minister of Germany." Further considerations include putting a pause on the process, starting an investigation into the committee—in essence, buying time to stop the downward spiraling reactionism that holds both the political and cultural sphere hostage in Germany and elsewhere. This would have been, perhaps, helpful in containing further divergence of opinions.

The publication of the curatorial proposal for documenta sixteen by Borja-Villel and Kortun on *e-flux* on December 14, 2023, went largely unnoticed. To one's relief, *e-flux* editors threw their weight behind the importance of the institution of documenta. Even the documenta organization team could take some pride in this—taking this as a sort of paparazzi moment rather than being prickly about possible non-disclosure agreement infringements. It was a moment

2 "Consulting and Support for the further development of documenta und Museum Fridericianum gGmbH," https://www.documenta.de.

of deflation, for both *e-flux* and documenta could have doubled down and exacerbated the situation.

These publicly-circulated moments should be coupled with "back-end diplomacy"—garnering support from domestic and international political and cultural actors. The establishment of an academic/artistic advisory board would be crucial, one that consists of people from artistic and curatorial fields, who are both good in their work and institutionally savvy. This was recommended in the organizational review[2] and ratified by the board of documenta half a year after the debacle. The role of critique is vital here but not without contradictions: exactly when the international image of documenta is tarnished, what can the critique of the "hegemony" of "Global North culture institutions" say about it?

The critique of documenta's hegemony, especially under the aegis of postcolonialism, could be interpreted in two ways. For one, it can debilitate the willingness to defend the project—which oddly resonates with concrete far-right demands. The critics might like it less when there is nothing left to critique. Alternatively, it can travel with its critique, accommodating the postcolonial perspective and the research on anti-Semitism in the history of documenta. The critique of documenta could lead to the defense of what is widely considered to be the last world-class beacon of critical, experimental and—at least for most of its history—daring art. And together with it, art as a practice for public reasoning. In reality, few in the non-West are interested in recriminalizing the West, certainly not when documenta is

3 Mark-Christian von Busse, Bettina Fraschke, Florian Hageman, "documenta-Geschäftsführer: "Wir sollten keine Notlösung erwägen", Die Hessische/Niedersächsische Allgemeine (HNA), November 21, 2023, https://www.hna.de/kultur/documenta/wir-sollten-keine-notloesung-erwaegen-92694107.html.

failing, even when or exactly when they are building their regional art projects. The position of the one selection committee member mentioned above clearly shows how much the non-Western part of the artworld cares about the institution. This is not a naïve propagation of universalism, but a universally important proof of what art can do in a society, and what it takes for it to institutionally endure.

This framing offers a different discourse than the hollow moniker of freedom of art. The latter is abstract, absolutist, universalist in the conventional sense of the term. Its absoluteness allows it to be deployed strategically in political discussions concerning basic rights. In the petition "#standwithdocumenta—Save the freedom of art!" launched on January 22, 2024 by a Kassel-based initiative, it is artistic freedom in the abstract that the campaign initiators saw as having been undermined. Insofar as artistic freedom can be defended in the abstract, the local Kassel-based initiators of the petition are fully in accord with the international art media. But then the demand is not clear as documenta und Museum Fridericianum gGmbH effectively does defend artistic freedom with their concrete administrative measures (to ensure "artistic freedom," no background check of artists will be made, but if individual artworks at documenta were to turn out to be anti-Semitic certain measures could be taken—first in the form of "dialogue" and "contextualization," and, in the last instance, works could be removed even against the wishes of the curators, but only if they are in violation of German law).[3] *e-flux* translated the German petition and published it on their website. The local campaigners are largely art aficionados who veritably have a sense of ownership of documenta, a historical civic education achievement unlike any other art project, to transform a good part of the local population to subscribe to art and to progressiveness. Hence, they bitterly disagree with national media and their accusations that documenta is anti-Semitic. The twist that escapes their self-conception is that the history of documenta they rightly take pride in is one that until now comfortably justifies a universalist understanding of art, making them a rather curious localistic cosmopolitan fellow to *e-flux* readers.

The positions presented so far—localist, liberal internationalist, social-justice minded cosmopolitan, critical postcolonial—are all phenomena of art from peak globalization. Where the artworld excessively focuses on more easily identifiable culprits such as the rise of the extreme right or the New Right, it fails to establish a larger-picture perspective, i.e., de-globalization, value-pluralism, the faltering of third-wave democratization. These effects of post-globalization I sketched out in earlier sections are acutely felt in the artworld in Germany, even though it has long been a norm for practitioners in other sociopolitical contexts. If we can acknowledge how any one of the positions pertains to the one pole among others in the multipolar world, then we edge closer to articulating critical *and* constructive positions. We will likely perceive the later development of Strike Germany with neither schadenfreude nor conviction. Strike Germany was started in January 2024 by an anonymous

4 Susan Neiman, interview by Sebastian Frenzel, "Das Kulturleben nimmt Schaden," *Monopol* (online), November 28, 2023, https://www.monopol-magazin.de/interview-susan-neiman-bds-antisemitismus-kultur.

group to garner support from cultural workers in refusing to work with German cultural institutions amidst the ongoing conflict in Gaza since October 7, 2023. Most German cultural institutions are public or receive government funding, and therefore fall under the banner of organizations that must abide by the International Holocust Remembrance Alliance's definition of anti-Semitism, which Germany adopts at the national level. To be sure, Susan Neiman already warned in her interview that German cultural institutions are being "boycotted" abroad.[4] The number of events impacted by Strike Germany is in the thousands and still counting.

When the discourse takes the form of a series of retaliations, it limits the space for deep-learning and respectful reasoning. Personally, I wish for a culture of political debate in which the collision of opinions is moderated and accommodated. Otherwise, both the right and the left are engaged in zero-sum political discourse, variously described with the simplistic friend-enemy divide. But politics is never zero-sum. And even the friend-enemy has a "pacifying" function according to Carl Schmitt's student Ernst-Wolfgang Böckenförde: it should precisely domesticate and channel the political within its realm into the friend-enemy divide to avoid escalation. This comes only with deep reckoning with the state of liberal democracies in the West, and their counterparts in various (il)liberal political cultures of the non-West. What is needed is the capability to navigate seemingly divergent poles and be intellectually resourceful in devising remedies, for

5 This is a synthesis of Friedrich Hayek's ideas by John Gray, based on Hayek's *The Sensory Order: An Inquiry into the Foundations of Theoretical Psychology* (Chicago: University of Chicago Press, 1952) and *Studies in Philosophy, Politics and Economics* (Chicago: University of Chicago Press, 1967). See John Gray, *Post-Liberalism: Studies in Political Thought*, 1st ed. (London and New York: Routledge, 1996), p. 38.

6 Michael Oakeshott, *Rationalism in Politics and Other Essays* (Indianapolis: Liberty Press, 1991).

instance, differentiating the gradients of conservatism all the way to extremism instead of labeling everything right of oneself right-wing. This is nothing new in the tradition of Western liberalism. No other person than the persona-non-grata of left-wing politics, Friedrich Hayek, described what could be called "unviable moralities"—systems of moral thought and sentiment incapable of sustaining any stable social order.[5] Amidst the collision of thoughts, is it possible to agree that what is sought is not truth but peace?[6] Or in a pragmatic fashion, to strive for a politics of the least-worst?

It is also noteworthy that there is a trend for political debates in liberal democracies to be supplanted by a legalist paradigm, in which claims and conflicts that are politically intractable are modeled in the jargon of rights and placed in the sphere of the judiciary. While post-liberal thinkers mostly focus on civil rights, recent events have put artistic freedom under the spotlight. The deployment of artistic freedom—in the negative—as a fundamental right could be tactical against allegations made in bad faith, i.e., when there is no constitutional law violation that can be established, is it acceptable to display art that diverges from public opinion? The legal scholar Christoph Möller, in his assessment on the "Admissibility of preventive measures to combat anti-Semitism and racism in state cultural funding," came to the conclusion that the state may have the right to tie art funding to secondary conditions of preventing racism and anti-Semitism but pointed out the political and administrative pitfalls of implementing a respective legal

7 Christian Rath, "Risiken bei Bekenntnispflicht," *Taz*, March 25, 2024, https://taz.de/Kulturfoerderung-und-Antisemitismus/!5999871/; Marcus Woeller, "Jetzt steht da schwarz auf weiss, was Claudia Roths Verantwortung ist," *Welt*, March 22, 2024, https://www.welt.de/kultur/plus250665025/Antisemitismus-Gutachten-Jetzt-steht-da-schwarz-auf-weiss-was-Claudia-Roths-Verantwortung-ist.html.

8 Isaiah Berlin, "Two Concepts of Liberty," in *Four Essays on Liberty* (Oxford: Oxford University Press, 1969).

9 Philip Oltermann, "'Free speech is a facade': how Gaza war has deepened divisions in German arts world," *The Guardian*, March 25, 2024, https://www.theguardian.com/world/2024/mar/25/free-speech-is-a-facade-how-gaza-war-has-deepened-divisions-in-german-arts-world.

clause. Furthermore, the state could not directly prescribe a program to art institutions, like documenta, which themselves are protected by the freedom of art and the practical assessment of works on a case-by-case basis would remain the responsibility of the institutions themselves.[7] Perhaps we need a more earnest discussion on freedom (e.g., freedom from vs. freedom to, à la Berlin[8]), without which all utterances of it will amount to kicking the can down the road, thereby shrinking the public culture for reasoning. This is especially worrying when the supervisory board of German art institutions are populated by politicians, which in times of rising globalization has contributed to a multicultural "vanilla liberal welfare state utopia," to quote Hito Steyerl.[9] While I'm not an "artistic freedom fundamentalist," I do think artistic non-fundamentalist views—that is, views informed by geopolitical conditions and hence not part of the defensive lamenting of the loss of the universalist claim over art—should be more represented at the institutional level. But if only this were a problem that organizational consultancy or organizational sociology could solve! If the conjunction of politics *and* legal interpretations overpower all the rest, then we will be cornered into a reactive position where we can only bemoan too much politics and violations of fundamental rights. There might be a sense of collectivity in the self-pity in the beginning, but in no ways can it propel active politics into being. If there are no adequate and clear-sighted engagements from the civic sphere as to "what can we do" beyond bemoaning and manicure amendments, then we will truly be doomed.

10 See Gray on George Santayana, *Dominations and Powers: Reflections on Liberty, Society, and Government* (New York: Charles Scribner's Sons, 1951), in Gray, 1996.
11 Nathan Gardels, "What Comes After Liberalism," *Noēma*, October 6, 2023, https://www.noemamag.com/what-comes-after-liberalism/.

In the long run, is the alignment of progress, liberty, and freedom, as expected in a democratic state, a contingency rather than a historical fate? Liberalism does not equate liberty with progress as the promise of the state; that it is what is strived for is another matter that makes left-wing politics worth pursuing. When post-Cold War globalization coincided with the high-water mark of Western civil society, the creed of liberty became a creed of progress expressed in welfare but also in the idea of freeing other people.[10] There is no more a variety of what is considered good, much less zealous negotiations between conflicting notions of good. Art became a normative aspect of the creed of progress, never drilling to the core of the social and institutional background from which its role is accorded. But it is a singular history, and its defining values may soon be rendered obsolete by its critics from the West and from those contending for their own uses of art. The unraveling of the liberal international order demands more rigorous engagements with liberty, individuality, community, progressiveness, democracy, civil society, and the state in realigned groupings depending on the context.

What could documenta do in anticipation of the multipolar world? There is some concrete "particular universal" to heed. A "modus vivendi" of liberalism for the future is based on recognizing the variety of human interests and the negotiation between conflicting interests in the name of civil peace.[11] This is in good order. Multipolar does not necessarily mean parallel universes or tectonic plates that do not interact with each other. On the contrary, we might find areas of overlapping territories and mixed allegiances. A curator, when asked to curate a biennale in Saudi Arabia, will need to negotiate what is possible within the sociopolitical boundaries and still strive to show art that can enrich the experiences and critical thinking of the locals. With similar consideration a curator for a future documenta will need to think how to bring genuinely critical positions into the show. Such would be the contribution of a realist and honorable art.

Chapter 3

China in Between Universalism and Particularism

1 Hans Belting, "Contemporary Art as Global Art: A Critical Estimate," *The Global Art World: Audiences, Markets, and Museums*, ed. Hans Belting and Andrea Buddensieg (Ostfildern: Hatje Cantz, 2009), pp. 38–73.

Chapter 3

China in Between Universalism and Particularism

In recent years, academia and the artworld have given rise to a marketplace that privileges the display and analysis of cultural particularities. To follow the routine of such formulaic knowledge production, it typically suffices to offer an alternative epistemology, a particular way of life. But there could be more at stake if practitioners approached this selective apparatus with more nuance. While the loss of local context in discourse and art production is generally attributed to the prevalence of global art, and though countermovements of "regionalism" or "tribalization" are perceived as contradictions to that global art,[1] a question remains to be adequately addressed in Western discourse: what happens when postcolonialism comes home?

This chapter moves beyond the mere critique of the local and the global by analyzing the context of China, where the magnitudes of political and historical complexities exceed such a particularizing tendency if undertaken from a purely formulaic method as described above. Applying a triadic analytical lens of politics, ideology, and economics, it becomes evident that cultural production in China follows a different path than it does in other post-Socialist or

Global South countries. The globalization of the artworld has given rise to strands of cultural production in China that align ideologically and, to some extent, economically, with Western practices. For example, much art writing focuses on works that sit comfortably in liberal perspectives (e.g., postcolonial perspectives on non-Han ethnic regions) or the New Left (e.g., the reappraisal of socialist illustrated science journals, and socialist art in general). Indeed, this kind of work typically interfaces with the West through the economics of biennales, art fairs, and Western—mostly institutional—collections. However, such work is produced specifically for Western markets/viewers and thus divorced from the contemporary political/social relations in China, doing little to help create a deeper understanding of that context. There are scarce conduits for the transfer of Chinese cultural and cultural theory production to that of the West (the opposite direction is more common), or for that matter, to its neighboring countries. Structurally, the invisibility of this intellectual and cultural production can be explained by the fact that these Chinese cultural producers are less likely to engage with politics and economics whether in China or outside. Thus, modalities and approaches to cultural production tend to remain in the lofty realm of idea-production, unlike, for example, counterparts in countries in the Global South that might receive targeted Western funding to produce "community" art (as discussed in the last chapter), or post-Socialist counterparts. In the latter cases, an underlying assumption holds that to accept such funding or support means being incorporated into liberal ideological canons of art, and necessitates accepting the impetus to make work that speaks to embodied experience for reception by spectators from the West.

In the last chapter I focused on the case of documenta, an institution that aspires to, which in turn encourages the production of, a deeply universalist dimension for artistic experimentation. I investigated some of the underlying assumptions of d15 from a "Western" or "liberal international" perspective, especially in the undifferentiated celebration of socially engaged art, notions of "traditional" worldviews, and community practice. I have also suggested that non-Western practitioners can do better in their curatorial and institutional practices, not least because their day-to-day experiences in negotiating cultural politics make them particularly savvy about the kind of cultural politics becoming dominant in the West. In this chapter, I offer a way that a non-Chinese reader can start to grapple with post-globalization by diving into the realities, parallels, and inconsistencies of globalization, by thinking with Chinese contemporary art. This deep dive into the political and cultural discourses of China is, in a practical sense, a form of overcoming particularity (rendering the universalist view of such particularity self-serving). This view seems to say: Europe does not need to be provincialized, because it already is. The question for European actors is: will Europe be defended from a universalist or particularist position, and by whom?

This chapter comes at this problem from the other direction to look at discourses and artistic production from what is typically (in the West) accorded only a particularist position. As with the last chapter, there is a cautious yearning for grounds on which *new* universals could be articulated. In other words, I propose we look for a benevolent and generative multipolarity, rather than a multipolarity rooted in contention (competing particulars that are inserted into a hegemonic universality). The provincialization of Europe is no premature self-congratulation on the part of China. It is due to the fact that there is less penchant for provincializing the West in China among intellectuals than China's concern with its own development path. This neutral, objective position is by no means a static and dogmatic one; it must be reconcilable when jumping from one context to another. If one exercises value neutrality in the Western context looking at illiberal societies and acknowledges the structural possibility of liberal art in them, as discussed in Chapter 1, then one must acknowledge that the same position can appear as apologetic within the context of China. Hence from the Chinese context, one must be acutely aware of the multiple challenges that come along with working through its political and social modernization. In a similar movement as the double critique of "community" in documenta (i.e., a critique of modern atomized Western society leading to calls for community practices, and no less a critique of the pre-modern tribalist notion of community), one must perform a double critique of the Chinese episteme when attempting to engage with concepts such as democracy and liberty. In other words, putting forward a critique of the West—be it a critique of modalities of governance, social

Xinyi Cheng
Losing Oneself, 2023
Oil on linen, 60 × 92 cm

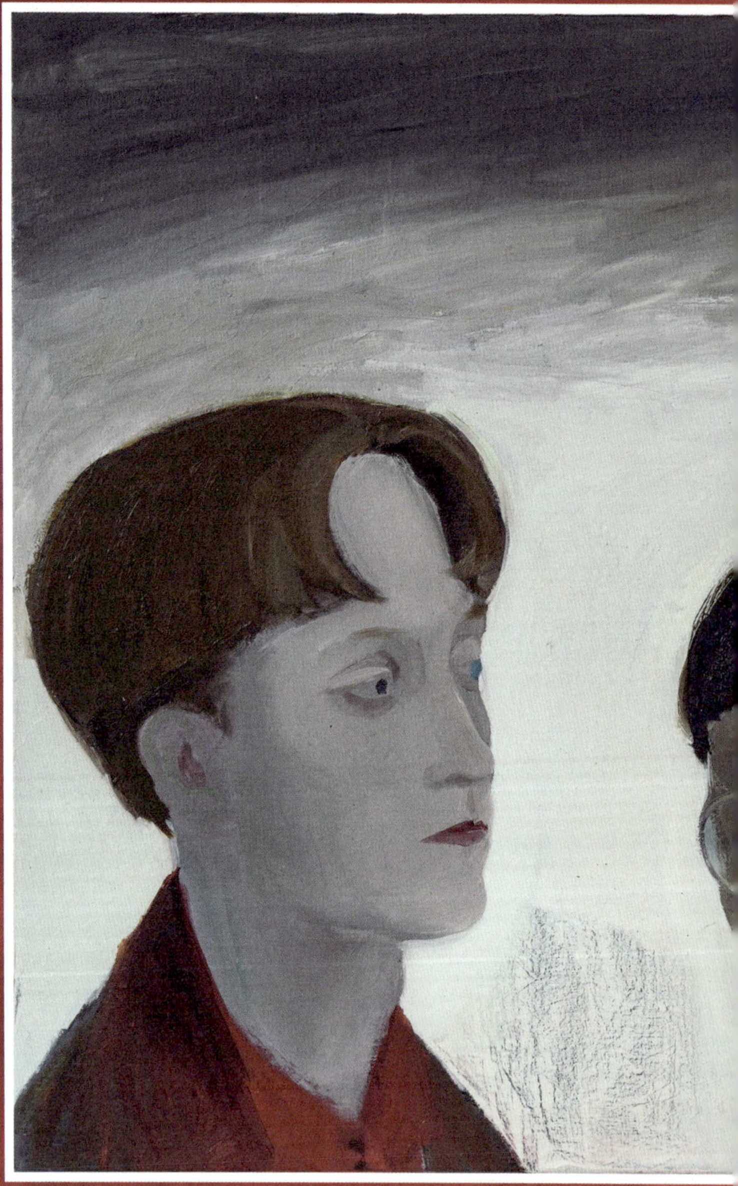

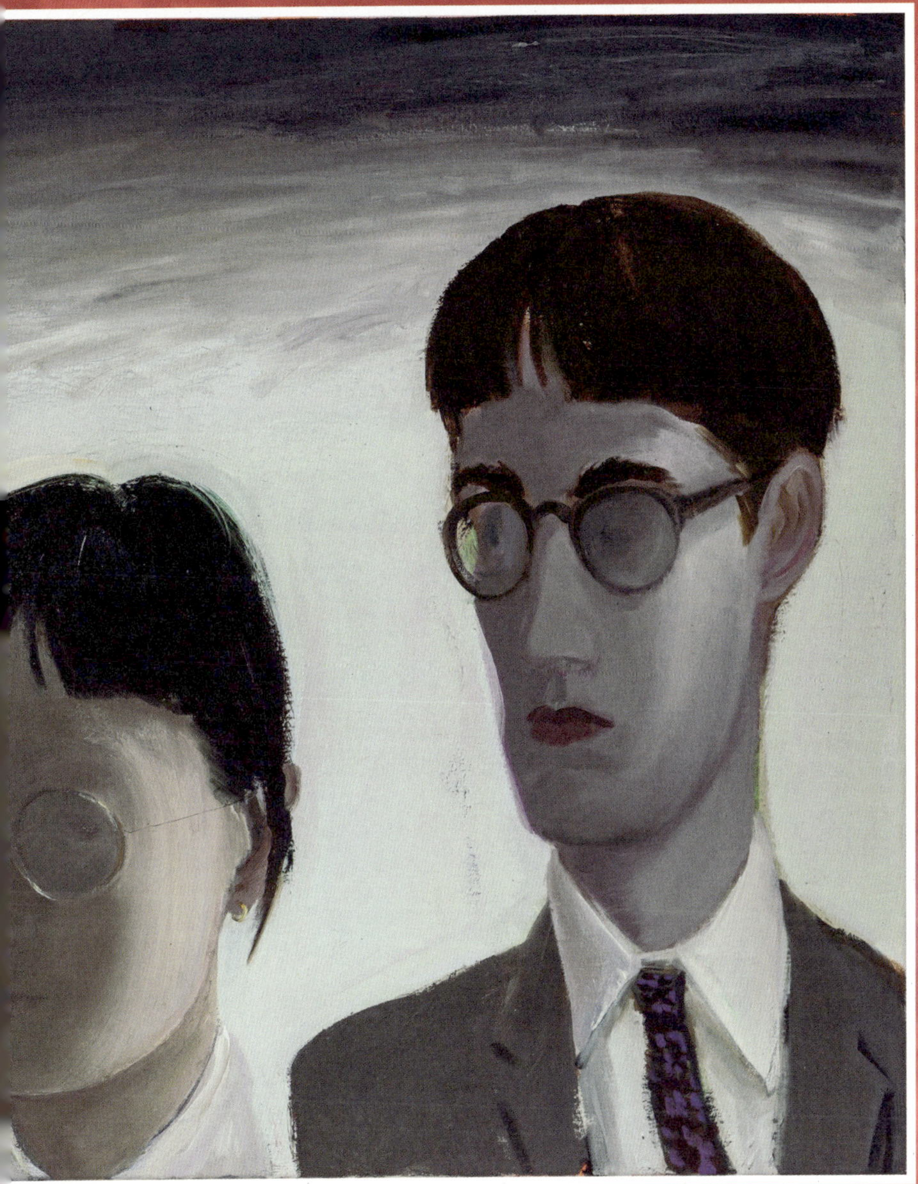

relational ontology, development, or artistic discourse—there must also always be a critique of the critique, staying attentive to how that critique can be instrumentalized politically. To write about the Chinese context requires a similar mode. What emerges at the end of the double critique would be a more concrete notion of politics that is both conscious of its own genealogy and of its contradictions.

In this chapter I present case studies that draw on a wide range of intellectual resources, from culturalist to materialist, from particularist to universalist, from conservative to revolutionary, from New Left to liberal, and from those produced for a self-sustained artworld and those with ambitions in the concrete political realm outside of aesthetic practice. These artistic/cultural projects are chosen on the ground that they reflect certain politics that are exemplary of the thesis of post-globalization: that there are fundamental discrepancies in traditional modes of understanding the role of state and market between progressive politics in China versus their Western liberal internationalist and leftist internationalist counterparts. The themes—Silk Road imaginaries and tech development—serve as examples through the "broken mirror" of comparison of contending with politics through art. While both China's cultural policy and tech policy demand in-depth surveys of their own, this chapter situates case studies from cultural and tech policy in intellectual discourses specifically. Further inquiry that could help develop this argument could look at environmental art, or art for workers' rights, but that is outside the scope of this discussion.

Before we dive into the case studies, I will outline broad considerations on the implications of thinking art and politics in post-globalization China.

The Role of the State

Following the hubristic neoliberalism of the last three decades, discourses abound in the West around the death of "the political." Whether it is the power of plutocrats, the advent of platform capitalism, climate catastrophe, or the Covid-19 pandemic and its mismanagement, democratic institutions are increasingly accused of inefficacy, cronyism, and navel-gazing. On the other hand, China's highly sophisticated and technologically advanced market economy demonstrates that political power is very much alive. The status of China as an "avant-garde nation" that had practiced actually existing socialism and has stridden the path of economic modernization without significantly changing its one-party political system makes it a good place for assessing the fundamental claims put forward by different pundits and activists coming from Western liberal, New Left, and conservative perspectives.

The progressives in the West, and increasingly, their liberal and conservative counterparts, have been quite ready to nominally accept the return of state-intervention and public ownership of industries. But what about economies that are taken to be an alternative to neoliberalism? In one sobering critique of Thomas Piketty's *Capital in the Twenty-First Century*, Chinese liberal scholar Qin Hui points out that the post-globalization paradigm shift is not one that trades

2 Hui Qin, "Dilemmas of Twenty-First Century Globalization: Explanations and Solutions, with a Critique of Thomas Piketty's *Twenty-First Century Capitalism*," *Reading the China Dream*, November 15, 2018, https://www.readingthechinadream.com/qin-hui-dilemmas.html.

on the binary between capitalism and socialism, but doesn't signal their convergence either. He argues that we need to understand the slippage between the two lefts:

> Leftists in Western welfare states should oppose globalization, while Leftists in China should welcome it, but at the same time should push for political reform, so that changes in the pattern of supply and demand caused by globalization should be able to truly realize the benefits of the Chinese working class and the disadvantaged, and thus promote the transformation of type-B into type-A [i.e., from an authoritarian socialist economy where rights are not protected to one that resembles a socialist market economy under social democracy], so that "socialism" and "market economy" can increase efficiency and equity.[2]

To be sure, liberals were in the intellectual mainstream in China from the 1980s well into the 2000s, with many promoting neoliberalism as the path for the country's economic development. A glimpse of the titles of publications—reading almost like a meme—include "Milton Friedman in Beijing" by Julian Gewirtz, *Adam Smith in Beijing* by Giovanni Arrighi, and "Ronald Coase in Beijing" by Christopher Connery, which exposes contradictions about the characterization of the contemporary Chinese economy. For example, Ludwig von Mises and Milton Friedman's emphasis on the private ownership of property, rather than the market, runs against the Chinese line of market reform in the late 1980s—as the reformist Ziyang Zhao famously said, "the state adjusts the market, and the market guides the enterprise."[3]

The Chinese New Left was bitter about the neoliberal swing of the country in the 1990s and early 2000s. Where they could, they stood with underprivileged communities such as migrant workers and peasants, through both street-activism and policy suggestions in consultation sessions. Over time, state capacity proved not only to be the driving force of economic rebuilding, but was targeted increasingly to address social equity;[4] examples include state-sponsored poverty alleviation programs which have effectively eradicated absolute poverty (measured against a standard equivalent of $2.30 per day in rural areas);[5] the state's steps to protect gig workers' labor rights;[6] and, contrary to common assumptions, data privacy.[7] Leading New Left thinker Hui Wang points out the indispensable role that the socialist past has played in the reform period, highlighting the legacy of land collectivization and the political mobilization of the masses.[8] Families, clans, and spatial governance relations were organized into new social relations in communes during the socialist period, on the foundation of which rural reform in the 1980s was organized. It is only through socialist political mobilization that the idea that the socialist state represents the interests of the majority of people is generally accepted. Without such acceptance, it would have been difficult for the different social strata to believe that the reforms promoted by the State represented their interests—why would anyone buy into Deng Xiaoping's "let some get rich first" without cynicism?

3 As cited in Isabella M. Weber, "Origins of China's Contested Relation with Neoliberalism: Economics, the World Bank, and Milton Friedman at the Dawn of Reform," *Global Perspectives* 1, no. 1 (April 9, 2020), p. 7.

4 Shaoguang Wang and An'gang Hu, *The Chinese Economy in Crisis: State Capacity and Tax Reform* (Armonk, NY: M.E. Sharpe, 2001).

5 See, for example, the Brookings Institute commentary, Maria Ana Lugo, Martin Raiser, and Ruslan Yemtsov, "What's next for poverty reduction policies in China?," September 24, 2021, https://www.brookings.edu/articles/whats-next-for-poverty-reduction-policies-in-china/?b=1.

6 See, for example, "Meituan to change delivery algorithm rules as China urges labour protection," *Reuters*, September 13, 2021, https://www.reuters.com/world/china/meituan-change-delivery-algorithm-rules-china-urges-labour-protection-2021-09-13/.

7 For more on this, see Chapter 3.2.

8 Hui Wang, "The Economy of Rising China," *Reading the China Dream*, originally published in *Beijing Cultural Review*, no. 2 (2010), pp. 24–35, https://www.readingthechinadream.com/wang-hui-the-economy-of-rising-china.html.

China can and should serve as a ground for practical reasoning without foreordained judgement and having to be anyone's client for the sake of a global critique of neoliberalism, either from the New Left or from the liberal camps. The ontological question of whether China is neoliberal or not is less pertinent than *how* and *when* Chinese is neoliberal.[9] Recent theoretical debates on the latter question concern the Chinese (economic) development model that delivers prosperity.[10] China's staggering economic growth is due to the government's policy directives and its related entities—namely, state-owned enterprises and banks that are deeply involved in both the production process and the allocation of economic resources. Land financing—again a legacy of socialism due to public ownership of high-value urban land—allows for the ability to use land as collateral to mobilize markets and leverage more funds for industrial investment.[11] Experiments in dismembering the "aggregated property" of land into the right to own, contract, and manage posit a reimagination of both radical left and liberal traditions.[12] After decades of high-speed development, local government debt has been exposed to risks.[13] But it has also produced assets such as infrastructures and industrial firms. There are doubts nonetheless—and not just from the liberals—as to whether this system promotes innovation in science and information technology. Ecological degradation is a grave consequence, but the resolve to address it is often coupled with optimism rather than desperation, unlike in the West.

9 See, for example, Isabella Weber, "Origins of China's Contested Relation with Neoliberalism: Economics, the World Bank, and Milton Friedman at the Dawn of Reform," *Global Perspectives* 1, no. 1 (April 9, 2020), pp. 1–14.

10 See, for example, Xiaohuan Lan, *How China Works: An Introduction to China's State-Led Economic Development* (Singapore: Palgrave Macmillan, 2024); Keyu Jin, *The New China Playbook: Beyond Socialism and Capitalism* (New York: Viking, 2023). See also venture capitalist Eric Li Shimo's TED talk, "Eric X. Li: A tale of two political systems," July 1, 2013, *TED*, YouTube video, 20:37, https://www.youtube.com/watch?v=s0YjL9rZyR0.

11 Philip C.C. Huang, "Chongqing: equitable development driven by a 'Third Hand'?" *Modern China* 37, no. 6 (November 1, 2011), pp. 569–622. Zhiyuan Cui, "从重庆领悟‘社会主义市场经济’：国资增值与藏富于民携手并进" (Coming to an understanding of "market socialism" from Chongqing: appreciation in value of state assets and wealth stored among the people go forward hand-in-hand) (2009), 文化纵横. www.cui-zy.cn.

12 See the "Introduction" to Roberto Mangabeira Unger, *Politics: The Central Texts,* ed. Zhiyuan Cui (London and New York: Verso, 1997).

13 See, for example, Zhang Yukun, Xia Yining, and Ding Feng, "In Depth: China's Trillion-Dollar Local Government 'Hidden Debt' Dilemma," *Caixin Global*, September 19, 2023, https://www.caixinglobal.com/2023-09-19/in-depth-chinas-trillion-dollar-local-government-hidden-debt-dilemma-102110275.html.

14 *Beijing Culture Review* is a bastion of rigorous scholarship on contemporary socialism and China.
15 赵鼎新：路径不依赖、政策不相干——什么才是中国经济成功的关键. Dingxin Zhao, Path Independence, Policy Irrelevance—What Holds the Key to China's Economic Success in Zhao, 2017.

16 See Dingxin Zhao, "State Legitimacy, State Policy, and the Development of the 1989 Beijing Student Movement," *Asian Perspective* 23, no. 2 (1999), pp. 245–84, http://www.jstor.org/stable/42704215.

Focusing on the economic side of things does occlude relevant issues. Indeed, these authors point out structural bottlenecks and fallacies. After China firmly withstood the shockwaves of the 2007–2008 global financial crisis, some scholars have increasingly gained confidence and propped up the models of Chinese development and modernization not only as an analytical discourse but as a normative one.[14] If this reflects the zeitgeist and serves ideological discourse both domestically and internationally, it does not become a self-fulfilling prophecy without facing academic scrutiny in China. One could debate, for example, whether the Chinese model is ontologically extant, or whether it pertains to a wider condition of path independence—in other words, whether the set of policies will necessarily lead to growth.[15] Or one can view these developments in the context from where state legitimacy is derived. Dingxin Zhao applies a state-society model in his research on historical and contemporary China, which include the behavior and capacity of the state; the nature of society as seen through, for example, the intermediate associations of social groups; and the linkages between state and society. For him, the latter entails three differing conceptions of legitimacy: legal-electoral, ideological, and performance legitimation, based on a critical expansion of Max Weber's model of traditional, charismatic, and rational-legal legitimacy.[16] The Mao era enjoyed ideological legitimation, the economic boom era performance legitimation. To what extent, then, is today's discourse production feeding into re-ideologization? There is an isomorphism between this explanatory model for state legitimacy and mine for interpreting cultural productions in a multipolar pluralist world; both consider politics/procedure of politics, ideology and economics.

If there are checks and balances in academic discourse, the state of cultural and artistic discourse can present an oversimplified picture of the present at best, and at worst lean into politics without realizing its liabilities. This will be further illustrated through case studies later in the chapter.

Chinese Contemporary Art Theory and Intellectual Practice

For all its impassioned artistic expressions, there is a lack of socio-politically minded contemporary art theory in China. This is in line with the limited sociopolitical rigor in contemporary art theory-writing in general, exacerbated by a loss of attention to context through linguistic and conceptual translation. Nonetheless, it is worthwhile to investigate certain cases of artistic production and art theory as demonstrative of a multipolar artworld. The plain and unvarnished reason why I emphasize viewing the development of Chinese contemporary art through intellectual history and sociopolitical theory is the lack of "checks and balances" in artistic and cultural theory production across different poles. While paying due respect to art history writing that periodizes stylistic tendencies, I am more concerned with how the Chinese art scene underwent ideological liberalization beginning in the 1980s through intellectual practice. In this regard, the stylistic differentiations in schools of art, such as the Chinese political Pop artists and the Conceptualists

17 Guoqiang Yang, “论新文化运动中的个人主义 (On Individualisms in the New Culture Movement),” 探索与争鸣 Exploration and Free Views, vol. 1, issue 8 (2016), pp. 12–22.

in their perennial contests with each other, may betray their underlying, common sociological and political sentiments and motives. Both artistic and intellectual practices have experienced transmutations and confrontations with their own contradictions, if not hypocrisy, and serve as a mirror for the Western-led, supposedly “global” developments in intellectual thought and art.

For example, while most contemporary Chinese artists from the 1980s onward profess some degree of subscription to individualism, it has never been clear which notion of individualism is being referred to. Recent Chinese scholarship has unearthed one plausible version of individualism's manifold intellectual history in China going back to the early twentieth century. In the modernization May Fourth Movement initiated in 1919, individualism appears in different forms. In the context of the confrontation with and opposition to the state, an anarchistic individualism emerged that was represented by the revolutionary Chen Duxiu. In actively drawing boundaries within modern society and its rules, an individualism influenced by John Dewey in the liberal and humanist sense was spearheaded by the scholar-politician Hu Shi and became popular among intellectuals. And, reflecting on the social form and culture of the collective, the community, and the mass, a discursive and critical individualism emphasizing freedom of thought was proposed and has remained present to this day, best articulated by the leading Chinese modern literary critic and writer Lu Xun.[17] Each of the three types of individualism has left its mark on artists and intellectuals in the 1990s and 2000s. Distinguishing between these three types of individualism, and potentially more, it becomes possible to reconcile why some of those artists who sought individualistic expression and "progressive" politics in the 1990s turned into statists in the late 2000s. They deploy tradition and a currency of unique development model that the state comes to champion. The specter of the unresolved third kind of individualism also returns to community practices, much of which has been valorized in similar ways as community practices from the "Global South" in the last documenta.

A major throughline in the development of contemporary Chinese art theory conforms with the global trend that performs a perfunctory critique between the geo-specificity of a place and the global networks of circulation. Today, the global art scene tends to assess artworks within frameworks indebted to poststructuralism's break from universalist assumptions and favoring of difference-oriented models of social emancipation.[18] Many scholars of global art have pointed out how "situatedness" can undermine individual artistic authorship through references to their "culture" or any other geo-specific context, but also how the notion of artistic agency can be retained. In the case of China, researchers identify that "Chineseness" implies competing, conflicting, or supplementing agencies,[19] presenting not only a form of cultural resistance in the postcolonial line, but also a form of commercialization, parallel to what Arif Dirlik describes as the self-orientalization of Chinese elites.[20] This has been criticized by both Chinese curators and scholars, as well as their non-Chinese counterparts.[21]

18 See Brian Holmes, *Escape the Overcode: Activist Art in the Control Society* (Eindhoven: Van Abbemuseum, 2009); Victoria Ivanova and Gerald Nestler, "Art, Markets, and Finance," *The Routledge Handbook of Critical Finance Studies*, eds. Christian Borch and Robert Wosnitzer, 1st ed. (London: Routledge, 2020).

19 See Franziska Koch, "'Chineseness' in Contemporary Art Discourse and Practice: Negotiating Multiple Agencies, Localities and Vocalities," *Journal of Contemporary Chinese Art* 3, no. 1 (June 2016), pp. 3–11.

20 Arif Dirlik, "Chinese History and the Question of Orientalism," *History and Theory* 35, no. 4 (December 1996), p. 96.

21 See, for example, Shiming Gao (ed.), 后万隆 (Post Bandung) (Shanghai: Shanghai Arts Publishing House, 2022); Paul Gladston, "International Curatorial Practice and the Problematic De-Territorialization of the 'Identity' Show: Deconstructing the Third Guangzhou Triennial, Farewell to Post-Colonialism," *Journal of Curatorial Studies* 4, no. 1 (February 1, 2015), pp. 6–32.

22 See, for example, Daniel F. Vukovich, *China and Orientalism: Western Knowledge Production and the P. R. C* (London: Routledge, 2012).
23 Hui Wang, *The Rise of Modern Chinese Thought (in Chinese)* (Beijing: Sanlian Shudian, 2004); Hui Wang, *China from Empire to Nation State*, trans. by Michael Gibbs Hill (Cambridge, MA: Harvard University Press, 2014); Hui Wang, *China's Twentieth Century: Revolution, Retreat and the Road to Equality*. ed. Saul Thomas (London and New York: Verso, 2016).
24 Gan Yang, *Tong san tong* (Unifying the three traditions) (Beijing: Sanlian Shudian, 2007).
25 Marius Meinhof, "Colonial Temporality and Chinese National Modernization Discourses," *InterDisciplines. Journal of History and Sociology* 8 (October 19, 2017), pp. 51–80.

In other words, as I asked above, what happens when postcolonialism comes home? How do geo-specificities, at the local, regional, and national levels, figure in their home context outside of the West? The possibility of a postcolonial/decolonial optics in China needs locally developed theory rather than being read purely by Western schools of postcolonial theory since it was not fully colonized by the West but instead has its own colonial histories and presents. Furthermore, the course of China's modernization is a glaring outlier compared to other historical empires: instead of dissolving into smaller nation states, it more or less retained its shape. Some Chinese studies scholars call for a postcolonial optics for the investigation of the Chinese context, in the multiplicity of forms of nationalism, Occidentalism, nativism, socialism, liberalism—all of which are reactions to semi-colonialism but are contradictory among themselves.[22] To this end, scholars both in China and worldwide have complicated the narrative of modernity, which is always already "colonial modernity," by drawing on the experience of Chinese revolutions[23] as mediated by the locally instantiated histories of socialism, political liberalism, and Confucianism,[24] or by zooming into the local experience of everyday modernity.[25]

An obvious candidate for an indigenous "postcolonial" or decolonial theory in China is a certain revived version of Confucianism. New Confucianists in the 1990s were marginal, if not considered fully heretical for proposals such as the establishment of a parliamentary system with a House of National Essence consisting of descendants of Confucius himself.[26] These views aside, Confucianism has enjoyed a steady revival since the 2000s. This galvanized the homecoming of Neo-Confucian philosophers working outside the country, such as Mou Zongsan or Tang Jungyi, through the publication of their works in China. The coupling of Neo-Confucian philosophy and questions of technology has also garnered much international interest, especially from the artworld.[27] At the same time, Hui Wang and thinkers from the New Left have returned to Confucianism to revitalize socialism for the present era.[28] Art practitioners, in turn, have consciously aligned postcolonial discourse with aspects of traditional cultural thought.[29]

While the postcolonial turn and anti-hegemonic claims for the liberation of knowledge have contributed to the legitimization of applying postcolonial and decolonial optics to China, some practitioners have reached a level of confidence in self-theorization that moves beyond mere historical recrimination of the West. Art scholars have called for a "post-West" society, as in Shiming Gao's writings that accompanied the Third Guangzhou Triennial *Farewell to Post Colonialism* (2008).[30] For him and his co-curators, the postcolonial "system of spectatorship" prevalent in the global artworld has a selective eye, and its particularist interest in identity and difference are not necessarily topics of concern for the Chinese artworld. The Chinese art community is keen to find, think, and create in a liberal environment—a practice that is firmly situated in "*bentu*" (native land), which is not to be confused with nationalism. In other words, instead of playing the game of localizing the

26 Jiang Qing, *A Confucian Constitutional Order: How China's Ancient Past Can Shape Its Political Future* (Princeton, NJ: Princeton University Press, 2012).

27 See Yuk Hui, *The Question Concerning Technology in China: An Essay in Cosmotechnics*, 3rd corrected edition (Falmouth: Urbanomic, 2022); Mi You, "Confucianism and Technology: Conceptual borders between tradition and modernity, Chinese and Euro-American modernity," in Paul Gladston, Beccy Kennedy, and Ming Turner eds., *Visualizing Chinese Borders* (London: Palgrave, 2021).

28 Kenneth J. Hammond, "The Return of the Repressed: The New Left and 'Left' Confucianism in Contemporary China," *The Sage Returns: Confucian Revival in Contemporary China*, eds. Kenneth J. Hammond and Jeffrey L. Richey, pp. 93–112 (Albany: State University of New York Press, 2015); Jun Deng and Craig A. Smith, "The Rise of New Confucianism and the Return of Spirituality to Politics in Mainland China," *China Information* 32, no. 2 (July 2018), pp. 294–314.

29 Many landmark artworks from the era could be read this way. For example, Huang Yongping's installation *Big Roulette* references *I Ching, the Book of Changes* was framed by curator Hou Hanru as "attacks" on the legitimacy of the Western-centric monopoly in intellectual and everyday life. See Hou Hanru, "Entropy, Chinese Artists, Western Art Institutions: A New Internationalism (1994)," in *Contemporary Chinese Art: Primary Documents*, ed. Hung Wu, pp. 249–52 (New York: The Museum of Modern Art, 2010).

30 Shiming Gao, "Observations and Premonitions of 'After Post-Colonialism,'" *Farewell to Post-Colonialism: 3rd Guangzhou Trienniale*, eds. Huangsheng Wang, Shiming Gao, Sarat Maharaj, and Zhang Songren, pp. 44–51 (Hangzhou: China Academy of Art Press, 2008). See also Shiming Gao, "The Dismantling and Re-Construction of Bentu ('This Land' or 'Native Land'): Contemporary Chinese Art in the Post-Colonial Context," in *A New Thoughtfulness in Contemporary China*, ed. Jörg Huber and Chuan Zhao (Bielefeld: transcript Verlag, 2011), pp. 103–20.

31 Xudong Zhang, *Cultural Identity in the Age of Globalization: Historical Reflections on Western Discourses of the Universal* (Shanghai: Shanghai Renmin Press, 2021).
32 Gao, "The Dismantling and Re-Construction of Bentu."

global vogue of difference and succumbing to the global capitalist "bentuing" strategy, one feels the need to reconstruct bentu, the base for cultural creation, from which one gets a continually changing, wearing and tearing as well as a development of history, an extending horizon. In a more philosophical approach, Xudong Zhang calls for conscious theoretical construction at the level of universality, which rationalizes the institution, value, culture, and lifestyle "particulars" of Chinese society to enrich the particular universals.[31]

Critical of the postcolonial syntax, this position opens a kaleidoscope of possible connections, many of which will continue to be metabolized by the postcolonial "system of spectatorship." One can indeed imagine an endemic discourse on the contemporary, a New Leftish interest in the Global South, or in the working class in China. All of these are expressions of art in a value-pluralist, post-globalization world and may or may not mean the same thing as their counterparts in the West. Admittedly, the cases presented in this chapter can also fall into one or another position in the range of positions. To capture a viable universal moment remains a major test for developing a locally workable understanding of present multipolarities. As Gao puts it, "the pressing need is to have a longer vision in which we could touch our different pasts and common future as much as possible and from a historical angle."[32]

1 See the author's previous texts and projects on the Silk Road and Eurasia: Curator (with Slavs and Tatars) of *Clouds and Power* at CHAT (Centre for Heritage Arts and Textile), Hong Kong and Tselinny Contemporary Art Center (Almaty) (2023–2024). See "Clouds, Power and Ornament—Roving Central Asia," *CHAT* (blog), https://www.mill6chat.org/event/clouds-power-and-ornament-roving-central-asia/. Curator of Silk Road: "Transgression, Syncretism," a festival of performance, performative lecture, art and screening program at Asian Cultural Center Theater as part

3.1

Silk Road: China's Geographical Imagination

The recent attention brought to the silk roads (networks of trade routes between Asia and Europe) via the Chinese supranational infrastructure project known as the Belt and Road Initiative (BRI) overshadows the fact that the Silk Road is not just one thing. I've worked on and in various parts of the Silk Road artistically and curatorially for over a decade, and still vividly remember the fringe status of the topic when I began my curatorial practice. Over the years, I have witnessed the mobility of people and goods through these infrastructure projects. I have cheered for the UNESCO listing of the Silk Road as a multinational initiative. And I have found myself having to explain that my interest and creative projects are not motivated by Chinese government–sponsored cultural programs.

The Silk Road is as much a series of historical trade routes connecting Europe and East Asia through Greater Central Asia as it is a contemporary political-economical trope for infrastructural projects. First popularized in German as *Seidenstrasse* by geographer Ferdinand von Richthofen in 1877, it is as much an expression of the lived realities of interconnected cultural spaces as it is an imagined of its inaugural season program, Gwangju, South Korea (2016). See "Transgression and Syncretism," *e-flux Education*, https://www.e-flux.com/announcements/105848/transgression-and-syncretism/. Curator, the inaugural Ulaanbaatar Media Art Festival, Ulaanbaatar, Mongolia (2016). See https://www.facebook.com/UBIMAF/. Co-initiator (with Binna Choi) of "Unmapping Eurasia" long-term research and curation platform at Casco Art Institute: Working for the Commons. See at "Unmapping Eurasia," Casco Art Institute, May 30, 2023, https://casco.art/projects/unmapping-eurasia/. Co-curator (with Binna Choi), "One Northeast" exhibition on Northeast Asia, Zarya Center for Contemporary Art, Vladivostok (October 2018). See at "ONE NORTHEAST," http://zaryavladivostok.ru/en/exhibitions/post/1864. "Unmapping Eurasia," a year-long study program, Dutch Art Institute (2018–2019). See "2018–2019 COOP Study Group: 'Unmapping Eurasia.' Tutor Team: Binna Choi, Mi You. Partner: Casco Art Institute: Working for the Commons," dai, http://dutchartinstitute.eu/page/11986/2018-2019-coop-study-group-unmapping-eurasia.-tutor-team-binna-choi. "Digital Earth" (as mentor) (October 2018–2019) "Unmapping Eurasia" walking exhibition and presentation, Media City Biennale, Seoul (June and September 2018) "Eurasia Steps," Roaming Assembly, Dutch Art Institute, Athens (June 2018).

2 See, for example, the New Silk Roads initiative based in the University of Leiden, https://newsilkroads.info/books-and-projects/.

3 Jonathan Holslag, "The EU's 'global gateway'—an answer to China, or a dead-end?" *EU Observer*, December 1, 2021, https://euobserver.com/opinion/153678.

4 Ruth Simao has done extensive field research in Zambia and describes such projects as having "embassy aesthetics." See her recent talk "Old Stories, Contemporary Politics, Shared Futures: Chinese Soft Power and Visual Narratives of Friendship in Zambia" delivered on December 1, 2022 at the conference "China's Cultural Diplomacy and Nation Branding" at Birmingham City University.

quasi-entity whose terminology coincides with the reign of European imperialism. Furthermore, it connects diverse and sometimes contradictory imaginaries and contexts, including those from before the emergence of the nation state where ways of life are considered to have been more community-oriented and attuned with nature; the aspirations of third-worldism in the 1960s and 1970s as a form of post-nation-state political alliance; and, most recently, the ambitions for rewriting Western-led globalization and its material and epistemological hegemony.[1]

Amidst the surging scholarship on the BRI, its cultural and artistic ramifications have slowly gained academic interest.[2] Granted, there are few cultural considerations from the Chinese government in this largely economic and geopolitical project,[3] if one doesn't take the kitschy, government-sponsored Silk Road-themed gala performances into account—an easy example of exoticization and (self-) orientalization. Other than song and dance festivals, the organization of bilateral painting exhibitions is another format that is frequently staged where there are Chinese infrastructural projects, such as in the case of Sino-Zambia Art Salon.[4] The geographical imagination of Silk Road finds its cultural and artistic expressions beyond the recent official ramp-up of cultural projects, and transgresses political, ideological, and artistic borders. In recent years, there has been a surge in artistic production from artists in both critical contemporary art and official academic art circles focusing on the regions along the Silk Road. What follows is a mapping of this dynamic field with contested, sometimes

Slavs and Tatars
Kitab Kebab (Transcendental Teets), 2016
Books, metal kebab skewer, 28 × 64 × 22.5 cm

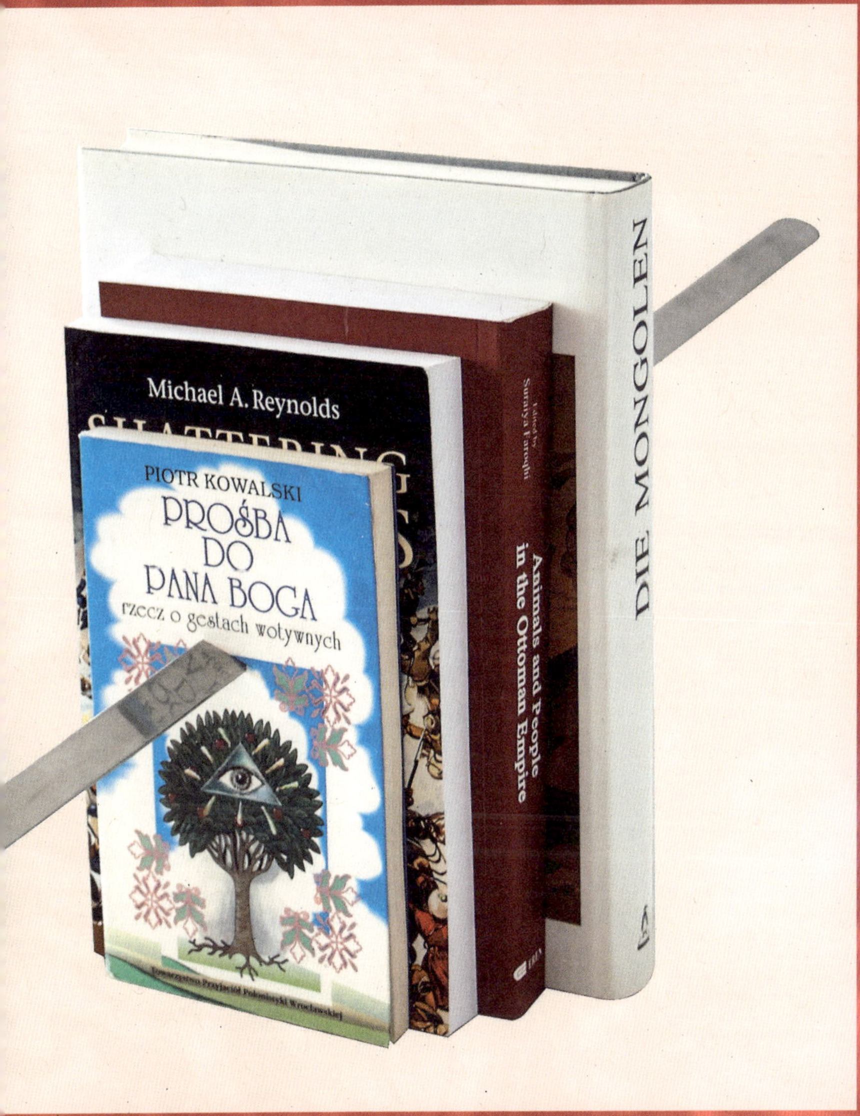
Michael A. Reynolds
PIOTR KOWALSKI
PROŚBA DO PANA BOGA
rzecz o gestach wotywnych
Edited by Suraiya Faroqhi
Animals and People in the Ottoman Empire
DIE MONGOLEN

contradictory positions. I reflect on how Silk Road-related art stands in relation to the broader intellectual landscape of China and, in turn, how the global or globalist aspirations written into its DNA come to bear in the post-globalization world.

Geo-Imagination: A Model

This section sets out to discern political orientations from the stylistic choices and institutional affiliations that constitute the reading of an artwork in art historical terms. Art historical analysis can often perform interpretations of social and political intentions and efficacies in artworks, but as the space of ambiguity sprawls beyond boundaries in the competitive market of meanings under post-liberalism, we need to acknowledge when a form of theorization becomes self-serving. What follows is a theoretical model developed with Nikolay Smirnov (a dialogue with him is included later in this chapter) to address the current limitations of art theorization on what we call geo-imaginations. The model comes close to explaining—rather than interpreting—factors that constitute choices in the nexus of art production and theoretical justification of these cultural productions, but we are mindful that this mechanism should not be mechanical.

We propose a "landscape" model to describe the field of geo-imagination. This borrows aspects from my analytical framework in this book and highlights the tension and transmutation within ideology, though always entangled with political and economic dimensions. Two main impulses

5 See the analysis of "New Right art" in Chapter 1.
6 Shiming Gao, "The Dismantling and Re-Construction of *Bentu* ('This Land' or 'Native Land'): Contemporary Chinese Art in the Post-Colonial Context," *A New Thoughtfulness in Contemporary China*, ed. Jörg Huber and Chuan Zhao (Bielefeld: transcript Verlag, 2011), pp. 103–20.
7 See, for instance, Doreen Massey, John Allen, and Phil Sarre, *Human Geography Today* (Cambridge, UK: Polity Press, 2007).

can be identified as acting in the field of the geo-imagination of the Silk Road: geo-specificity and internationalism. This gradient model depicts how artistic works are positioned in relation to—and at the same time affected by—the two impulses. Geo-specificity signals the turn to the locally specific context, often connected to traditional knowledge, lifestyle, and other characteristics of a particular group of people. It has been a leading force in the arts for decades, starting with the neoliberal turn in the 1980s and up to the recent neo-conservative turn worldwide. It can be perceived as "emancipatory" and "progressive" if it concerns the case of ethnic minorities and non-independence, or "nationalist" and "reactionary" when taken up by a sovereign state. Likewise in the arts, the impulse to geo-specificity can be applied as a tool to advocate for progressive politics, but it can also lead to right-wing political art.[5] This double-meaning of geo-specific as "bad" or "good," "reactionary" or "progressive" is similar to the pair of interpretations of *bentu* (native land) in Shiming Gao's writings: one based on the identity "*bentuing*" logic of global capital to become a "multi-local"/"multi-*bentu*" as opposed to an anti-essentialist, anti-traditionalist performative and relational creative and never-ending re-construction of *bentu* as a process of self-understanding.[6] It is also close to the rethinking of "place" that was taken up in critical human geography in the 1990s in which place was theorized as a concept through which to instantiate an essentialized identity versus place theorized as purely relational and performative.[7] The counterpart of the geo-specific is the internationalist impulse which is committed to an internationalist politics with its roots in twentieth century anti-imperialist, anti-nationalist, and anti-colonial struggles. They attack the neoconservative turn in politics and geo-cultural relativism in cultural-political discourses prevalent today. The internationalist impulse is opposed, firstly, to essentialist geo-specificity which is tied to nationalist and traditionalist ideologies. But in its turn, internationalism can be both a generic force as globalization unifying oppression of localities and an emancipatory one as progressive reconstruction of *bentu* and place.

While both impulses appear and are applied in multiple contexts, the former is anti-universalist (relativist, inward-looking, essentialist) and the latter universalist (sharing common struggles and aspirations). In art theory, artworks are variously positioned along the axis between them to track the artists' historical and ideological affinities. Sometimes, they might be situated closer to one pole while gravitating toward the other. For example, critical contemporary art in the West traditionally has its footing closer to the "internationalist" pole, while the sector experiences headwinds that push it toward the "geo-specific" pole. In China, the impulse to internationalism is prevalent in both historical and contemporary art that strives for an internationalist alliance in shared struggles, yet they are not uprooted from the geo-specificity of China due to its socialist heritage, which in turn becomes an item in the global "market of identities." This shows how the two impulses can transmute into each other. Thus, what follows is a mapping and

8 Thomas S. Mullaney, *Coming to Terms with the Nation: Ethnic Classification in Modern China* (Oakland, CA: University of California Press, 2011).

9 See Hera Chan and Alvin Li, "Becoming Ethnic in China: A 'Good Story' Told in Painting and Dialect," *Afterall* 53 (September 13, 2022), pp. 158–73; Mingjun Lu, *'Revolution of Art' and Modern China: Radical Origins of Chinese Contemporary Art* (美术变革与现代中国:中国当代艺术的激进根源) (Beijing: Commercial Press, 2020).

analysis of the diverse artistic positions that thematize the Silk Road in this dynamic field of geographical imaginations. They are grouped broadly into two camps while, as suggested already, shapeshifting and crisscrossing the borders.

Geo-Specific Imaginations

Following the not unproblematic ethnic classification project in China during the 1950s, official artists in the art academies championed ethnic minorities as a theme, which coincided with the "nationalization of oil painting" movement.[8] Many of the key artists emerged from the "frontier plein-air painting" movement during wartime in the 1930s and 1940s, when artists resided in safer Western China and were in contact with local indigenous cultures.[9] In the early 1940s, the painter Pang Xunqin spent four months walking in the mountainous region of Guizhou. The painter Dong Xiwen copied medieval wall paintings in Buddhist grottoes in Dunhuang during the war. In the 1950s, he traveled the route of the Long March in rural Western China to make plein-air drawings.

If ethnically Han artists incorporated ethnic motifs into the nascent national academic painting tradition in the nation-building days, the works of non-Han Chinese academic artists continued to be promoted today as official academic art. Often serving as members of regional artist associations, their works feature recognizably ethnic motifs, such as singing and dancing scenes, costumes and postcard landscapes, as in the oil paintings by the Uyghur artist Abdukerim Nasir. Over the last years, such works have populated government organized art exhibitions celebrating BRI but are panned by artists from the critical contemporary art tradition. However, if we juxtapose this with internationally recognized Neo-Realist painter Liu Xiaodong who captured life in Hotan, Xinjiang in his series of paintings as part of the *Hotan Project* (2012–2013) depicting Muslim jade-diggers and the bare landscape on the brink of the Taklamakan desert, what makes them so different? The stylistic characteristics between official academic art and contemporary art are not so clear. It seems that the determination hinges on whether the work serves "minoritarian" or "majoritarian" politics in the eyes of contemporary art critics, if not the milieu the artists find themselves in. But even this characterization does not convey the full picture.

Recently, a number of internationally acclaimed contemporary Chinese artists have ventured into the Western Regions to observe life, glean knowledge, or refine their artistic skills in what could be called "frontier plein-air art 2.0." For example, in his video installation, *Bitcoin Mining and Field Recordings of Ethnic Minorities* (2018) and the sequel *Can Sound Be Currency?* (2020), artist Liu Chuang brings to attention bitcoin mining sites in rural Western China, which is also home to several minority groups such as the Muya Tibetans. Contextualizing questions of capital investment within histories of science and popular culture, the work critiques the deployment of cutting-edge technology at the expense of ecological and minority intelligences.

While taking the side of a "minoritarian" political position but through aesthetic sensibilities from somewhere else, one could speculate that the artist's position is rather detached from the context in which they are themselves mining information.[10] Furthermore, the drift toward the geo-specific favors a divergence of epistemology, for example on the question of technology in Liu's work. The pitfall of this however, as Benjamin Bratton argues, is that divergence can become both the means and ends, while we lose sight of technological viability of bringing divergent tech epistemologies into actual design. Importantly, the relation between convergent and divergent instrumentality and convergent and divergent epistemology (or cosmology) are not the same. Thinking with his notion of the "stack,"[11] Bratton writes that they are "technologically diverse but cosmologically monocultural and we can imagine Stacks which are technologically isomorphic but animated by diverse cultural imaginaries (and presently, we have them)."[12]

In their video *Counting Blessings* (2014), artist Shen Xin documents their painter father's quest for an authentic way to represent Tibetans in his paintings. Shen follows their father's journey to Tibet and interviews him about the photo archive he keeps, largely in a tone critical of his orientalizing gaze. The artist wanted to work through their relationship with their father, which at the same time amounted to a postcolonial critique applied to geographies of the "internal other." However, there are caveats. Years later, Shen corrected their own overtly critical position. Shen has come to realize that there might be something there in their

10 Simon Frank, "Does Liu Chuang's new film challenge the colonial gaze or merely reproduce it?" *Frieze*, June 1, 2019, https://www.frieze.com/article/does-liu-chuangs-new-film-challenge-colonial-gaze-or-merely-reproduce-it.

11 The stack is a concept proposed by Bratton to describe technical and political reordering of societies at a planetary scale in the image of interconnected and interdependent layers that make up a stack: earth, cloud, city, address, interface, and user. This has been expanded by other thinkers to describe specific stacks, and Bratton has since cast the geopolitical conditions into an image of the hemispheric stacks.

12 Benjamin Bratton, "The Stack at the Edge of Planetarity: Notes on Convergence, Divergence and War," *Vertical Atlas* (Arnhem: ArtEZ Press, 2022).

13 Xin Shen, TRANSMISSIONS TV, Episode 3, 2021, https://www.transmissions.tv/season-three/.

14 Alvin Li, "West Side Stories," *The Contest of the Fruits*, eds. Guangtian Ha and Slavs and Tatars (Cambridge, MA: The MIT Press, 2021).

father's fascination beyond the simplistic determination of orientalism.[13] What makes the reassessment more complex is the fact the Shen Xin later realized their late father had Tibetan DNA. This raises an uneasy question: in the current regime of identitarian politics, at what point does one feel entitled enough to speak about the "other"? Why might some feel that Shen's father could only make art about Tibetans if he shared DNA with them? A space of ambiguity is thus opened in research into geo-imaginations.

In another of these constructive openings, curator and writer Alvin Li examines how ethnicity becomes a site of one's own negotiation and imagination in popular culture, such as the genre of Uyghur hip-hop which has enjoyed stardom as a result of being featured on TV hip-hop contest in China.[14] Li engages with a close listening of the song "Ependi" by Uyghur group Yiltiz (meaning "roots" in Uyghur), which, with lyrics both in Uyghur and Mandarin Chinese, cloaks its sharp critique of state-capitalism as experienced in Xinjiang by evoking the folkloric figure of a wise man as an anti-capitalist hero. At a time of massive sinicization in the cultural sector along with the ruthless exercise of necropolitics in Xinjiang, their strategic use of Mandarin is not just a formal compliance but a cunning dissimulation of a critical message which aims to convey the struggle of Uyghurs through deploying both minoritarian and majoritarian means.

These phenomena do not lend themselves easily to an analysis through the lens of postcolonial theories, not least because in much of this theory, it feels as though

15 Tingyang Zhao, "A Political World Philosophy in Terms of All-under-Heaven (Tian-Xia)," *Diogenes* 56, no. 1 (2009), pp. 5–18.
16 Cai Menghan (2017) "论天下——超越天下主义的困境" (On tianxia: Overcoming the dilemma of tianxia), 文化纵横 *(Beijing Cultural Review),* no. 2 (2017).

the answer is preordained as it searches for a question, or context in which to apply its answer (in Shen Xin's case, for example). Thus, postcolonial discourses can be applied both to the nation (China versus the West) or internal colonization (Xinjiang, Tibet, etc.), and the subject of critique may subsequently shift in contradictory ways. This is why Shiming Gao has proposed the geo-specific episteme of *bentu* (native land) as discussed earlier. More emphatically though, he has called for a "post-West" society in his writings accompanying the Third Guangzhou Triennial, *Farewell to Post Colonialism*, which was co-curated by Gao, Sarat Maharaj and Chang Tsong-zung in 2008.

This is paralleled by the steady revival of Confucianism since the 2000s. In the context of BRI, the Confucian notion of *tianxia* is often evoked, meaning "everything under heaven." Historically, it denotes a hierarchical world system wherein the Chinese Empire was at the center. Theoretically unequal, the tributary states would nevertheless gain benefits from this hierarchy. Scholars like Tingyang Zhao have argued for *tianxia* as an ideal form of global governance beyond "international politics," based on the harmony and common wellbeing of all peoples.[15] Scholar Cai Menghan has brought caveats to the generalization of the term by tracing its intellectual history. Importantly, Cai has shown that *tianxia* discourse faded in Song and Ming dynasties, only to be revived in the early Qing dynasty around mid-seventeenth century via intellectual debates. It was believed that even if the Manchu overlord conquered China, they could never defeat the *tianxia*.[16] In other words, *tianxia*

17 See, for example, Yongle Zhang, *Remaking An Old Country: 1911–1917* (Beijing: Peking University Press, 2011); Yongle Zhang, *The Rivalry of Nations: Kang Youwei and the Decay of the Vienna System* (Beijing: Commercial Press, 2017); and Hui Wang, *The Rise of Modern Chinese Thought*, ed. Michael Gibbs Hill (Cambridge, MA: Harvard University Press, 2023).

18 Duncan M. Yoon, "Bandung Nostalgia and the Global South," *The Global South and Literature*, ed. R. West-Pavlov (Cambridge, UK: Cambridge University Press, 2018), pp. 23–33.

encapsulates a Chinese culturalist, albeit emancipatory, proto-nationalism during in early-Qing Dynasty, and shows that such discourses are forms of knowledge rallying certain politics or political thinking as the time called for it. Other scholars have reinvested late-Qing reformist intellectual and statesman Kang Youwei's *datong*, a Confucian utopia where all are democratically ruled by one central government.[17]

Here, the impulses between geo-specificity and internationalism become dynamically dialectical. Revisiting the faded legacy of internationalism is a crucial step to unravelling this.

Internationalist Geo-Imaginations

Critiques of geo-cultural relativism by scholars and artists presuppose commitment to internationalist, anti-imperial, anti-colonial struggles, often connected to the legacy of the socialist era in China. The Bandung Conference in 1955, which aimed for cultural decolonization among non-aligned countries, remains a fundamentally unfinished project.[18] After officially establishing Sino-African relations at the Conference, Chinese premier Zhou Enlai's 1963–1964 state visits to ten African countries consolidated non-aligned principles and promoted solidarity and cooperation among third-world countries. At its height, there were extensive internationalist revolutionary cultural production promoted by China. For example, in the spirit of Bandung, the Oriental Song and Dance Ensemble was established in 1962 to promote cultural exchanges between non-aligned countries.

Emily Wilcox, *Revolution- Bodies Chinese Dance the Socialist Legacy* (Oakland, CA: University of California Press, 2019). Rossen Djagalov, *From Internationalism to Postcolonialism: Literature and Cinema between the Second and the Third Worlds* (Montreal: McGill-Queen's University Press, 2020). Masha Salazkina, *World Socialist Cinema: Alliances, Affinities, and Solidarities in the Global Cold War* (Oakland, CA: University of California Press, 2023). Kuan-Hsing Chen, *Asia as Method: Toward Deimperialization* (Durham, NC: Duke University Press, 2010); Kuan-Hsing Chen and C. B. Huat, "An Introduction," *Inter-Asia Cultural Studies* 1, no. 1 (2000), pp. 9–12; Sun Ge, "How Does Asia Mean? (Part I)," *Inter-Asia Cultural Studies* 1, no. 1 (2000), pp. 13–47; Sun Ge, "How Does Asia Mean? (Part II)," *Inter-Asia Cultural Studies* 1, no. 2 (2000), pp. 319–41. Arif Dirlik, "The Bandung Legacy and the People's Republic of China in the Perspective of Global Modernity," *Inter-Asia Cultural Studies* 16, no. 4 (2015), pp. 615–30.

23 See, for example, "China-Africa: Performing the Image of Migration and Migration of Image," *Entangled Histories of Art and Migration: Theories, Sites and Research Methods*, eds. Cathrine Bublatzky, Burcu Dogramaci, Mona Schieren and Kerstin Pinther. (London: Intellect, 2024).

24 Melissa Lefkowitz, "Revolutionary Friendship: Representing Africa during the Mao Era," *China-Africa Relations*, eds. Kathryn Batchelor and Xiaoling Zhang (New York and London: Routledge, 2017), pp. 29–50.

The repertoires saw music and dance from Asia, Africa, and Latin America, and the ensemble's Chinese actors studied in several African countries.[19] Elsewhere, the Soviet-sponsored Tashkent Afro-Asian Writers' Conference[20] and Tashkent International Film Festival[21] are exemplary cases of such non-aligned cultural collaboration. Up until now, scholars have mostly focused on inter-Asia dialogues to cross-reference shared experiences in anti-imperialist struggles and modernization.[22] This third-worldism of the 1960s and 1970s in China enabled a network of cultural transfers including revolutionary literature, film, music, and art, and kindled a lasting geo-imagination of third world countries.[23]

On closer examination, much of the poster art from the era depicts solidarity pictorially: Africans and Chinese locking arms together in a gesture of collective struggle. Notably in revolutionary paintings, as anthropologist Melissa Lefkowitz observes, the African figures are often depicted wearing traditional robes, while the Chinese appear in their worker, peasant, or military outfits, suggesting that China incorporates Africa into an imagined global community.[24] Looking back, perhaps one should not apply the experiences and material residues of the common struggles involving the staging of ethnic identities too readily to postcolonial studies or to cultural appropriation discourse—indeed solidarity movements could be said to give rise to the latter. In a compelling study on cinema and literature between the second and third worlds, Rossen Djagalov documents how proponents of postcolonial theory, such as Ngũgĩ wa

25 Djagalov, *From Internationalism to Postcolonialism*.
26 According to a private conversation with filmmaker Danial Shah, May 22, 2022.
27 "Khudozhnik Iz Uzbekistana Gotovit Ogromnui͡u Kartinu, Posvi͡ashchënnui͡u Velikomu Shelkovomu Puti" (An Artist from Uzbekistan Is Preparing a Huge Painting Dedicated to the Great Silk Road), *Podrobno.Uz*, August 26, 2019, https://podrobno.uz/cat/uzbekistan-i-kitay-klyuchi-ot-budushchego/khudozhnik-iz-uzbekistana-gotovit-ogromnuyu/.
28 See Maximilian Mayer and Karolina Pawlik, "Politics of Memory, Heritage, and Diversity in Modern China," *Journal of Current Chinese Affairs* 52.2 (2023), pp. 139–62.

Thiong'o or Ousmane Sembène, were shaped by experiences of the third world exchanges ranging from physical convenings to literary circulation networks, only to later be assimilated into Western academia where the field of postcolonialism became specialized and institutionalized.[25]
Fifty years on, official art celebrating China-Africa partnership still retains some of the same sentiments, gestures, and composition, such as in Wang Yiguang's depiction of black workers and Chinese workers dancing on a railway construction site in the style of Socialist Realism. To honor the Belt and Road Initiative, official bilateral artist residencies and exchange programs have been organized, for example, with Pakistani and Chinese artists.[26] The Uzbek news agency *Podrobno* reports that China has proposed to create a gallery of paintings reflecting the history of the Silk Road and the significance of its further development.[27] Uzbek academic painter, member of the Academy of Art, Sabir Rakhmetov was chosen by a Chinese committee to make an oil painting that depicts a buzzing market scene along the Great Wall of China in a historical Romantic style not unlike the above-mentioned Soviet-influenced, ethnically themed paintings seen in China.
But the underlying discourses in such artistic exchanges initiated by China have shifted dramatically from a socialist, anti-imperial, solidarity-based internationalism, to a renewed engagement with *tianxia*. Domestically, *tianxia* is a project of essentializing and homogenizing to fix collective political memory[28] and, internationally, it is the promotion of a re-styled Confucian world order that propagates for a

29 Emily Verla Bovino, "Nation Branding by Evasive Curation: The Case of Q Art Group—A Hong Kong-made Image of China through Central and Eastern European Art," presented on December 1, 2022 at the conference "China's Cultural Diplomacy and Nation Branding," Birmingham City University.

supposedly universalist empire without imperialism. The inclusion of Rakhmetov into the BRI "gallery" is thus paradoxically many things at once: a nod to the socialist era in style and technique, a tribute to the historical Silk Road in content, but with adherence to the neo-Confucian, neo-*tianxia* aspirations of China today.

While many working in contemporary art may have a categorical distain for such "propaganda art," an inconvenient question emerges: what if China had adopted critical contemporary art in its cultural mission in the BRI? What would Western critics of art and cultural policy have to say? We do not have to speculate too much to answer this question. As much as it appears unthinkable from today's perspective, China smartly deployed critical contemporary art in the early 2000s by supporting international exhibitions with Chinese contemporary art—an exercise of soft power that willingly assimilates critical positions not dissimilar to Cold War–era programs for promoting post-war Euro-US hegemony via cultural production.

If analyzed closely, an otherwise inauspicious case raises alarms. Q Art Group, with seats in Hong Kong and Budapest, presented a neatly curated exhibition of modern and contemporary Eastern European Art in Hong Kong in 2021. As researcher Emily Verla Bovino unveiled, however, the foundation is connected to a Hong Kong-based property developer, which is expanding its commercial arm in Eastern Europe under the umbrella of the BRI project, not to mention that it subtly exercises political influences on Hungary.[29] This marks a new and much more insidious form

30 For more grounded studies, see Deborah Brautigam, "A critical look at Chinese 'debt-trap diplomacy': The rise of a meme," *Area Development and Policy* 5.1 (2020), pp. 1-14. Pádraig Carmody, "Dependence not debt-trap diplomacy," *Area development and policy* 5.1 (2020), pp. 23–31.

of cultural diplomacy that actively engages with contemporary art with its inherent progressive values if not critical virtues, while masking political and economic intentions. For those committed to an updated version of non-aligned internationalism, *tianxia* will have a hard time vindicating itself from charges of cultural relativism in the eyes of critical cultural workers. The leftist arm of the critical contemporary art scene in China positions itself largely in opposition to the regime, and by extension to the BRI projects which are overwhelmingly read as imperialist by commentators on international political economy.[30] One way that artists in China have responded to this is by revitalizing the internationalism of the 1960s and 1970s and creating works that side with the underprivileged in what used to be China's third world allies. For example, artist Hu Wei's film *Long Time Between Sunsets and Underground Waves* (2020) focuses on labor history from the 1990s and memory in Malaysia. Feng Junyuan, and Zeng Jiahui's video essay *Two Three Kinds of Heat (Chapter One)* (2018) critiques Chinese state-sponsored infrastructural projects in Sri Lanka that seem detached from the local urban context. Sometimes the attempt to activate a political subjectivity through an internationalist geo-imagination spills over into the social realm, such as in the "Babur Garden" movement, an artistic/social happening, in which a park in Beijing was temporarily claimed by a group of feminist artists and activists to align with the Babur Garden in Kabul, calling attention to gender inequality—explicit and implicit—in both countries. The possibility of such an internationalism existing in

31 Peter Osborne, *Anywhere or Not at All: Philosophy of Contemporary Art* (London and New York: Verso, 2013).

general, let alone in artistic practice confined to certain institutional parameters, is perhaps the most profound challenge to critical practitioners in the global artworld today. Some artists are attempting to cultivate internationalism anew even when the sociopolitical conditions necessary for such a political movement are no longer present—whether socialism at the state level or socialist-inspired movements such as the World Social Forum. Instead, what one typically sees in the artworld is the internationalization of aesthetics rather than the aesthetics of internationalism, or as we have already seen, the Osbornian "First Transnational," by which he wryly appropriates the socialist and communist First, Second and Third International.[31] In Chapter 2, I discussed how the NGO-ization of art has been unfolding in the Global South, perpetuating certain forms of NGO aesthetics. It seems that a genuinely critical position must challenge not only statist propaganda and NGO aesthetics, but also its own categorization of all the above.

Synthesis of the Geo-Specific and Internationalist Into Particular Universals

So far, I have presented a range of contested geographical imaginations that are evident in relation to the Silk Road, where the presentation of traditions and specificities of a locality, just as the depiction of international alliance, solidarity, and friendship can be motivated by divergent, if not contradictory political, cultural-symbolic, and economic calculations. While recognizing the efficacy of documenting and commenting on social ideals or transformations through art and cultural practices, we are nevertheless confronted with the limit of theorizing social change through the prism of art history and endemic discourses in art alone. Instead of adhering to distinctions that art discourse takes for granted, such as critical contemporary art and (socialist) artist association art, the model I propose aims to ascertain more fundamental mechanisms to the political claims of art. Macrostructures like economy and ideology co-exist in the field of art—that's why sometimes the same images produced in different time and social contexts could be interpreted differently when they align to different macro structures (realist paintings in the socialist era and in global contemporary art market), or the same work could be incorporated into different value regimes that do not cohere (critical contemporary art in liberal internationalist art circuit and in official exhibitions). Under such macro structures, the impulses defined here—"international" and "local"—are microstructures, or mechanisms, that describe how certain artistic inclinations reflect in a certain type of work. In such a way, structural causal relations could be suggested. That is, under a set of control conditions, that which can be observed, and can equally be deducted, has a determined relation. Though this is by no means determinism as nothing in the cultural world—certainly not diplomacy—is based on mechanical calculations, the motive of establishing such mechanisms is to overhaul the current interpretive lenses that tend to be ad hoc and self-fulfilling prophecies, like reading art that references socialism in a liberal Western context as political.

32 Bob Jessop, *State Power: A Strategic-Relational Approach* (Cambridge, UK: Polity Press, 2010); Johannes Suitner, *Imagineering Cultural Vienna: On the Semiotic Regulation of Vienna's Culture-Led Urban Transformation*, (Bielefeld, Germany: Verlag, 2015).

Complimentary to the lens of macrostructures and mechanisms there are also actors and agents. Actors in art and cultural policy and institution building have agency in shaping the orientation of specific geographical imaginations. In the tradition of critical geography and cultural political economy, materiality not only determines certain discursive formations, but competing social imaginaries shape public institutions and in turn influence the material planning policy and culture-led development through discursive construction of culture where certain art events, signs, and texts have "institutional power." Much of it focuses on "imagineering" and "branding," capturing the dynamics of culture-led social transformation in a specific cultural context.[32] Domestically, this can be seen in the cases of Silk Road-themed art events, not to mention other cultural festivities which primarily serve domestic audiences. But viewed internationally, there is an uneven distribution of power and no concerted effort in the state interaction with art. Sometimes rising political and economic power does not translate into cultural power. For example, countries such as South Korea are aware of how to build cultural power that it goes hand in hand with increased economic power. If BRI embodies an aspiration for post-globalization globalization, then the cultural imaginations of the Silk Road should be able to synthesize "divergent" elements, both produced in China and elsewhere, into a system of thinking toward new universals. As with the case of documenta, once again we find ourselves confronted with the dialectic between the universal and the particular.

33 James M. Buchanan, *The Limits of Liberty: Between Anarchy and Leviathan* (Chicago: University of Chicago Press, 1975), p. 210.

Although on closer inspection, the historical Silk Road was rather analogous to an ideology-free infrastructure, perpetuated by market actors who spread culture which resulted in value-pluralism. This image of the Silk Road is akin to the ultimate public good as defined by liberal thinkers, i.e., a specific operational procedure itself, an infrastructure that maintains the social architecture to provide freedom of choice to everybody.[33]

Perhaps the lack of such an apt (trans)cultural edifice that could boost China's soft power is heartfelt among scholars who become self-appointed cultural policy advocates. A student of Fredric Jameson, Xudong Zhang, analyses Western culture and intellectual thoughts as following "self-negation," and the conflictual processes of deconstruction, the incorporation of the other into the self, and finally, a new synthesis. Equally, Chinese scholarship must go through these processes of deconstruction, reconstruction, and synthesis. It should search for, contribute to, construct, and continuously improve the concept of universality through different forms of particularity as "particular universals." If we apply such thinking to this discussion, then the historical images of the Silk Road, *tianxia*, and even third-worldism cannot be transposed to today's art and cultural production without going through deconstruction and then reconstruction. In all three historical moments, there was an aspiration or concrete vision of universalism, but in order to renew the discussion on universalism their contexts are different, and their meanings need to be updated. Elsewhere, there are similarly ambitious projects that evoke ancient, civilizational or transnational traditions for modern cultural policy, such as India with its mega-exhibition, *Ancient Sculptures: India Egypt Assyria Greece Rome* at the Chhatrapati Shivaji Maharaj Vastu Sangrahalaya museum in Mumbai, and Saudi Arabia with its Islamic Biennale in Jeddah.[34] It remains to be seen whether any of them can conjure up an operational combination of good politics, value claims, historical memories, and contemporary culture.

Zhang's thinking, at an abstract level, concurs with that of other Chinese intellectuals such as Wang Hui[35] and Sun Ge.[36] What is unique is that Zhang endeavors to map this thinking onto the current state of affairs in China and the world, and makes a less utilitarian and more foundational proposal of "cultural politics," which for him means that culture can fundamentally equal politics. Following Carl Schmitt's Hegel-inspired insight that a non-political domain can turn political analogous to a jump from the quantitative to qualitative, Zhang analyses that religion, culture, economics, law, science, education, aesthetics, and so on are not "opposites" to politics, but rather integrated into the dialectics of substantive politics as "neutral" or "autonomous." Wherever there is tension, it can become a dialectical site where politics emerges.[37] Zhang's analysis implies that what cannot be resolved in culture (i.e., competition of cultures) and the material competition/warfare are parallel, though it does not implicate going further down the Schmittian reading that the political necessarily leads to war, whether cultural or political.

34 Neil MacGregor, "An Ambitious Mumbai Museum Project Sets Indian History in a World Context," *Financial Times*, December 30, 2023. The first Islamic Arts Biennale in Jeddah brought together a mix of ancient artefacts and contemporary art about Islam, see https://www.oma.com/projects/islamic-arts-biennale.

35 Hui Wang, and Matthew A. Hale, "The Politics of Imagining Asia: A Genealogical Analysis," *Inter-Asia Cultural Studies* 8, no. 1 (2007), pp. 1–33.

36 See, for example, Naoki Sakai and Sun Ge, *Universality and Particularity: What is Asianness* (Berlin: Archive Books, 2020).

37 Xudong Zhang, *Cultural Identity in the Age of Globalization: Historical Reflections on Western Discourses of the Universal*, 3rd Edition. (Shanghai: Shanghai Renmin Press, 2021).

Tuo Wang
Tungus, 2021
Single channel 4K video (66 min),
video still

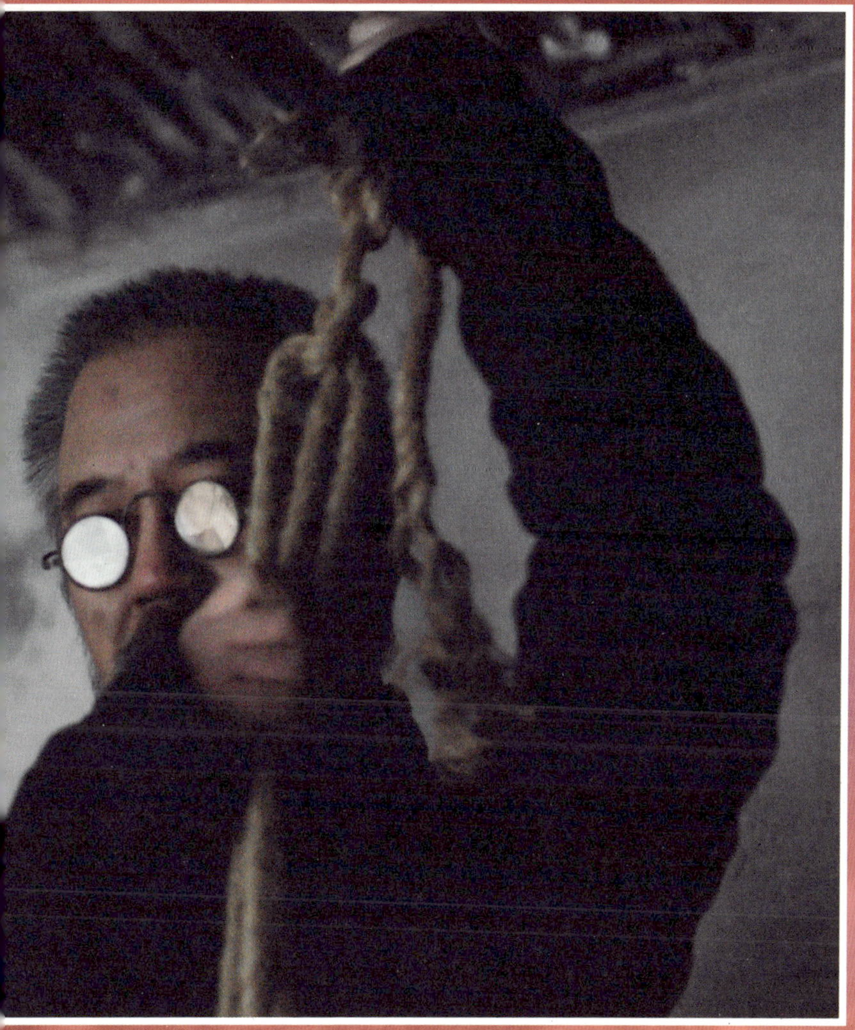

1 See Mi You, "Manchukuo, Capitalism and the East Asian Modern: Transhistorical Desire in Kishi the Vampire," *Southeast of Now: Directions in Contemporary and Modern Art in Asia* 2, no. 2 (2018), pp. 93–117; Mi You, "Silk Roads, Tributary Networks and Belt and Road Initiative," *Tidal Thinking: What comes after nations?*, eds. Rana Dasgputa, Nanna Heidenreich and Katrin Klingan (Berlin: BerlinHaus der Kulturen der Welt and Matthes & Seitz Berlin, 2020); Nikolay Smirnov, "The Island Imagination of Tamagne," essay-exhibition, Golubitskoe Art Foundation, 2020, https://golubitskoefoundation.com/imagination-of-taman; Smirnov, "Left-Wing Eurasianism and Postcolonial Theory," *e-flux Journal*, no. 97 (2019), https://www.e-flux.com/journal/97/252238/left-wing-eurasianism-and-postcolonial-theory/.

The Shared Futures of Eurasianism and Tianxia

In 2020 Nikolay Smirnov and I collaborated on a dialogue for the online journal *EastEast*. Throughout our discussion, we reflected on the underlying philosophical discourse in Russian and Chinese cultural and geopolitical spaces respectively. At the time, Nikolay was working on geographical imaginaries and left-wing Eurasianism, and I was investigating Silk Road projects and Panasianism.[1] We were keen to understand the connections between these intellectual spheres. A comparative study today would probably raise many eyebrows. But back then, much less attention was given to some of the primary figures which we remark on below. For example, the far-right political philosopher Aleksandr Dugin's visit to China in December 2018 was high-profile enough to become something of a social media sensation among academics in China, and yet scarcely drew attention from the Western academic world. At the same time, the big Russian oligarchic-funded art foundation V-A-C, run by a progressive leftist team of curators, organized a discussion between Dugin and Yuk Hui which, although walking an ambiguously thin line between celebrating non-Western philosophy and building an anti-Western philosophical alliance, was thought-provoking. Anyone familiar with Dugin knows that his neo-Eurasianism is partly fascist and at best, an ambiguous philosophy. In the context of a broad decolonial sensibility, where the search for "other" epistemologies, anti-hegemonic and often anti-Western rhetoric is fashionable in

2 See a recent discussion on decolonialism and the far right: Miri Davidson, "Sea and Earth," *New Left Review Sidecar*, 2024, https://newleftreview.org/sidecar/posts/sea-and-earth. The point on *Grossraum* is cogently covered in this piece.

radical progressive circles, sometimes there loomed an illusion that his constructions may illuminate dialectics and dangers of decoloniality. Since the Russian invasion in Ukraine and his daughter's death finally turned Dugin into a fanatic and militant maniac, it has become crystal clear that some of these non-Western epistemologies that progressive art and academia has an appetite for can be ill-founded and deeply problematic.[2]

Back in 2020, we hoped that by discussing *tianxia* and Eurasianism together, we could contribute to the discourses of multiple non-Western onto-epistemologies. Our shared interest was manifold: to understand their genealogy and their deployment in intellectual and political spheres; to assess them as indigenous or geo-specific answers to postcolonial discourse; and to compare Eurasianism and *tianxia* as placeholders for the pre-post-colonial systems of thought and answers to the postcolonial; to highlight some internal dialectics and dangers of decolonial and emancipatory rhetoric, especially in claims for geo-specificity in political practice and theory; to demonstrate that there is a nebulous zone where it is often impossible to measure precisely to what degree the art and thought are progressive or reactionary, left-wing or right-wing (themselves Western concepts that don't necessarily describe how reactionary or revolutionary ideologies function in other contexts). We didn't want to generalize the dialectics, pitfalls, and dangers of decolonial thinking and rhetoric. Is there "good" and "bad" decolonization, or "true" and "false" decolonization? Where is the border between "progressive" resentment and "fascist" calls to arms?

In each of our curatorial practices, we were thinking with artists who could articulate this nebulous space and ask these questions rather than become a symptom of it. We tried to understand what maximally non-reductive ways of talking about complex and ambiguous phenomena could be possible. Of course, we understood that we were playing with fire, especially to talk about Eurasianism which to a certain extent almost instantly merged with Dugin's Neo-Eurasianism—but we undertook this intellectual exercise openly, making our progressive intentions clear.[3]

In retrospect, there are many considerations we left out at the time, some of which I have written into this book. One glaring omission perhaps is Carl Schmitt's notion of the *Grossraum* (Greater Space): a principle that orders the world into blocks, each dominated by a hegemon and characterized by a cultural, economic, and political coherence, to which Dugin's thinking, not to mention Russian's post-2012 "Eurasian turn" in foreign policy, is associated.[4] What this line of thinking leads to is a contentious multipolar world built on cultural spheres—in Dugin's project for example, they are the Atlantic, Eurasian, and Asian spheres. At a time when the world is dangerously heading toward a place that resembles this schema, that inflection point is exactly what both of us and this book want to move beyond. But in doing so, we would have needed to sift through the cultural philosophical ideas and political visions—and sometimes gruesome political consequences—that are

3 We were not the only ones who tried to do so. See for example, Benjamin Bratton's piece touching on the interrelations of Dugin's and Hui's thinking. For Bratton, Dugin's brutish worldview of divergent cultural and political blocks is a theory of multipolar hemispheres, but not all multipolar hemispheres or divergence are Duginian. "Just because cosmotechnics identifies convergence with a problematic modern technological present and champions divergence based on revived cultural specificity does not mean that it is compatible with Duginism," Bratton writes, "Nor does it mean that it is incompatible." Divergence as ideal means and ends leads him to critique the divergence in epistemology in relation to (actually existing convergence in) instrumentality. Benjamin Bratton, "The Stack At The Edge Of Planetarity: Convergence, Divergence And War," *Vertical Atlas*, March 2022, https://verticalatlas.net/#benjamin-h.-bratton1.

4 See for example David G. Lewis, "*Grossraum* Thinking in Russian Foreign Policy," *Russia's New Authoritarianism: Putin and the Politics of Order Edinburgh Scholarship Online,* September 17, 2020.

5 See, for example, Perry Anderson, *American Foreign Policy and Its Thinkers* (New York and London: Verso, 2015). See also John J. Mearsheimer, "America Unhinged," *The National Interest* 129 (2014), pp. 9–30; Mearsheimer "Why the Ukraine Crisis Is the West's Fault. The Liberal Delusions that Provoked Putin," *Foreign Affairs* 93, no. 5 (2014), pp. 77–89.

often compounded. As mentioned above, there are several cultural philosophical concepts and images that Dugin works with that are not far from discourses in the Western, liberal, even progressive left humanities today. Schmitt too, worked with metaphors of land and sea. In the conversation, we should have mentioned not just this coming-together of Schmitt and Dugin, but also the fever for Schmitt's ideas in China. We should have considered the evidence *Grossraum* thinking in the history of US foreign policy.[5] And we would have to be clear-headed about the "friend-enemy" distinction, which posits that a central feature in politics is the distinction between those that share a common identity, values, or existential concerns with one's group than those that appear to threaten it. Though much derided by critics on the left and right, and though often simplified by those applying it to geopolitical contestations, the "friend-enemy" distinction is less pertinent here for our discussion—admittedly, Mao was more absolutist than Schmitt in applying friend-enemy thinking to politics. To do justice to the cultural philosophical features in Schmitt's thinking, we need to acknowledge his emphatic critique of liberalism. For Schmitt, Catholic culture holds a different juridical logic that guides human social life as opposed to Protestant instrumental rationality, which finds resonance in China with Confucianism. To connect this to contemporary post-liberal discourses in the West and places like China will be a timely endeavor.

With these disclaimers made clear, below is our conversation in full as a way of bridging two parts of this chapter which investigate different modalities of postcolonial epistemology. The conversation has been lightly edited for clarity.

—Mi You and Nikolay Smirnov, March 2024

Nikolay Smirnov: I would like to talk about non-Western philosophies. In particular about Russian attempts to create such a system of knowledge. The most well-known case is Eurasianism. While in China, it would be *tianxia*. Shall we compare them a little and try to consider what kind of philosophical and ideological operations lie behind these undertakings? Maybe we can also talk about the re-emergence of these philosophies in the contemporary geopolitical conditions in Russia and China, most likely in relation to postcolonial ideologies.

Mi You: Thank you very much, Nikolay, for the introduction and for the invitation. And I look forward to the dialogue.

Nikolay Smirnov: Let me begin with Eurasianism. It was a philosophical and political current that emerged in the 1920s among the Russian diaspora in Europe. Radically criticizing European cultural hegemony, Eurasianism subsequently attempted to conceptualize a theory of Russian-Eurasian identity and its universal mission, reaching its peak in the 1920s and 1930s. However, Eurasianism's origins lie earlier with the rise of nationalist romantic ideologies prominent at the beginning of the nineteenth century. In this way, this twentieth-century Eurasianism was not "original" because many European nations formed ideologies of a so-called "third way" in the first half of the twentieth century. Developing ideas which first appeared during those nationalist romantic movements, they tried to elaborate their own ideologies, their own unity, and their own philosophies.

Russian Slavophiles discovered this path before Eurasianism. In the first half of the mid-nineteenth century, they had already formulated quite original interpretations of non-Western philosophy. In particular, I want to mention Alexei Homyakov's concept *sobornost.* In general, *sobornost* is an analogue of the term *Catholicity*—the idea of the universality of the Catholic Church. But Homyakov split this term and claimed that Catholicity is a repressive notion and that it is proper for the Western world, to the Catholic Church. Even though Russia was a center of the Orthodox world, according to him, it also expressed *sobornost*—an ideal of non-repressive and not formal cooperation between people—which is neither equal to Protestant individualism, nor to Catholicist unity. For Homyakov, Catholicity was a "wrong," or in other words, a repressive and formal unity organized by the Catholic Church, and *sobornost* was a "proper," non-repressive unity that as not formally organized but instead according to the religious "spirit" of the Orthodox Church—a "true" unity. One could say it was the first example of such a duality: one part good, another bad. One is ours and the other one is foreign.

Later, in the beginning of the twentieth century, Eurasianists repeated this modality. In general, Eurasianism was formulated after the October revolution, when certain intellectuals and scientists ended up in exile from the Soviet Union. They tried to reflect on what had happened

6 Nikolai Trubetskoi, "On the Turanian Element in Russian Culture," *Anthropology & Archeology of Eurasia* 37, no. 1 (July 1998), pp. 8–29.

in the country and to formulate a philosophy of "Russia-Eurasia," a specific "geographic personality," which is not equal to the East nor the West. They did not consider Russian-Eurasian religiosity to be institutionalized clericalism. To the contrary, they thought of the rites and mundane lives of people as interconnected. They assumed that Russian-Eurasian people do not need institutional hierarchy because their life is full of mundane religiosity or, as they called it, "everyday confessionalism." They said that people who lived in this Russia-Eurasia geographical entity did not distinguish between the ideal and profane. So these two realms penetrate each other and people try to implement the ideal in every minute, in every gesture of their existence. In connection with this, they also spoke about the orthodoxy of folk, which they contrasted to the orthodoxy of the elite. According to them, the religion of everyday people or folk is different from the religiosity of the ruling classes.

Another concept, developed by these philosophers, is the so-called "Turanism."[6] They dreamed about Turan, which is a strip of the land between South and East Asia and North Asia, somewhere in the steppes. Turanians' consciousness is very concrete and not abstract. Turanians and Russian-Eurasians as successors of the Turanian psychological type just borrow abstract concepts, change, and then implement or realize this modified concept in everyday life. And this is, in short, what the Turanian psychological type, according to Nikolai Trubetzkoy, was.

In general, one could speak of the ideocracy—the rule of the idea in all spheres of life, whether science, art, ideology, or state structures. In fact, Eurasianists talked a lot about different features of Russia-Eurasia, but here I just highlighted a few key points to demonstrate how they formulated this theory of specific geographical identity. Moreover, they understood the world as very diverse in a geocultural sense. So Eurasianism championed cultural relativism. In the beginning Eurasianists criticized the cultural hegemony of the West and later they began to define the specificity of Russian-Eurasian geoculture as one of many others in this global palette of geocultures. And they marked all these points that I already mentioned: about everyday confessionalism, Turanian psychological type, and so on. Thus, during the 1920s and early 1930s, classical Eurasianism was formulated around these principles.

Later this group of intellectuals split into left- and right-wing factions. The left wing was more interested in socialism, and tried to unify Karl Marx with Nikolai Fyodorov (the founder of Russian Cosmism), while the right-wing maintained a classical, orthodox version of Eurasianism. But in general, they all agreed on the idea of geocultural diversity. Maybe the main idea of all currents of Eurasianism was that the world should be unified and diverse simultaneously.

You: Thank you, Nikolay. Let us compare and discuss the various thoughts proposed by thinkers from both contexts. I would just briefly discuss the ideology of *tianxia* or the philosophy of *tianxia*, that may in some strange ways, resonate with Eurasianism.

tianxia literally means "everything under heaven." It is an ideological system that depicts a hierarchical world system where the Chinese Empire stays at the center and sort of controls or manages everything under heaven with this heavenly mandate. In terms of foreign policy, for the centuries that predated the modern era it meant that countries on the periphery of the Chinese empire had to enter into a tributary relationship with China. I will return to this question of tributary relations a little bit later, as I have been keen in reading archival records to understand how such relationships actually worked.

What binds the tributary relationships is a kind of symbolic order. When all these other countries sent their missionaries to China, they had to perform very elaborate rituals. They had to kneel down or bow down to the Chinese Empire and to present gifts and recognize that they were lower down the order than China. Usually, they got gifts that were worth much more than the gifts they had brought. And they would, of course, have to recognize the Chinese Emperor as the universal ruler.

The real use of this term begs our attention because you hear about *tianxia* these days a lot in the last ten to fifteen years with the rise of China on the global stage, and there has really been a surge of scholarship on *tianxia*. Scholars like Tingyang Zhao who has published books on *tianxia* and whose books have been translated into many languages really proposed this ideal form of global governance. This global governance is beyond international politics as we know it today, because international politics is based on theoretically equal nation states, whereas *tianxia* is based on the harmony and common well-being or a common destiny of all peoples. Such recent scholarship has excited people on both the left and right. And so I ask: is it actually a historically accurate practice, and if not, then how was *tianxia* actually used and theorized historically?

Another snapshot of *tianxia* came much earlier in the eleventh and twelfth centuries with the esteemed Confucian scholars Zhang Zai and Zhu Xi who felt that China was going through some kind of bureaucratization. They felt the country had lost their spirit. They lamented the fact that they were no longer living in this system of *tianxia* where sage kings reigned with rites and music, but now we had only schools and exams. I mean, it is not so bad to have school and exams—it depends on what kind of school or exams you have. According to them, it was better when society was not organized around these technocratic or bureaucratic systems, but with rites, rituals, and music. That would be when all the peoples and "everything under heaven" can come to harmony together. This point—rites and music—somehow reminds me of what you just have said about "everyday confessionalism" in the geosophy of Russia. This is how *tianxia* as a term and as a concept was actually used by intellectuals in history.

Another crucial moment was before the modern era, at the beginning of the Qing dynasty, which was the last imperial, non-Han-Chinese dynasty where the Manchus ruled China for almost three hundred years. When they first conquered China around the mid-seventeenth century, many Chinese scholars committed suicide to show their loyalty the Ming dynasty, and other scholars argued that even if Qing could take over China, they could never win the *tianxia*. It implies that *tianxia* is kind of a more abstract idea than the actual physical country that you conquer and encompasses a cultural sphere. In that sense, it was kind of a prototype of emancipatory nationalism. This was the most explicit case. We could compare the curious trajectories of *tianxia* and Eurasianism, and whether they could potentially harbor emancipatory potential sometimes. But it can also be distorted and co-opted to justify neo-Imperial practices, at other times—perhaps in some sense we are seeing it become possible today.

Smirnov: Yes, I would like to compare them. The situation is much clearer for me with Eurasianism: it has the big contradiction and big intellectual discursive contrast within itself. But I would like to ask you, first, what part of *tianxia* ideology appears in modern political philosophy?

You: I think it is fair to say that *tianxia* had a much longer lineage and it is really not up to us to judge if it is "good" or "bad." We could reflect at what times and to what purposes it has been evoked. So if you look at the most recent surge, as I already pointed out earlier, it really coincides with the rise of China as a military and economic powerhouse. It also comes at the time of the Belt and Road Initiative (BRI).

Part of that "package" is building roads, oil or gas pipelines, airports, and ports, but it also comes with a political bargaining power so that, as you know, some countries would turn to the side of China if they had to vote on certain issues. Western liberal democracy seems to be in trouble or seems to be running out of steam. And then you have this discourse of *tianxia* as a kind of modern political system. It works in the same way as what you just described in terms of how Eurasianism was designed to be.

When it comes to military and economic questions, things get complicated. For example, if you look at how *tianxia* contributed to peacemaking in the region both in the case of the nomadic tribes and the Chinese Empires in pre-medieval and early medieval times (albeit at great costs for China), and also in early modern time between the Ming and Qing dynasties and its East-Asian and Southeast Asian neighbors. It is true that these relationships did contribute to regional peace. There are numbers and statistics that demonstrate that there was really very little major warfare between China and these countries. This tributary relationship is equivalent to today's trade delegations and trade treaties. In a way we can argue that something like that is going on with the BRI and with all these trade agreements and bilateral investment treaties, basically involving China lavishly giving money to other nations. Answering your question, hard power is always behind this kind of discursive, theoretical, and philosophical soft power in the modern and contemporary context of struggle for power, that is something that makes *tianxia* quite a dubious concept.

Smirnov: Thank you. You touched on a really important question about the connection of these ideologists with a contemporary situation. But when I asked you about the modern implication, I meant Modernity in general, beginning with national romanticism of two hundred years ago, because in the case of Eurasianism it was very important. In this regard I also think about Kyoto school, it also was a case of political modernism. They had some traditions in the past, in particular, Buddhism, and wanted to create non-Western original philosophy in modern political situations. Returning back to *tianxia*, I am curious about the construction of contemporary *tianxia*: what percent of the ancient original ideology there is on the one hand, and how much of modernist political thought and the contemporary struggle for geocultural hegemony is on the other?

You: I appreciate this jumping back and forth in history, geography, and ideas. I think you are really showing the complexity of this intellectual landscape. And there are many points that I could raise in this regard. It is true that *tianxia* as a modern political ideology or a system was not synchronous with the modern version of Eurasianism, the classical Eurasianism, because that was the time when China was really busy fighting its anti-imperial wars. There were very few formulations beyond this national liberation discourse itself, save for the very short-lived attempts such as Pan-Asianism proposed by Sun Yat-sen, the founding father of China. And then of course there was a very rapid

7 Vivek Chibber, *Postcolonial Theory and the Specter of Capital* (London and New York: Verso, 2013).

embracing of the communist ideology in the 1920s and that the oppressed people of the world should unite.

I could also relate to what you said about Eurasianism as prefiguring post-colonial discourse if we follow the ideas of Vivek Chibber, for example.[7] Building this kind of unified, but also diverse—so in a word, maybe pluriversal—worlds seems to be only a possibility of something that is actually universal. Because you can only view such a pluriversal world if you have gone through and you are situated in a kind of Western tradition, be it in the elite Western universities or in the sort of universalism of the global ruling elites. I am interested in whether a non-Western philosophy is possible. Was it possible before? Is it going to be possible in the future? Does it feel almost as if that it is only possible within a certain universal structure and that is maybe the most frustrating part of being a thinker from a non-Western country and trying to understand where we are. I know you are still interested in how much of *tianxia* as a modern political theory is viable. I think the most recent manifestation is not actually *tianxia* itself, but the concept that is connected to it which has been adopted by the Chinese Communist Party as a model not just for foreign policy, but for their general policy—in the slogan "community with shared future for mankind." This is the idea of the common future of the humanities. Curiously enough, I think they changed the English translation from "shared destiny" in the original rendering because they felt "destiny" sounds a bit fatalist ideological or it just doesn't evoke the right feelings. So this common future of humanities is connected to the ideology of *tianxia* and they profiled it as an original idea as a proposition for international governance and also as a goal for society, domestically and internationally, but they never quite looked into similar ideas that had been already in place, for instance, in Germany around the circles of Carl Schmitt. It is a really complex situation: mentioning any of these concepts would evoke very different reactions or associations depending on who you are talking to and what is the context of where you are speaking.

Smirnov: We began with the definitions of particular ideologies such as Eurasianism and *tianxia*, jumping between different points of view and comparing them. But finally, I think the relevance of this discussion and of further inquiry into those theories is a question of how to build this unified and diverse world which they tried to conceptualize. And this requirement should work as a regulative idea or regulative fiction, I think.

You: Yeah, that is a very good point. I think that is almost a hinge on which everything hangs. *tianxia* offers those kinds of different perspectives rather than a unifying perspective.

1 For one example, see Jeremy Daum on China's social credit system, "China through a Glass, Darkly," *China Law Translate* (blog), December 24, 2017, https://www.chinalawtranslate.com/china-social-credit-score/.

3.2

Tech and Ideologies: Chinese Tech Legacy in Art Production

As with Silk Road, technology and its incumbent culture in China is a topic that deserves intercontextual attention for the cultivation of a theory beyond particularism. It didn't take long for a topic that was rather niche to become a household concern under the banner of "tech war" and its variations such as "chip war," that are gaining historical bipartisan support in the US and elsewhere in the West. Numerous books have been written on the development of the Chinese tech stack, one of the most important hemispheric stacks. For topics such as "surveillance state" and the social credit system, the purported national program that uses data to monitor, assess, and regulate the behavior and trustworthiness of individuals, businesses, and government entities, international researchers in the tech field have cautioned that we need to base our judgement on practical research on the ground instead of falling into sensationalism.[1] Artistic production that thematically or conceptually refers to Chinese technology both from inside and outside of China has largely ignored this gap of evidence-based research and tends to follow critical theory with a touch of culturalist assumptions, sometimes

2 Sinofuturism is a popular artistic genre which turbo-charges futuristic tech imaginaries of China.

repeating techno-orientalist "sinofuturist" patterns.[2] It is admittedly difficult to steer clear of taking such positions when it dominates the discourse. As such, I am also self-critical of my own work and see a need to arrive at a meta-critical position.

What follows here and in the following chapter are case studies that introduce different modes of engaging with technology and the history of science and technology in China. As with the Silk Road, the underlying motivations of cultural productions around tech present a range of ideologies and pragmatisms. What is considered critique of technology in the West and in China may carry different connotations and may converge on points that are under-emphasized. In a place where multipolarity is almost embedded full-stack—by which I mean from the raw materials to software and regulations—let me refrain from chanting multipolarity and instead put forward some avenues of inquiry for pragmatic ways of speaking to a possible universal.

Case Study 1: The Wandering Earth

The Chinese sci-fi blockbuster *The Wandering Earth* (2019) is based on the novella by award-winning sci-fi writer Liu Cixin. Set in the near future, the solar system has become uninhabitable and the Earth's population forms the United Earth Government. A plan is devised to move the Earth out of the solar system to the Alpha Centauri system. Planetary engines are built across the planet, underneath which are underground cities to house the human population. The engines, running on fusion power, stop the rotation of the Earth and propel it away from the sun. As the film starts, the Earth passes by Jupiter, whose gravitational spikes cause devastating earthquakes on the Earth and international rescue teams risk their lives to keep the Earth engines running. However, Earth is drawn in by Jupiter's gravitational pull to the point of no return. The artificial-intelligence-controlled international space station deems Earth impossible to save and turns on an escape mode to continue searching for inhabitable planets to populate. The young protagonist, Liu Qi, suggests igniting Jupiter's hydrogen-rich atmosphere to propel Earth, but the most powerful engine on Earth falls short of igniting Jupiter. At this critical moment, astronaut Liu Peiqiang, Liu Qi's father, destroys the command system in the space station and drives his spacecraft to the cloud between Jupiter and Earth, helping the ignition by sacrificing himself. Earth is propelled out of Jupiter's orbit and continues its migration to another galaxy.

Sci-fi ends where science begins. Tech-optimism is in the air in China: from government officials to state-sponsored futurologists, from the private sector to the public, the importance of scientific development is a shared consensus. With *The Wandering Earth* grossing the second highest profits in Chinese box-office history, a sci-fi boom is catapulted into being. Public and private investments are pumped into sci-fi "industrial zones" to support creative economy companies banking on sci-fi IP spin-offs. Sci-fi

3 Smriti Mallapaty, "China's Five-Year Plan Focuses on Scientific Self-Reliance," *Nature* 591, no. 7850 (March 18, 2021), pp. 353–54.

4 Jacob Dreyer, "China Dreams of a Palace in the Sky," *Noēma*, 2022, https://www.noemamag.com/china-dreams-of-a-palace-in-the-sky/.

5 This is a remark made by Jacob Dreyer during a private conversation.

expos attract high-profile media features and large audiences. Elementary school children are enrolled in sci-fi writing competitions. There is any number of space travel themed amusement parks and art exhibitions across the country. The latter phenomenon is concurrent to a nationwide rollout of STEM or STEAM education, where kindergarten kids start learning computer programming. The Chinese state is doubling down on its spending in basic sciences, an area until recently overshadowed by applied sciences.[3] It may appear to be a moment when speculation and rationality are coupling, but going deeper it is debatable if both can be reduced to instrumental uses. The appearance of sci-fi on steroids veils not only the tendency to reinforce the known, including the best and worst of our morals, but also the incapacity to change the present. This is a classical dystopia as utopia, where solidarity becomes possible in the worst of all scenarios. Too often it serves as a fantasy ride into an accelerated future so viewers and readers in the crumbling present can derive comfort from the knowledge that future realities are still livable, alarmism aside. Or, following techno-optimism, the liberating possibilities of science and technology seems to contribute to "the pursuit of quiet, conformist prosperity," one that is situated in a general cultural optimism of the Chinese middle class.[4] Geopolitically, the space mania in popular culture generated at the high altitude of the Cold War may be less fitting a comparison for its "loudness," but there is an acute sense, as some have remarked offhandedly that "the US is the problem, [and] science is the answer."[5]

6 However Liu is not the first to propose this scenario of taking the Earth on an exile. Tianxiao Bao (1875–1973), a novelist and publicist, wrote a short story "世界末日日记" (Stories of the End of the World) in the 1900s in which the moon is approaching the Earth, and people debate ways to save the planet. One of the proposals is to use all scientific means to force the Earth to fly out of the solar system. It also resonates with Buckminster Fuller's *Operating Manual For Spaceship Earth* (1969), a philosophical treatise that emphasizes the idea of Earth as a single entity.

7 Yuk Hui, "For a Planetary Thinking," *e-flux Journal*, no. 114 (December 2020). https://www.e-flux.com/journal/114/366703/for-a-planetary-thinking/.

8 Lorenzo Marsili, *Planetary Politics: A Manifesto* (Cambridge, UK: Polity, 2021).

9 See Benjamin Bratton's planetary computation thesis in *The Stack: On Software and Sovereignty* (Cambridge, MA: The MIT press, 2015).

10 Nathan Gardels, "Planetary Politics When the Nation-State Falters," *Noēma*, 2021, https://www.noemamag.com/planetary-politics-when-the-nation-state-falters/.

One of the most striking features of *The Wandering Earth* is the premise of the Earth as a spaceship,[6] as opposed to the biblical (and earlier Mesopotamian) image of Noah's Ark or typical Hollywood narratives in which a few humans survive atrocities on Earth by performing a grand escape (based on a Western colonial notion of space into which Earth can always be extended). The story turns this on its head by taking an inward or intensive image of Earth. Conveniently, the film was released to coincide with the popularization of China's slogan 人类命运共同体 ("a community of shared future") in an attempt to articulate the need for global cooperation. At various global summits, Chinese leaders emphasize concrete policy issues such as development, security, and sustainability, as well as intangible ties, such as those established via culture. A high-flying idea, it does however strike a chord and comes close to a "planetary politics" that many argue is needed to save us from the climate crisis, from cultural theorists,[7] left-wing political theorists,[8] tech culture luminaries,[9] as well as think tanks such as the Berggruen Institute.[10]

If this speculative fabulation renders such a political message palpable, and in doing so, becomes wittingly or unwittingly the best piece of cultural diplomacy China has produced in recent years, the original novella presents more than disconcerting details about the organization of this future society under the guidance of the technocratic United Earth Government. Education is practically reduced to astrophysics and engineering, love is rare though couples do marry and reproduce, and elders are sacrificed so

11 Mi You and Federico Ruberto, "Sg_Dao.Inc," *Lonely Vectors*, eds. Mi You, Joella Kiu, and Kenneth Tay (Singapore: Singapore Art Museum, 2022).
12 Cixin Liu, *The Three-Body Problem* (New York: Tor Books, 2016).

that the young can survive instances of technical failure. There are certainly some degrees of objective necessity in suppressing the liberal individual tradition in the face of an insurmountable catastrophe, but even there, softer forms of social engineering are imaginable.[11]

If all of this is an unsettling nod to Aldous Huxley's *Brave New World*, then the chill goes even further in Liu's dazzling interstellar epic, *The Three Body Problem.*[12] In this dangerously competitive universe, "dark forest rule" prevails: any civilization will annihilate other lifeforms before they have a chance to do the same. The most powerful weapon that Earthlings have against a higher intelligence civilization is deterrence, since the Earth can reveal both its own galactic location and that of this predator civilization. In the third book of the *Three Body Problem* trilogy, both Earth's and the invading Trisolaris's coordinates are ultimately revealed, resulting in the annihilation of both by a yet higher intelligence civilization. This operationalized distrust, against the background of a zero-sum game, betrays the fact that Liu was raised during the Cold War and Cultural Revolution. Of his childhood Liu likes to tell a story from when he was seven years old when the whole village gathered to watch Dong Fang Hong 1, China's first space satellite, passing in the starry night. The person behind the satellite project that inspired Liu to embark on a sci-fi career was no other than Qian Xuesen, whose life uniquely embodies science and speculation, though of a quite different kind.

On Qian Xuesen

Chinese cybernetician Qian Xuesen's legacy remains somewhat enigmatic and can be claimed and reactivated by a variety of intellectual spheres. A towering figure in the history of Chinese cybernetics, he was an aerodynamicist who spent the 1930s and 1940s training in the US, where he worked with Theodore von Kármán to develop rules characterizing supersonic and hypersonic airflow. In the 1950s, at the height of the Second Red Scare in the US, Qian returned to China as part of a prisoner exchange (for eleven US pilots captured in Korea) to oversee China's nuclear weapons, missile, and space programs. During the 1950s and 1960s, Qian became the chief propagator of cybernetics in China. His work advanced a particular branch of cybernetics, which he called "engineering cybernetics," that emphasized the design principles of systems and urged scientists to be aware of the theories of the systems themselves.

After initiating the Open Reform process in 1978 (the so-called economic reform with "socialist characteristics"), Deng Xiaoping pulled the brakes on heavy military industry and sought to decouple political mobilization from technological development. Revolutionary subject-formation (class consciousness and proletarianization) were no longer given priority. Instead, the aim was to kickstart China's economy by ramping up consumer industries and allowing decentralized developments driven by self-motivated local agents. "科学是第一生产力" (science is the first productive force) became the motto. At this historical juncture, Qian continued to promote cybernetics, suggesting, like his

13 David A. Palmer, *Qigong Fever: Body, Science, and Utopia in China* (New York: Columbia University Press, 2007).
14 Qian Xuesen, Yu Jingyuan, and Dai Ruwei, "A New Discipline of Science—The Study of Open Complex Giant System and its Methodology," *Journal of Systems Engineering and Electronics* 4, no. 2 (June 1993), pp. 2–12.
15 Orit Halpern, *Beautiful Data: A History of Vision and Reason since 1945* (Durham, NC: Duke University Press, 2014).

British contemporary Gregory Bateson, that it be used to study agriculture and ecology.
What Qian became most drawn to, however, was the supernatural functions of the human body that he saw manifesting in Qigong practices and the development of somatic sciences, which, during the 1980s and 1990s, were booming in China in what has come to be known as a period of *qigong* Fever.[13] In October 1982, at the third plenary session of the Preparatory Committee for Human Science, Qian wrote a report entitled "Does this Breed a New Scientific Revolution?" where he declared that *qigong* and supernatural capabilities were a kind of human science worthy of in-depth study, and that they might lead to a new scientific revolution. Their significance, he speculated, could be as profound in the twenty-first century as quantum mechanics and relativity were in the early twentieth century.
It was around this time that Qian proposed the Open Complex Giant System (OCGS) as a research field in systems engineering.[14] This was meant to offer an alternative path to computation, where expert knowledge, databases of knowledge and information, various AI systems, and computers would form a giant human-machine integrated intelligence system. In the West, cyberneticians like Warren McCulloch were interested in how to turn mental processes into cognition, in line with what they perceived as an algorithmic rationality. The reformulation of cognition in cybernetics as patterns that link thought to action marks the abandonment of the concern with the real. In its place, an interest in predicting future interactions took precedence.[15] This shift

16 Ruwei Dai, "从工程控制论到综合集成研讨厅体系——纪念钱学森归国50周年 from Engineering to Hall for Workshop of Metasynthetic Engineering: Commemorating 50th Anniversary of Qian's Return to China," 复杂系统 与复杂性科学 *Complex Systems and Complexity Science* 3, no. 2 (2006).

17 Hongzhe Wang and Yuan Jiang, "Seeking a Cybernetic Socialism: Qian Xuesen and the Transformation of Information Politics in Socialist China," *Resurrecting Cybernetics* (Shanghai: CAC publication, 2019).

heralded a whole new field of methodologies and practices that make computation more powerful to the point that they—fast forward a few decades—could co-shape our reality more than previously thought.

Qian embarked on a different—and ultimately more ontological—inquiry into intelligence. His OCGS does not just hinge on a set of experts, a series of formulas, or an abstract framework built on the back of a few axioms. Rather, he sought to create a holistic system, synthesizing technology with the capacity of the human. The successful application of this methodology hinges on the holistic and integrated strength of the human mind and computational performance.[16] Qian's wish has always been to integrate 灵感 (*linggan*, inspiration, intuition, and creativity) and figural thinking into computation. If the formal system based on logic alone fails to simulate the emergence to human level intelligence, Qian speculated that the pragmatic alternative was to create a symbiotic human-machine intelligent system. Given Qian's interest in supernatural events, one can speculate if the capacity of the human can be activated or attuned through *qigong* and Chinese medicine. His work on complex system design has not been given enough attention, especially in the current tech race of computational power, which is often based on the same foundational design and architecture.

Due to his near canonization in the Chinese history of technology, Qian has often been superficially interpreted as the patriotic scientist. This leaves a vacuum for different intellectuals to project what they want onto his legacy.

There is a "New Left" milieu that wants to revisit policies of the socialist era to make a case for grassroots technological politics, or for the "mass line"—a Maoist political concept which encourages education and mobilization of the masses to participate actively in political processes, the distinctive Chinese method of technological development until the end of the 1970s, which later gave way to industrialization and economic reform. They cherish the experiences of Chinese scientists, who went down to concrete production sites in villages and factories and taught cybernetics, mathematics, and data sciences during the Great Leap Forward and the Cultural Revolution. Through this process, the villagers and workers learned to optimize their production and the scientists engaged with the local grassroots. In other words, this experience amounts to political mobilization through technology.[17] It even garners attention from those involved in actual grassroot organizing in tech sectors today.[18] Meanwhile, a comprehensive overview of Qian's life published on *Palladium*,[19] a US-based journalism platform pushing a post-liberal governance futurist agenda, lambasted the way cybernetics was applied to giving "scientific" proof for the one-child policy with violent consequences. Eventually, the application of cybernetics in planning social systems such as price reforms and management of public security, seems to converge with post-liberal statecraft.

The liberal optics of individual rights stands in stark contrast to the New Left upholding of mass line politics. We would be well-advised to embrace both readings in a form

18 See Jack Linchuan Qiu and Hongzhe Wang, "Radical Praxis of Computing in the PRC: Forgotten Stories from the Maoist to Post-Mao Era," *Internet Histories* 5, no. 3–4 (October 2021), pp. 214–29. Jack Qiu spearheads the Platform Cooperativism Consortium movement in Asia, which leverages tech to organize labor and social movements in cooperative ways.

19 Dylan Levi King, "The Genealogy of Chinese Cybernetics," *Palladium Mag*, October 17, 2022, https://www.palladiummag.com/2022/10/17the-genealogy-of-chinese-cybernetics/.

of intellectual gymnastics appropriate to a post-globalization constructive politics and notice how they can be united in a productive tension. If Wang Hongzhe's version takes historical dynamism and paradoxes into consideration in line with New Left discourse on Chinese development, it shuns addressing the other side of the coin, namely that this interpretation can only be possible as a retro-justification, rather than serving as a normative prescription at any point in history. Conversely, the liberal position remains consistent with the timeless liberal yardstick—there is little historical dynamism. Each interpretative framework can be an interloper for the other.

Case Study 2:
Qian Xuesen and the Yangtze River Computer

My exploration of Qian's legacy began in 2020, when I commissioned an essay film by Chinese artist Shi Qing for the 13th Shanghai Biennale. Exploring how Qian Xuesen's work could inform our ideas about computation, the theoretical-fictional film speculated on a hypothetical "Yangtze River Computer" as a model for artificial intelligence, where somatic science and *qigong* are "written back" into computation, uniting "nature" and "artifice," human and machine. *Qian Xuesen and the Yangtze River Computer* (2021) is a one-hour-long, retro-futuristic sci-fi film. It draws on real historical figures and events in the history of cybernetics in China, while also adding fictional details, thus conjuring a speculative past and future of computation alongside Qian's biography. The film is made up of mostly black

20 Peggy Wang, *The Future History of Contemporary Chinese Art* (Minneapolis: University of Minnesota Press, 2020).
21 Matthew D. Johnson, "The Science Education Film: Cinematizing Technocracy and Internationalizing Development," *Journal of Chinese Cinemas* 5, no. 1 (2011), pp. 31–53.

and white or faded color archival footage. The narration switches between a matter-of-fact socialist TV anchor-like narrator, the protagonist Qian Xuesen, and an additional commentator. Chapter titles, keywords, and phrases are shown on screen in a red font, using a typeface that resembles propaganda posters from the Cultural Revolution era. The film's collage of large text blocks and images is reminiscent of socialist *Heibanbao*, or "blackboard newspaper," a grassroots form of newspaper-making on current affairs, arts, and culture that uses blackboards in public spaces or classrooms for maximum exposure, thus serving as a tool for mass engagement with art. Scholars have noted the rich visual and material culture present in contemporary art in China, which energizes interpretations of the Political Pop Art scene.[20]

The visual and narrative style of this work evokes the genre of a scientific education film, which dominated Chinese cinema from the founding of the People's Republic of China to the 1970s. These films covered topics as diverse as hygiene, modern machinery and production methods, pesticides in agriculture, and communal organization. They were often technical and painstakingly detailed, while conveying a sense of collective progress. Some films targeted specific audiences, such as peasants, factory workers, miners, and students, and were closely tied to Maoist views of development and scientific education.[21] To an unsuspecting viewer, *Qian Xuesen and the Yangtze River Computer* may appear to be a scientific documentary. Narrated by stoic, objective voices, the film follows Qian's journey back to China and

22 Qing Shi, "Qian Xuesen and the Yangtze River Computer," exh. cat. (Shanghai: 13th Shanghai Biennale 2021).

23 Benjamin Peters, *How Not to Network a Nation: The Uneasy History of the Soviet Internet* (Cambridge, MA: The MIT Press, 2016).

24 See Hongzhe Wang and Yuan Jiang (2019).

his invention of the fictitious "Yangtze River Computer"—a supercomputer that uses the collective organization of the masses to achieve optimal computation results.

In the film, Qian visited the construction site of the Shisanling Reservoir in Beijing in 1958. He was struck by the orderly organization of four hundred thousand volunteer workers and thought: "This is like a mass collaborative physical computer! Compared to the instrumental nature of Western computers, it was the consciousness and discipline of these workers that made real computing possible."[22] Although it may seem outlandish, the ontology of the Yangtze River Computer as a "computer of and for the masses" is an extrapolation from the mass movements that the Chinese cybernetic program was rooted in. China did not follow the same path as Soviet cybernetics, which was largely controlled by a technocratic elite and thus presumed a high level of centralization. The Soviet cybernetic program ultimately failed due to fierce competition and self-interest among the numerous research institutes, technocrats, and specialists involved.[23] In China, on the other hand, especially during the Great Leap Forward and Cultural Revolution, Chinese scientists worked on cybernetics, mathematics, and data sciences at local production sites such as villages and factories in a mass line tech politics.[24]

At this point, the film takes a detour to Salvador Allande's Chile, where a (fictional) Chinese delegation visited the (real) Project Cybersyn in the early 1970s. Cybersyn, designed by cybernetician Stafford Beer, aimed to support the management of the national economy by processing

25 See Lawrence Lek, *Sinofuturism (1839–2046 AD)*, HD video essay, 2016, https://vimeo.com/179509486; and Virginia L. Conn, "Sinofuturism and Chinese Science Fiction: An Introduction to the Alternative Sinofuturisms (中华未来主义) Special Issue," *SFRA Review* 50, no. 2–3 (2020), pp. 66–70.

production input and output data in real-time while involving workers in the management. The film aptly identifies similarities between the Cybersyn principles and the Angang Constitution of 1960, a set of management principles derived from experiences of the Anshan Iron and Steel Complex. The core elements of the constitution were the participation of cadres in labor, and workers in management; the reform of rules and regulations that prove unreasonable in the production; and the integration of workers, leading cadres, managers, and technicians.

Later in the film, Shi Qing connects Qian's deep interest in *qigong* with the work of compatriot Jack Parsons at the California Institute of Technology, who was a rocket engineer under von Kármán and allegedly practiced black magic. The film takes a speculative leap of faith here, suggesting that both *qigong* and the supercomputer are the result of energy shifts generated by quantum leaps under anomalous conditions. Qian claimed to have developed a quantum computer that runs on this parallel computing model, where the computing masses are not eliminated but incorporated.

Through a mix of real and fictitious events, and by evoking an alternative history of computation, *Qian Xuesen and the Yangtze River Computer* presents itself as a retro-futuristic film that complicates how we imagine tech in relation to "sinofuturism." With a touch of cyberpunk noir, sinofuturism typically emphasizes the speed and velocity of tech development, ultra-efficiency as a mantra of statecraft, and bottomless obedient crowds as human resources.[25]

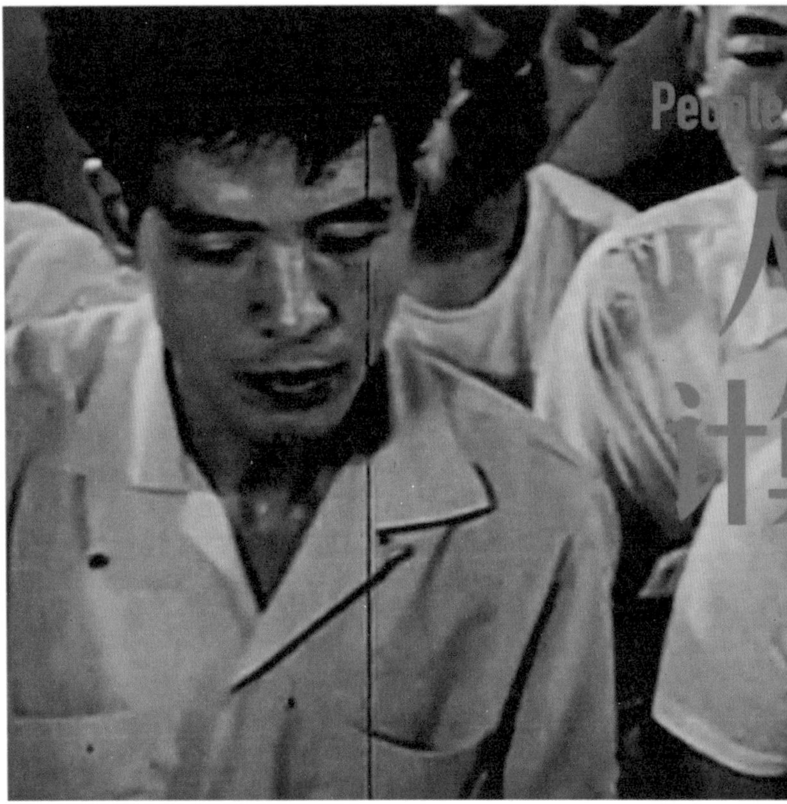

当时被人们亲切地称为“

was affectionately known as the “

Shi Qing
Qian Xuesen and the Yangtze River Computer, 2021
Single channel video (60 min), video still

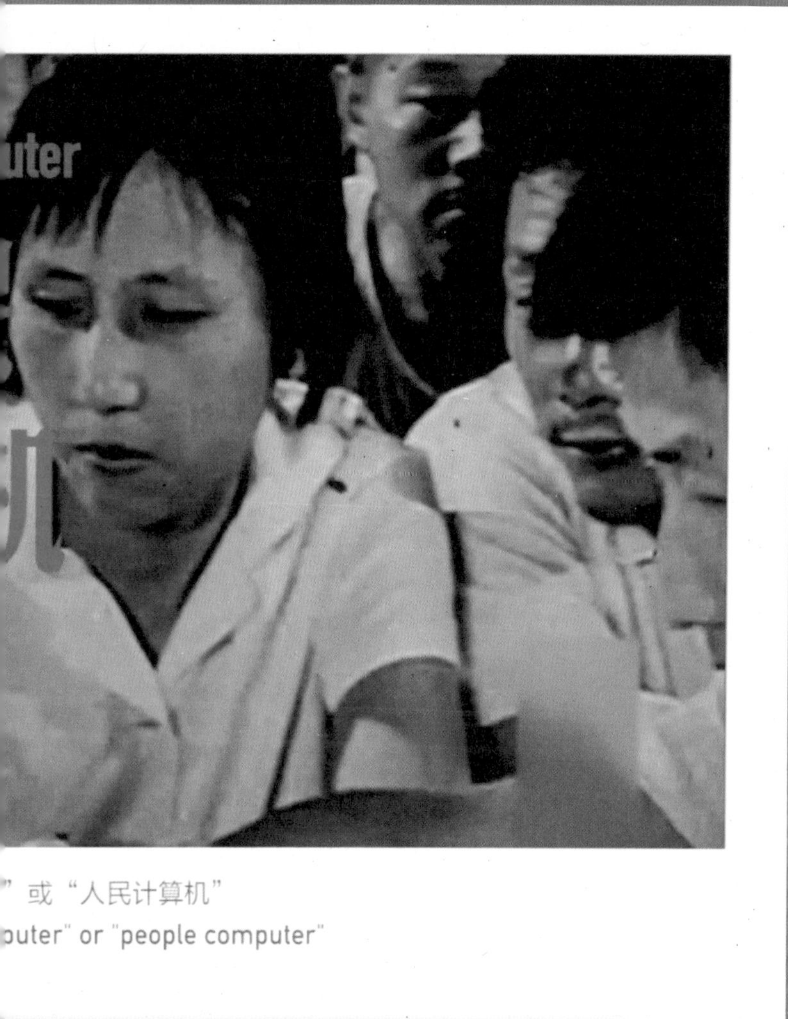

26 Gabriele de Seta, "Sinofuturism as Inverse Orientalism: China's Future and the Denial of Coevalness," *SFRA Review* 50, no. 2–3 (2020), pp. 86–94.
27 See Benjamin Noys, *Malign Velocities: Accelerationism and Capitalism* (Winchester: Zero Books, 2014).

It operates with an aesthetic repertoire that is legible to audiences both inside and outside of China, evoking a sense of fascination, anxiety, and national or cultural pride. However, it reproduces the same tropes and narratives of techno-orientalism, premised on a "denial of coevalness," in Gabriele de Seta's words.[26]

One cannot deny a New Left sense of exceptionalism in the tech vision put forward in Shi Qing's film, from the aesthetics to the pivotal role of the masses. Is the leftist vision of technology distinct from sinofuturism or is it another version of it? I lean toward the latter, on the formal ground that the leftist precept of Qian's legacy is only one side of the story. But there are more extreme visions of leftist technophilia. This idea that China exists on a different timeline from the rest of the world, one marked by a mechanical type of mass mobilization, unifies sinofuturistic imaginations with twentieth century Western leftist fascination with communist states as supposedly non-individualistic, such as interpreting the excessive labor input and fusing the living labor of human bodies and the dead labor of machines to create "living machines" in the Stalin era as a form of left accelerationism.[27] It is also present in some imaginations, such as the already infamous—arguably techno-orientalist—analogue computation scene in the blockbuster science-fiction trilogy *Three Body Problem* mentioned earlier. In a simulated world, Qin Shi Huang, the First Emperor of China in the third century BCE, orders his thirty-million-man army to carry out "computation." Each soldier signals a binary value with a white flag for "0" and a black flag for "1," collectively

28 Cixin Liu, *The Three-Body Problem* (New York: Tor Books, 2016).
29 See David Harvey, "Rate and Mass: Perspectives from the *Grundrisse*," *New Left Review*, no. 130 (2021), pp. 73–98.

forming an enormous motherboard circuitry in space. The penalty for a soldier making a mistake and causing the computer to abort would be execution, in typical Qin Shi Huang fashion.[28] These imaginations of the human mass as a giant machine or a robot horde only replicate the trope of "yellow peril," if not fundamentally misunderstanding the paradoxical relation between living and dead labor.[29] Those on the left should indeed be cautious about ideas from those further left of themselves.

Perhaps to supplement the Qian's leftist interpretation we need—for want of a better word—humanism. Qian Xuesen's work—especially his interest in collective *qigong* practices—suggests an alternative conceptualization of mass culture, collectivity, and computation. Rather than a throng of mindless labor or politicized Maoist workers, how might we think of a human mass that has *agency?* This idea is related to Qian's intuition and creativity, and involves a speculative leap of faith that this notion is possible. Intuition itself can be seen as a grassroots problem-solving mechanism linked to collectivity. This is, in some ways, a metaphysical claim. But Qian's study allows us to venture beyond narrow Western science fetishism, lending itself instead to "cosmotechnics," a term coined by philosopher Yuk Hui that recognizes the unification of cosmic and moral orders through technical activities. The vision of artist Shi Qing highlights this salient feature in Qian's work; neither advocating for technological dominion over humanity nor arguing to scale it all back to the human. His vision does not amount to a grounded, "local," cosmological episteme and

30 Yuk Hui, *The Question Concerning Technology in China: An Essay in Cosmotechnics*, 3rd corrected edition (Falmouth: Urbanomic, 2022).
31 Yuk Hui, "Cosmotechnics as Cosmopolitics," *e-flux Journal*, no. 86 (November 2017). https://www.e-flux.com/journal/86/161887/cosmotechnics-as-cosmopolitics/.
32 *Sreda*, "Technical Issues with Yuk Hui and Aleksandr Dugin," podcast, 2020, https://www.youtube.com/watch?v=-ZZFxM50w7Q.

corresponding practices that are often small, analogue, and communal but neither does he advocate for a man-machine assemblage that leads to subsumption, servitude, and alienation. In the film, technology does not have to be emptied of speculative dimensions to be viable; indeed, practicing somatic technologies or political mobilization of masses are nothing short of cosmological speculation. At the same time, Qian's story shows how these practices can be lived and translated into concrete design.

Yuk Hui's cosmotechnics is intended to overcome the conceptual dualism of techne and nature.[30] Cosmotechnics can be seen as a reunification of technics (器 *Qi*, tools) and the cosmic order (道 *Dao*, the way, order). He also takes issue with the idea, which he sees as embedded in the very notion of technics, that there is a single, universal nature, whose telos can be supposedly revealed via technology. Instead, he argues that such conceptions of the progress of reason belong to a specific political order of western modernity.[31] Thus, Hui advocates for a great plurality of technics, or cosmotechnics, to reinvigorate cosmopolitics beyond this stale Western technological monoculture. In a conversation with philosopher and far-right Neo-Eurasianism ideologue Alexander Dugin, Hui suggests that if the Western model of technological singularity or "AI takeover" marks the moment when human *Dasein* is destroyed, then instead of viewing the singularity as a synchronized endpoint, we should diversify the endpoint and have different singularities.[32] Computational pluriverses can be conceived of by working backwards from the kind of endpoints that we

33 Jordi Vallverdú, "Matter, Spirit, AI," *Vertical Atlas*, 2022.
34 Benjamin Bratton, "The Stack at the Edge of Planetarity: Notes on Convergence, Divergence and War," *Vertical Atlas* (Arnhem: ArtEZ Press, 2022). Available at https://verticalatlas.net/#benjamin-h.-bratton1.

want. We may, for example, look to traditional wisdom, such as the Japanese *kami* (god, force of nature), to counteract the alienation caused by AI by means of re-humanization.[33] In Hui's further work, it becomes clear that cosmotechnics is not necessarily related to computation but works as a sort of analogy, with Hui describing Chinese medical practice as cosmotechnical, expanding the definition of technology to encompass "smaller" practices.

On the other hand, this solipsistic retreat into a pre-packaged cosmology is at best endearing and at worst an operationalization of traditional knowledge. Benjamin Bratton warns of how the divergence becomes a value in itself, especially how decentering has a tendency to be centered in the West (a romantic embrace of all the things that Europe believes that it is not, but that Others are). A genuinely productive cosmotechnics for a cosmopolitics would be both convergent (because planetary) and divergent (because human), and in all senses viable.[34] The work of Qian Xuesan diverges from today's dominant tech systems both at the instrumental and at an epistemological level. However unlikely, he clearly had an interest in "viable" reconfigurations of tech systems design. Given that a small number of Chinese computer scientists are still working on implementing his legacy, this speculative computation is therefore not just symbolically significant—the aim is to rearrange the material assemblage of data-man-computation.

Qian's design for open complex systems, as elaborated and reimagined by the artist Shi Qing, where human intuition and decision-making is reintroduced into the system alongside somatic science, presents an alternative paradigm for computation. It debunks at once the universal computer, the fetishistic, "localist" sinofuturistic supercomputer, and the artworld's fascination for a certain analogue pre-computer. Playing with truth and speculation, the film allows the intensities of the present to emerge, rather than being locked into a barbaric past or heading towards a fully automated machine era with malignant speed and velocity.

Case Study 3:
Sci-(no)-fi

The last case study in this section is a curatorial project that walked the "redline" of politics and expanded the imaginations of what is politically possible. I curated the exhibition "Sci-(no)-fi" for the Akademie der Künste der Welt (Academy of the Arts of the World) in late 2019, which told a speculative story about China and Hong Kong. The democracy protests broke out in Hong Kong just days before the opening. The title is a play on words: science fiction, science non-fiction, science is not fiction, or sino-fiction, a Chinese story of the system and society in the digital age since China's rapid rise to global superpower is also happening technologically.

The exhibition featured newly commissioned and collaboratively produced works with a colossal hologram installation as its centerpiece titled *The Master Algorithm*, a social sci-fi located in a reasonably foreseeable future in Shenzhen and Hong Kong that questions the influence and

35 The Academy of Arts of the World published the texts in its magazine *Hybrid Transactions*: Mi You and Royce Ng, "News from Nowhere," *Hybrid Transactions*, p. 13, September 13–December 15, 2019, https://www.adkdw.org/en/article/1844_hybrid_transactions.

confluence of future technologies with social togetherness. The installation was developed by Shenzhen-based Swooding Architects, a young, radical and no less commercially successful and publicly recognized architecture firm that designed the fictional city in the work, the Hong Kong-based artist collective Zheng Mahler, who penned short stories about the city together with me, and materialized the stories through their signature dazzling aesthetics and use of technology. While both sides have developed into its own version of utopia, a joint information-technology-city was constructed, hovering over the border yet disguised through sophisticated hologram technology, hence not visible to the eyes. In the tacky but also mesmerizing hologram, the audience encounters snippets of life in this third space, a non-site beyond ideological differences, a catalyst for projects envisioning new social values where people find ways to address questions of social relations, care, trust, kinship, and legacy under the omnipresent regime of technology.

The stories were part critique, part accelerationist speculation, and part earnest inquiry into future social forms.[35] For example, it reveals a hidden political layer of the Chinese Internet space: "A movement called neo-litlit (somehow inspired by forerunners in the May Fourth Movement in the twentieth century) compose the great netizen *bildungsroman*. Not adopting the platform of literature—now a marginalized subgenre serving the games industry—the work is collectively composed in epic verse across the comments sections of Daipong Dianping restaurant reviews and Baidu

36 Mi You and Royce Ng, "News from Nowhere."
37 Mi You and Royce Ng, "News from Nowhere," p. 9.
38 Mi You and Royce Ng, "News from Nowhere," p. 10.

maps."[36] It sketches out a macroeconomic condition where the state lives in symbiosis with the private sector, pursuing the same social vision. "Many quantifiable qualities are standardized for job applications, but employers are most inventive in teasing out the unusual qualities of their potential employees. This includes interviewing the candidate on tinder."[37]
There is a story on the common destiny of data and AI despite current divergent paths:

> ... in the Great Overfitting Pandemic ... overfitting produces the hallucinatory effect of drawing patterns where none exist when data sets are too large and the algorithm makes connections between wildly dissonant categories of data. A convolutional neural network trained to recognize the threat of terrorists through facial recognition algorithms is accidentally given data sets from skin cancer epidemiology databases and hallucinate the faces of a million terrorists in the patina of pores on a person's skin. In order to combat this problem, both the autonomous and dependent militaries have their vision augmentation set to manual mode and then given psychedelic drugs in order that their 'wet' vision match the machine hallucinations.[38]

And there is a story about border crossing.

> In the 2030s, tokenization of one's legacy has become commonplace. "*Wealth lasts three generations.*" Family

39 Leslie Cheung was one of the best known and beloved Cantonese pop singers, and Mei Lanfang was the most celebrated Peking Opera performer. Mi You and Royce Ng, "News from Nowhere," p. 10.

40 Another demonstration that we were putting visionary narratives in the real was after the project, Swooding added elements of the story in the design brief for the headquarters of an education foundation in Shenzhen, where they asked designers to reflect "what it means to sense colors, see sounds and play with gravity" as set forth in the scenarios.

> run conglomerates die off from a combination of personal corruption and taxation. Yet it pushes people to question the real meaning of personal legacy. A consensus was reached, first by a small group of people, that legacy should be a shared and socialized practice. People began voluntarily tokenizing their legacies—artifacts, skills, knowledge, secret stories. The fictive value of the tokens skyrocketed when Leslie Cheung's music was tokenized. Later, the Chinese side started a similar tokenization of Mei Lanfang.[39]

Note that this came two years before NFTs took off. And just as with previously hyped technologies, NFTs are rooted in fetishistic individualist ownership. Whereas with the technological infrastructure and mechanism, it is more crucial to question what such distribution networks mean for the art, like questions about the collective caretaking (conservation) of an artistic idea, whether in the form of adaptation, annotation, or further development.[40]

When I received the invitation to curate an exhibition about China and technology, I was determined not to make a group show based on existing works, many of which I consider techno-orientalist, even if that is not the artist's intention. Looking back at this exhibition at the time of writing this in 2024, its message still appears quite balanced: it neither blindly condemned nor naively celebrated any particular tech vision that could be attributed to China or Silicon Valley, as a current or speculative extrapolation into the future. The decision was then to make a vital new production constructed in a collaborative way that would allow in-depth explorations of the topic, to which I contributed not just curatorially but also dramaturgically.

Already in the late 2010s, the West reacted to China's prowess in technology with awe, suspicion, cynicism, or crackdown. The exhibition was walking not just one redline; as just before the opening, as already mentioned, protests broke out in Hong Kong, sparked by widespread opposition to a proposed extradition bill and soon evolved into a broader movement for greater democratic freedom. In the end, we were able to advance a message that the exhibition should speak for itself. No allegation could be made that the exhibition was cheerleading one side, for it tried to bring them together through people-to-people collaboration. Additionally, the audience realized the exhibition was not about taking sides in the present moment. It was more invested in striking a balance between techno-optimism and solutionism, as well as between techno-pessimism and nihilism. I told the public and media that it was, in the end, a show about Europe. It asked what is the future role of Europe with its declared commitment to the social, vis-à-vis the US and China? How could a public culture of sci-fi stimulate imaginations of and discussions on society in Europe? The associated programs, including a "Sci-fi-a-thon," a twenty-four-hour writing marathon, game session, and workshop sessions, became an engine for future sci-fi social scenarios, social relations, and operational models.

In the three distinct cases of artistic and cultural production presented in this section, sci-fi takes on various forms, each with respective historical depth and ideological reverberations, depending on its use as an artistic mode. In this sense, the topic of tech and the Silk Road are not dissimilar: no infrastructure today is without intentions. Taken together, they present how tech or cultural historical discourses could be shaped and continue to shape the multipolar world, and crucially, how a position that moves beyond the current contested multipolar order could be possible, whether by articulating a humanist universal or a sensible leverage point. Succumbing to dominant discourses, voluntarily reducing complexities, going for harmlessly low hanging fruits may be a safer choice, but it will truncate the spectrum of art in a multipolar world in the long run. Lastly, "Sci-(no)-fi" offers a good segue into the final chapter on experiments in a multipolar world, where I examine real world implications of artist collaborations with tech, corporations, public policy, or transnational bodies in ways that refigure the logic of different participating partners.

Chapter 4

Experiments

4.1 Tech Pragmatics in Artistic Experiments

4.2 Designing Institutions: Art After a Multipolar World

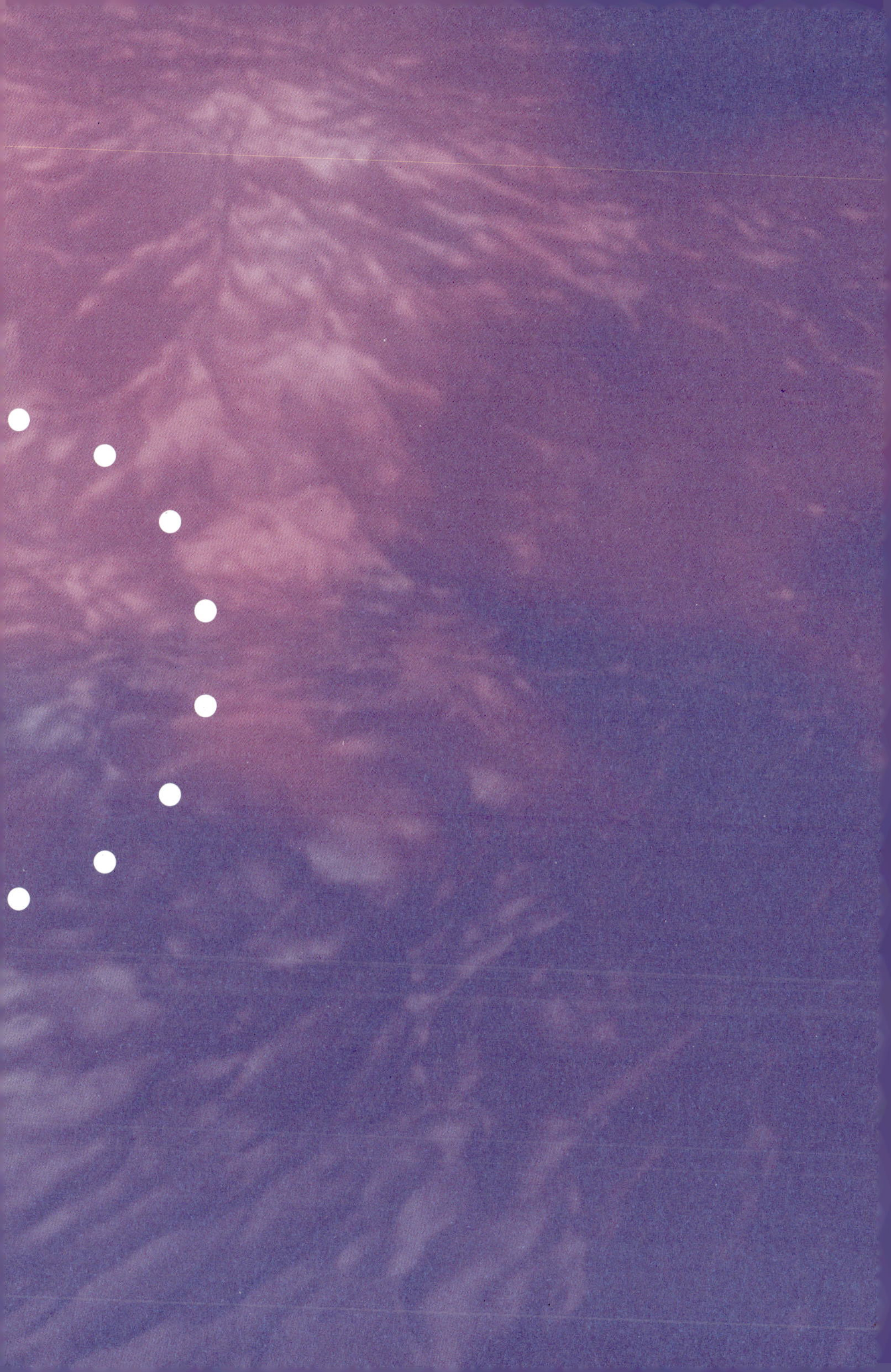

Chapter 4

Experiments

The previous chapters have reworked political theories that inform ideological perspectives prevalent in artistic production in the Global North and South, including the reappraisal of (post-)liberalism and the emergence of locally instantiated New Left tendencies in the West and in China. I'm aware that at first glance and given the present conjuncture (characterized by rearticulating colonial violence, the rise of right-wing support across much of the world, and impending climate catastrophes), such concerns might feel a bit like flexing the wrong muscles. However, it is my contention that working through them is necessary, if only to acknowledge that many practitioners and theorists are guided by certain ethics in their political and theoretical projects without articulating them or even acknowledging the ethical impetus.

I invoke China to articulate the role of the state or a vertical stack of actors of middle and high ranges in a way that contrasts starkly with the habitual thinking of the Western Left, which posits the state must reign in capital. This is not the same thing as cheerleading a particular mode of governance, as it might be assumed. To be sure, no one can know whether the Chinese system of state management, tech, and social development work, would work elsewhere, or indeed what is meant by "work" without exercising good

1 See Gideon Rachman, "America breaks global rules as it defends the free world," *Financial Times*, May 27, 2024, https://www.ft.com/content/8249cd96-bda3-48c9-bf91-005df4125f9d.

2 We might also recall the conceptual artist Douglas Huebler's famous line: "The world is full of objects, more or less interesting; I do not wish to add any more."

critical reasoning in thinking across disparate contexts. As mentioned in Chapter 1, several transitional societies share similar experiences; some are developing civil society and civic consciousness, while shunning abrupt revolutionary change. If the lessons learned from the effects of apologetic exceptionalism of the state is anything to go by, we should not take China as an external entity outside of one's political, social, and cultural context, as often happens with a range of actors, from the political camp of the "rules-based international order,"[1] to postcolonial guilt-ridden academics, to the New Left, eager either to lecture or be lectured. Critically minded reckonings with structural issues of one's own society and those of others under and after globalization should allow a much more intercontextual picture of (particular) universals. We need to do better in the post-globalization era. For those interested in the building of cultural/political institutions and for devising multivalent political approaches, I have endeavored to prepare a foundation of intellectual resources and tactics. In this chapter, I will start to address several experiments that are already underway. Given my focus in this book, we might well call them "art of a multipolar world."

A note on the use of the word "experiment." There continues to be something of a fetish for the notion of "the experimental" in the art and culture sector inherited from the twentieth century. The term is typically associated with practices that appear to add something ontologically *new* to the world. It is my argument that it is more necessary today to understand what is already there.[2] Could the

3 Gilles Deleuze and Félix Guattari, *A Thousand Plateaus: Capitalism and Schizophrenia*, trans. Brian Massumi (Minneapolis: University of Minnesota Press, 2007), p. 160.
4 François Laruelle, *Principles of Non-Philosophy*, trans. Anthony Paul Smith (New York: Bloomsbury Academic, 2013).

additive, associative mode of poststructuralist thinking be a result of globalization? The art and culture sectors thrive on this logic of the accumulative: "and more, and more, and more." More finance, more indigenous or non-Western epistemologies (but under a Western framework), more unmediated communications, and so on. The potential speculative formulations go on and on. And yet there is a lack in much artistic production and theory of a clear explanatory structure that sets a limit to the incessant "destratification" of theory. That is, a deconstructive move against the congealing of objects, subjects, and desire into fixed identities and rather for a permanent movement that brings new elements into alliances. Indeed, as Gilles Deleuze and Félix Guattari noted, "staying stratified—organised, signified, subjected—is not the worst that can happen; the worst that can happen is if you throw the strata into demented or suicidal collapse, which brings them down on us heavier than ever."[3]

François Laruelle's notion of the "generic," that one equals the one, resonates with such thinking, positing itself against the endless "and, and, and."[4] Under such a notion, there is no identifiable difference between "generic" and "ordinary" entities. Especially in the face of natural or man-made catastrophes demanding collective action, this notion can be conducive to visions of a social order whereby selfhood is subdued so as to champion a multiplicity, a common collective good. This might seem to leave little room for artistic expression. Or does it?

Many working in the arts today are categorically against

systems and technologies that render one a "generic" entity, which appear counterintuitive to the poststructuralist vogue for relentless differentiation. But maybe this is exactly what has been missing: an understanding of systems and systematic use of political institutions and technological tools that is not directed towards the endemic field but toward society in general. Counterintuitive for those opposing "neoliberalism" wholesale, quantification, according to left accelerationists Alex Williams and Nick Srnicek, "is not an evil to be eliminated ... network analysis, agent-based modelling, big data analytics, and non-equilibrium economic models, are necessary cognitive mediators for understanding complex systems like the modern economy."[5] Proposals for computational management of the planet's energy resources, or the functions of an economy may take many forms, including Tektology,[6] cybernetics,[7] and more recently, various calls to take over the feedback infrastructure.[8] With geopolitics in mind, the possibility of calculating a "planetary optimum," facilitated by novel quantum sensors and data compression methods can nevertheless be entertained.

If institutions are indeed necessary for addressing complex social needs, then a great deal of imagination and skill is required to identify and manage those needs. Looking beyond the false binary of patriarchal control vs neoliberal abandonment and deregulation, might it be possible to imagine useful institutions if we take certain technical realities seriously? If technological advancements and experiments in a deregulated space concerned mainly with

5 See "Accelerate Manifesto for an Accelerationist Politics," *Critical Legal Thinking*, http://criticallegalthinking.com/2013/05/14/accelerate-manifesto-for-an-accelerationist-politics.

6 See Alexander Bogdanov, *Tektology: Universal Organization Science*, 1912. See also Bogdanov's influence on the "social utility" concept developed by Alexander Chayanov and its later repercussions in ecological economics, in Eric Magnin and Nikolay Nenovsky, "Calculating without Money. Theories of in-Kind Accounting of Alexander Chayanov, Otto Neurath and the Early Soviet Experiences," *The European Journal of the History of Economic Thought* 28, no. 3 (2021), pp. 456–77.

7 See Stafford Beer's Project Cybersyn, and in general, his theorization on how to tame complexities in Stafford Beer, *Designing Freedom* (Toronto: CBC Publications, 1974).

8 Evgeny Morozov, "Digital Socialism? The Calculation Debate in the Age of Big Data," *New Left Review* 116/117 (2019), pp. 33–67. See also Daniel Saros, *Information Technology and Socialist Construction: The End of Capital and the Transition to Socialism* (New York: Routledge, 2014).

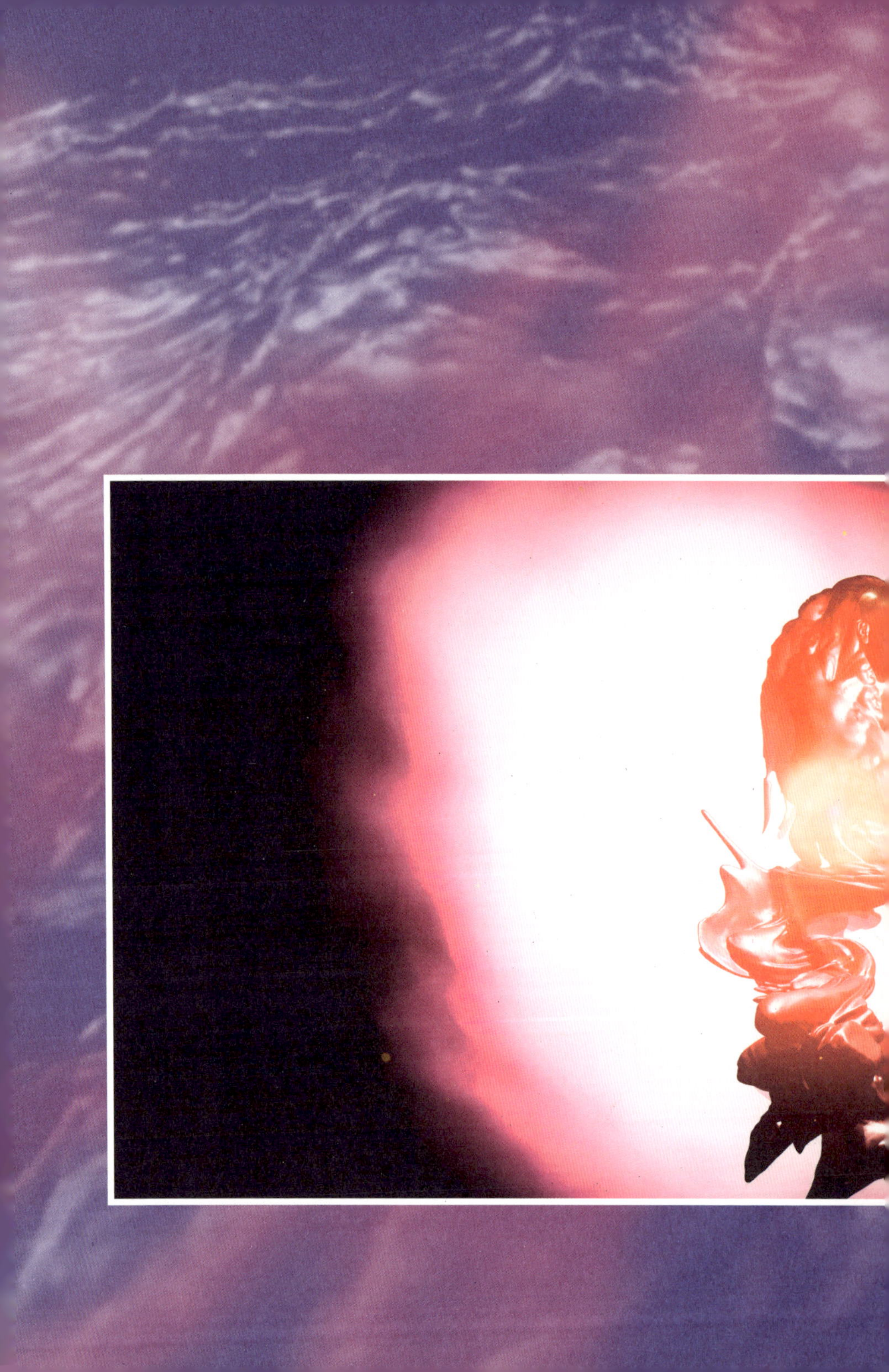

Zheng Mahler
The Master Algorithm, 2019
3D animation, 9 holographic ventilators, blue tooth sound, video still

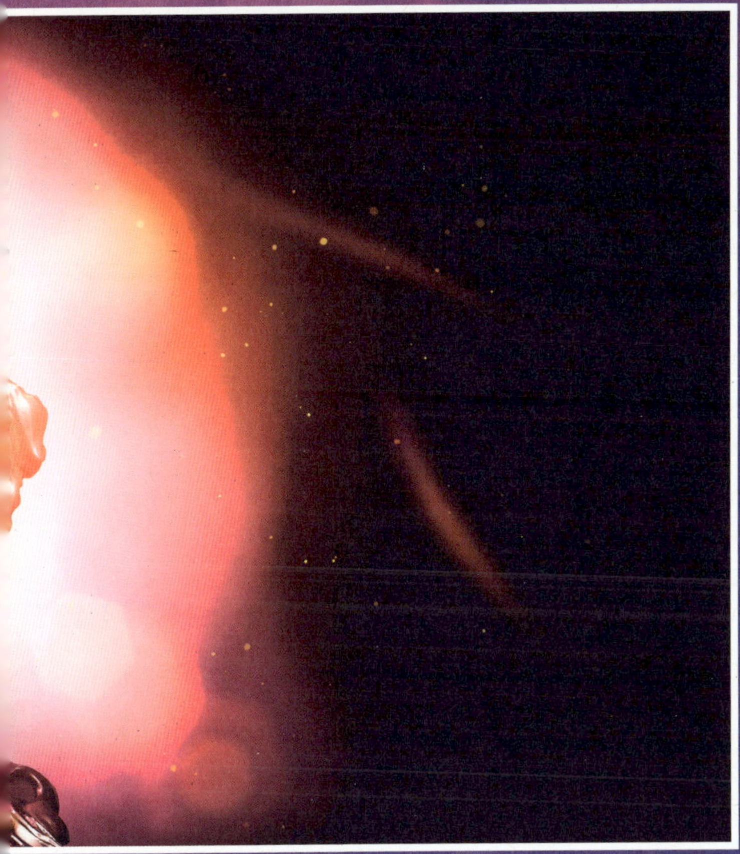

capital (and therefore blocked from attaining legitimacy as social institutions) were radicalized by an actual social subjectivity, would something new become apparent? And could such systemic innovations bring something to the self-understanding of art today?

This chapter tests some of these thoughts in projects that have art and culture as means rather than ends. They all deliberately suppress the unbounded speculative drive, as seen in artistic case studies in the previous chapter, in pursuit of the real, i.e., real social movements or practices. While these projects still speak to the multipolarity thesis, the book concludes with what could be on the horizon: art after multipolarity.

1 Mi You, "Future Art Ecosystems: Focus on China", Serpentine Galleries, August 18, 2020, https://www.serpentinegalleries.org/art-and-ideas/future-art-ecosystems-focus-on-china/.

4.1

Tech Pragmatics in Artistic Experiments

In 2020, I was commissioned to pen the Art and Advanced Technology Report by Serpentine Gallery's Research and Development program. Serpentine Gallery is one of the few institutions which question what new technologies mean for art's infrastructures, the supply and demand side of prototypes, and business model innovations. I produced a report that included a macro-historical appraisal of technology in China; a survey of different institutional actors in art, tech, and adjacent fields; and broader societal dynamics that could create opportunities for art and tech collaborations in hitherto unthought of places and ways. In a summarizing interview,[1] I spoke about China's digital economy where new social infrastructures emerge.

> The digital economy is the new driving engine of China's economy. It is estimated that in 2019, the internet economy reached the size of 313 trillion RMB (44 trillion USD), or one-third of Chinese GDP.
> Digital economic models are being deployed by internet platforms beyond e-commerce, and are increasingly recognized as "new social infrastructures." Kuaishou, China's leading video sharing app, is a pioneer in this.

As opposed to its rival TikTok/Douyin, Kuaishou targets third-tier city and countryside users, and allows users to see diverse contents by way of its flatter algorithmic design. For example, farmers started livestreaming their daily production routines and became hugely popular. The platform built in an e-commerce function and worked with farmers to sell their produce peer-to-peer. This in effect created a poverty alleviation program, now adopted as one of the pillar programs of Kuaishou.

There is also an "economy" around intangible goods: transmission of cultural heritage in the form of teaching how to play traditional instruments, grassroot performance of acrobatics, DIY/self-invention of useful or useless objects.

Similar changes are happening the other way around. E-commerce platforms are embracing the culture of live streaming. In the early days of the Covid-19 crisis when thousands of tons of vegetables were left to rot in rural farms due to shutdowns of agricultural wholesale markets throughout the country, Pinduoduo, a popular e-commerce platform for group buying deals, launched a campaign to help farmers distribute their produce directly to group buyers in cities. Farmers livestream from their storage and showcase their products to buyers nationwide—this has been a popular feature on Chinese e-commerce platforms for a while, though this time this personal touch is especially welcomed by users due to the unusual social condition.

2 Meanwhile, the tech sector has gone through major overhauls. See Lorenzo Marsili and Mi You, "China and the West Can Build a Better World, Together," *Al Jazeera*, October 30, 2021, https://www.aljazeera.com/opinions/2021/10/30/china-and-the-west-can-build-a-better-world-together.

The Pinduoduo grouping mechanism encourages buyers to share their reviews of products among real-life friends, creating a network of trust and a sense of participating in a social cause. The New E-Commerce Research Institute People's Daily has given official recognition to these organizational and business models for stabilizing agricultural supply chains in its latest report issued in March. Beyond business, it is the social relationships Pingduoduo creates that may outlast the epidemic and become elements for future social projects.
For the future art and tech ecosystem, I would see potential in emerging fields rather than concrete projects. For example, art can enter into more structural engagements with agents in technology by way of sci-fi, STEAM education and social and ecological causes. Artistic practices in the broader sense can help co-create community life in urban regeneration projects, or co-shape new social relations with the rise of "new social infrastructures," i.e., internet platforms working increasingly in cross-sectoral ways.

Looking back, the fields I have identified are still bourgeoning. The social claims I identified in the tech sector continues to hold true.[2] The report remains rather idiosyncratic in its attempt to identify creative and social potentials that are neither evident to market watchdogs nor art folks. My interest in placing art and culture in a place that does not sit squarely with art's traditional rationales and concerns may indeed be counterintuitive since I focus on art's critical propensity in my curatorial and theoretical practices. While the tech section in Chapter 3 presents how I think through technology and society in relation to ideology, this section adds materialist concerns to the mix: technical, economic, and organizational. In this section, I illustrate the processes and multi-scalar collaborations that emerge as part of the response to the Covid pandemic by the civil society in China and later mediated by the government. I aim to demonstrate the emergence of a novel synthesis of public-private-society and organizational structures that work beyond ideology.

Chinese Big Tech and Pandemic Responses

In the West, scrutiny on China's tech policy is frequently focused on a critique of a "surveillance state" than on Big Tech companies, with the recent grilling of TikTok by the US government is an exception. On the other hand, critiques of Big Tech, whether political economic or ideological, are more ubiquitous in the West, echoing from public media to academia. Cursorily, one could say the academic theory in the West today is preoccupied with critiquing rogue states (China) or rogue capitalistic companies (Big Tech). But what, specifically, is the critical perspective by Western commentators and academics on Chinese Big Tech?

The Chinese tech world, like the Chinese artworld, is much more globalized than the Western public may be aware. This goes beyond China's role as a major node in the supply chain for global tech companies. There are two primary

3 See for example, Nick Srnicek, *Platform Capitalism* (Cambridge, UK: Polity Press, 2017); Shoshana Zuboff, *The Age of Surveillance Capitalism: The Fight for a Human Future at the New Frontier of Power* (New York: Public Affairs, 2019).

reasons. Firstly, global investors are incredibly well represented in Chinese tech companies. And secondly, Chinese and US tech companies have similar business models and corporate cultures. This means that critical theory about tech in the West should also apply to the Chinese context. For example, Western critique focusing on how Big Tech leverages affect to attract more users, capitalize on user data, shape user behaviors, and disrupt traditional labor markets could and should apply in China as well.[3] To my mind, the biggest obstacle to this, or in other words, the biggest difference between the US and Chinese contexts, is that in certain ways, the Chinese state actually collaborates with users in fighting against those types of extractive tech policies mentioned above. This poses a dilemma for analysis similar to that of the "two lefts." Thus, the theoretical playbook of the critical left media and tech studies in the West may not apply in China so clearly. As noted in the introduction to this chapter, this should not be mistaken for cheerleading. Rather, my point is that because the articulation of players (tech companies, legislative bodies, individual subjects) is different, the epistemological basis for critical theory must also be rearticulated.

A glaring case to demonstrate the divergence in contexts is how contact tracing was implemented in the early days of the Covid pandemic in China as opposed to grassroots mutual aid efforts in the West. Panicked, the Chinese public anxiously waited for Big Tech companies like Alibaba and Tencent—that run the country's most popular e-payment and everything-apps—to roll out a contact tracing

4 Excellently discussed in the Sinica podcast with Kendra Schaefer, Jeremy Daum, and Kaiser Kuo. See Kaiser Kuo, "China's draft regulations on generative AI, with Kendra Schaefer and Jeremy Daum," *The China Project* (podcast), May 11, 2023, https://thechinaproject.com/podcast/chinas-draft-regulations-on-generative-ai-with-kendra-schaefer-and-jeremy-daum/.

warning system to curb the spread of infection. However, initially, Big Tech companies were silent, and the government clumsily put together a tracing system using the geolocation data provided by state-owned telecom companies, which only had a resolution of 50 meters. Key background information here is that in China, Big Tech companies act as gatekeepers of vast user data and are wary of sharing it with the centralized government. In the EU, privacy policies include laws that stands between the user's data and the government marketers, hackers, and bad actors. In Chinese privacy policy, on the other hand, it's the government and user that form a united front for consumer data protections from hackers, marketers, and companies that in many ways are stronger than Western countries have instituted.[4]

If the Western Left falters in marshaling state capacity to contain (in the US) or foster alternatives (in the EU) to Big Tech, existing critiques of Big Tech often seem ineffectual and invite us to ask whether small tech is necessarily better? For example, does decentralization necessarily serve the social good? I am sympathetic to—and have engaged with—data commons, fair data economies, and platform cooperativism movements in Europe and the US. Advocates for these movements propose portability and interoperability of data shared across different service providers as key features of a potential next generation of data economies, enabling collaboration and co-creation of value and services. But when it comes to China, one cannot not be ideological or doctrinal about horizontality, because it risks ignoring existing or emerging vertical partnerships, where good values could still be possible given that it is different from the West, as already noted.

In the early days of the pandemic, citizen initiatives in China bloomed. While the West also saw the rapid growth of mutual aid and collectivist movements, in China, it is my feeling that because not all such mobilizations can necessarily find technological solutions for scaling up, and because China demonstrates a unique relationship between civilian and state-run information networks, we can perhaps identify a method for state, civil society and business infrastructures to be used in scaling up such efforts. At the beginning of the pandemic, the Internet and hacker communities were particularly quick to respond with information and network powered solutions, including open-source initiatives that establish real-time data service for hospitals, factories, procurement, and donations, linking those in need and those with capacities to help. It is important to note that not all grassroot solutions need to be powered by sophisticated tech and information infrastructure. With basic chat group functions, volunteer drivers created a fleet to provide transportation to medics, restaurants offered working meals, and hotel owners self-organized a network of hotels that gave rooms for nearby medics to rest—days before the government made official requisitions.

If self-initiated networks function mainly on the information and service platforms, then businesses in China with a stake in supply chains and logistics have contributed their part in integrating the supply of goods in increasingly collaborative ways. For one example, the online retailer

Pinduoduo started a campaign during the pandemic to help farmers sell directly to group buyers in cities. The Pinduoduo grouping mechanism, as mentioned earlier, encourages buyers to share their reviews of products among off-line friends, creating a network of trust and a sense of collective participation in a social cause. The personal touch to Pinduoduo further accelerated sales. Another encouraging example came a couple of weeks into stringent lockdowns, when restaurants running low on cashflow and fresh foodstuffs and grocery delivery platforms short of delivery staff decided to join forces, sharing storage, food-processing, and delivery capacities.

The state can be a partner too. During the most hazardous time in early February 2020 in Wuhan, when many were infected yet had to stay home due to a massive shortage of care units in the hospital, the medical sector was acutely understaffed and short of personal protective equipment. At this critical moment, a volunteer team organized vertically and horizontally engaged in relief efforts. They repurposed the online magazine channel *Guojia Renwen Lishi* (National Humanity History) of *People's Daily* on social media platforms WeChat and Weibo into a contact channel that allowed people in desperate situations to report needs, and a group of around 2000 volunteers, named Yaya Volunteer Group, worked 24/7 to verify cases by directly speaking to people on the phone. The most urgent cases were reported to the supervision team of the central government thanks to the backing of *Guojia Renwen Lishi*. They made crucial contacts between local hospitals, wellness,

5 See, for example, how Dayu Community, a community co-creation initiative in Shanghai, reflects on the post-pandemic reproduction of relational networks in a community through online tools, "疫情下的社区互助经验 | 社区团购、互助就医、握手平台、行动转化 (Community Mutual Aid Experiences under the Epidemic | Community Group Purchase, Mutual Aid for Medical Care, Handshake Platform, Action Transformation)," https://c.m.163.com/news/a/HMASQ16V0525D88B.html.

and psychological support teams and created a lifeline for thousands.

The world witnessed China's sweeping centralized measures against the coronavirus, sometimes with awe and sometimes with criticism. This gives a picture from various levels from below, in a matter of speaking. In a similarly low-resolution way, one can always be critical of the platform economy. Yet we witnessed tech platforms sharing capacities and data from across the supply chain and businesses matching the business value network (instead of single value chains) with social values and emerging social collaborative networks. These are vertical and horizontal social networks of support in the broadest sense of the social, where no one is categorically against collaborations with social, business, and state agents at other levels. Even when life returned to "business as usual" in China, some of the social networks interwoven during this time continue and take on new meanings.[5]

The divergent relations between the constellation of actors identified above means that Western critiques of Big Tech extractivism and accumulation or of the carceral functions of state surveillance might not work when applied in China. However, this does not mean the control of grassroots or cultural action to platforms or state actors should be ceded. Rather, my argument puts forward that because of this different relationality between the state, corporations, and individuals under multipolarity, there can be alternative approaches to mediating and utilizing existing infrastructures for other aims. Artistic thinking and projects can

6 Trebor Scholz and Nathan Schneider, *Ours to Hack and to Own: The Rise of Platform Cooperativism, a New Vision for the Future of Work and a Fairer Internet* (London: OR Books, 2016).

identify and demonstrate how this can happen and open pathways to actualizing networks that organize everything from play to collective care.

Curating Platforms

Thinking through the lenses of multipolarity and deep pluralism, one can recognize the possibility of tech platforms in China as something of a middle-range actor between the state and individual, akin to how civil society functions in a liberal society. Thus, inductive theorizing and concept-building are necessary for practices on the tech platforms because they do exist as a horizon for mediating social relations.

What comes after the critique of Big Tech platforms? Platforms are also places where subjects hang out, work, tinker, create solutions, and generate value (even if that value is not evenly distributed). Surely platforms can be recast or repurposed if users replace the predatory logic with cooperative, community, city, or inventive union models.[6] Or, as seen in the cases above, they can become crisis lines in a time of emergency—which begs the question, how could such practices be sustainable? In conceiving platforms differently, art and curation can enter the seemingly tumultuous field of tech platforms, sometimes by staging provocations and sometimes by building testing sites for different platform models. There may indeed be no art with capital "A" (art for art's sake) at the end of these processes, but there can be an appreciation for the creative characteristics that are evident in public culture, or in the very systems logic of platforms design. Working with the expanded notion of platforms way before our imaginations capitulated to Big Tech, Olga Goriunova has perceptively analyzed cultural productions on the Internet as "art platforms." These phenomena may not be self-conceptualized as art but rather point to art as a "collectively distributed social practice that forms society."[7]

I would like to think about artistic and cultural production on and through platforms in such a way. Rather than focusing on works *about* platform economies (common to the art sector in the West), here I will reflect on two artistic projects that tap into the infrastructural conditions of platforms and demonstrate alternate possibilities for both critique and practice. I curated both projects as part of the 13th Shanghai Biennale (2020–2021), where the role of curator extended beyond contextualizing and exhibiting and involved the organization of social processes and technological infrastructures.[8] More specifically, in these projects I strived to address the following questions through curatorial engagement: if platform capitalism creates new forms of social coordination, replacing legal norms and supplanting the fundamental logic of markets, what kinds of alternative social coordination can art help imagine?[9] Vis-à-vis platforms backed by deep-pocketed investors, how can art bring out other kinds of value, abundance, and liquidity? And, how can curating focus not only on content, but also on infrastructures?

7 Olga Goriunova, *Art Platforms and Cultural Production on the Internet* (London: Routledge, 2012), p. 9.

8 Under the theme "Bodies of Water," the Biennale looked at how water mediates and interconnects bodies of diverse scales, from the planetary to the microscopic, from biological, ecological entities to collectivities or social bodies, thereby activating forms of liquid solidarities.

9 See, for example, Katharina Pistor, "Rule by Data: The End of Markets?," *Law and Contemporary Problems*, 83 (2020), pp. 101–24; Evgeny Morozov, "Digital Socialism? The Calculation Debate in the Age of Big Data," *New Left Review*, 116/117 (2019), pp. 33–67.

10 Miao Li, Chris K. K. Tan, and Yuting Yang, "*Shehui Ren*: Cultural Production and Rural Youths', Use of the *Kuaishou* Video-Sharing App in Eastern China," *Information, Communication & Society* 23, no. 10 (August 23, 2020), pp. 1499–1514.

Artistic Case Study 1: Jimeimen

The first project is by playwright Sun Xiaoxing and a multidisciplinary team (playwright Qiu Zhen, researcher Kunfang Zhao, and architect Huang Siyao). *Jimeimen* (Gate of Sisters) talks colloquially from the platform Kuaishou used for sharing short videos, and where an eccentric grassroot culture has emerged. Unlike its rival TikTok, Kuaishou utilizes a much less targeted algorithm, and tends to push more diverse content to its users. It is embraced by the vast populace in small cities and rural China and is most widely associated with content that focuses on the wretchedness but also the earthiness of countryside or small-town life, featuring unapologetically raw content such as excessive eating, village youths ranting about their schools, farmers doing acrobatic stunts and inventing absurdist instruments.

One hugely popular format is the so-called *shenhui yao* (society shake): a brute form of dance to lo-fi disco music. The term *shehui* (society) signals the characteristics of life for many small-town youths. They are forced with shouldering responsibilities at a premature age and on the app don "tough guy" looks and demonstrate the use of brute force to solve problems and survive against all odds. Studies of these social genres have focused on the way these subcultures are inherently embedded in the urban-rural class divide.[10] Certain colloquial choices of words, often spoken with an exaggerated accent and forced puns, make their way through Kuaishou as a new *lingua franca*, such as

11 William Davies, "The Politics of Recognition in the Age of Social Media," *New Left Review* 128 (March/April 2021), https://newleftreview.org/issues/ii128/articles/william-davies-the-politics-of-recognition-in-the-age-of-social-media.

the mispronunciation of *jiemeimen* (sisters) into *jimeimen* (gate of beauties). Once invented, these dances, props, and language are widely adopted across Kuaishou, where one video can be viewed by hundreds of thousands of people, with many of the viewers mimicking and sharing their own versions, thereby triggering a network effect.

Sun Xiaoxing and the team have chosen a series of symbols from Kuaishou viral videos and turned them into sculptures, including a "flower hand," a gesture taken from a *shehuiyao* dance, tacky LED shoes for shuffle dances, and a RSZ motorcycle, an economical Yamaha model that is often tricked out on the cheap. For their project, these sculptures are displayed on pedestals in a purpose-built black-box space, lending them a certain artistic aura—from digital platform to material (artistic) pedestal.

Critics might rightly point out that these Kuaishou trends, seemingly meaningless, feed into the attention economy—seeking recognition based on an "inwardly generated identity."[11] Other critics may rail against the platform altogether for predatory behavior as an extractive technology that could only be resolved by making data user-owned or socializing tech platforms. Both modes of critique assume the primacy of the individual, as the producer and harbinger of "me, myself and my data," and as the arbitrator of good for oneself. But what if instead of the inwardly generated identity, there is something "outward" and communitarian going on? What if participation on Kuaishou attains a social dimension because the app's algorithm and design encourage exploring rather than reinforcing preferences? What if

12 I use the term subaltern in the way it has been theorized in the Subaltern Studies Group in postcolonial studies, which denotes people of lower-class background with little access to cultural power.
13 Xiaoxing Zhang, Yu Xiang, and Lei Hao, "Virtual gifting on China's live streaming platforms: hijacking the online gift economy," *Chinese Journal of Communication* 12, no. 3 (2019), pp. 1–16.
14 Marion Fourcade and Daniel N. Kluttz, "A Maussian bargain: Accumulation by gift in the digital economy," *Big Data & Society* 7, no. 1 (2020), pp. 1–16.
15 Arjun Appadurai, "The Wealth of Dividuals," *Banking on Words: The Failure of Language in the Age of Derivative Finance* (Chicago: The University of Chicago Press, 2016), pp. 101–24.
16 Randy Martin, *Knowledge LTD: Toward a Social Logic of the Derivative* (Philadelphia: Temple University Press, 2015).

the collective data the community produces can generate an abstract kind of social value, a weak form of social movement where one comes to see and relate to each other in a hitherto impossible way?

Philosophically, I want to suggest a consideration of this appreciating, mimicking, and making of content as the self-expression of a subaltern collectivity.[12] In such a reading, the forms of content-making on Kuaishou can be read through the notion of "the gift." When users of Kuaishou remake an object, a dance, a certain stunt, they are receiving and passing on a gift. This gift here is not an easily monetizable exchange under the pretense of gifts.[13] It is not the mechanism of give-to-get that underlies the design of many online platforms, Kuaishou included.[14] Rather, the abstract gifts in question are affects pulsating from one screen to another, while the users scrupulously copy a dance movement, or creatively reinterpret and remake an object, edit videos, and pass them on in a community that they feel they are part of. As Arjun Appadurai argues, a gift in this sense creates ties not between two individual entities but rather between "dividuals." Each of them is joined by the gift to form new subjectivities.[15] Rather than acting like an object of alienation (i.e., the commodity in a Marxist framework), this performativity of the gift allows the subaltern participants to collectively explore volatility and establish a sense of collective subjectivity.[16]

Of course, it is a stretch to claim any political efficacy just from a theoretical analysis. Appadurai, for example, can only point to a politics of the dividual in a discursive way. Looking for a political agenda from movements like Occupy Wall Street, one is likely to end up with an artistic understanding of politics by association. In this sense too, Kuaishou users are not too dissimilar in forming a "temporary collective body" that, at the very least, shows resilient and creative tactics to the challenges of small-town life. But there is more to it—creativity cannot be the excuse to deny them a better life. Kuaishou itself never set out to appeal to a particular taste or community but was shaped by its own users after-the-fact. Banking on its success ad hoc, or in other words, seeing the forms of connection that its platform was able to foster, Kuaishou rolled out a customer-to-customer business model for farmers to sell their products as part of a poverty alleviation program. Though nothing close to a redistribution, the organizational aesthetics that have been produced by "dividuals" compelled Kuaishou to support some of its users—demonstrating what is perhaps a preliminary step to alternative forms of online connectivity made possible in a multipolar world.

The artists of *Jimeimen* were well-aware that their polished objects could not on their own convey the social meanings of Kuaishou. That is why, in my dialogue with the artists, we were focused on the social dimensions of the platform. One of the team members came from a grassroots theater background and worked extensively in a migrant worker's theater on the eastern outskirts of Beijing. She was previously headhunted by Kuaishou to join their project development team, which she rejected for personal reasons.

In view of this, I asked the artists at the outset to take a social and infrastructural turn by expanding the artistic manifestation into the realization of the "real" social spaces of Kuaishou. The artists originally came up with a proposal to collaborate with Kuaishou on a quasi-competition of short videos that would be marketed to all Kuaishou users. However, if we would communicate the competition as an art competition, it would only reinforce the perceived elitism of the artworld and betray the spirit of Kuaishou. I then came up with idea to frame the campaign under the banner "Is it art?" The rationale followed the premise that we needed something in line with Kuaishou's ethos and that plays into the double bind of senselessness and seriousness. This rhetorical question would shake off the burden of institutionalizing art, and instead encourage unexpected and aberrant reactions. Kuaishou's massive user-base would then participate as themselves, not as aspirational artists. We expected all kinds of eccentric manifestations that would potentially expose art to its own discontents. Thinking along the organizational form of grassroots creativity, repetition, and gifting, the network effect would augment this social moment to attract more repetitions and mutations, and a collective exploration of art embedded in life might emerge.

The Biennale organizers were not keen on this idea. They counter-proposed to launch their own thematic video contest but ended up abandoning it. Instead of utilizing the infrastructure of a platform for the purpose of art dissemination, what I proposed as a curator was an organizational aesthetic engagement *with* the platform. These platforms

17 See the *ReUnion Network* website: https://www.reunionnetwork.org/.

are in fact malleable and designed by someone. For example, Kuaishou has a geolocation function that allows users to click on hotspots on a map and see recent videos posted from the chosen location. Given the app's user base and my interest in the Belt and Road Initiative, I have been browsing short videos from Chinese construction workers in the Middle East and Africa, documenting in no particularly systematic ways their worksites, food, and markets, along with assorted local curiosities. This not only creates a stockpile of materials for anthropologists to engage with BRI "from below," but it also becomes a potential site of artistic or creative interventions. If the geolocation function is designed and maintained by a project manager, what other social functions could be plugged along that network infrastructure to connect people, stories, and desires? I will continue to think creatively with platforms, in the same way that the "Sci-(no)-fi" exhibition mentioned in Chapter 3 did not shy away from involving real-world partners. This requires considering the experimental social and organizational forms thriving on Kuaishou as significant in their own right.

Artistic Case Study 2: ReUnion

ReUnion Network is an art and social design project initiated by artist Aiwen Yin that aims to "reunionize" people through peer-to-peer care.[17] While utilizing digital infrastructures, it imagines a different kind of platform that is commons-oriented. At the Shanghai Biennale, this

18 Marie Fare and Pepita Ould Ahmed, "Complementary Currency Systems and Their Ability to Support Economic and Social Changes," *Development and Change* 48, no. 5 (September 2017), pp. 847–72.

imaginary was prefiguratively enacted through a role-playing game.

ReUnion Network initially started from an artistic curiosity: How could society be organized if blockchain became the technological infrastructure and decentralization became the ruling ideology? Our answer was to design a system that considers interpersonal relationships as the basic unit, instead of individuals or imagined communities created by given narratives, to create a commons-oriented approach for socio-economic organization. While the allocation of care continues to be put in crisis, it is also a form of labor that everyone does (to varying degrees) every day, one that demands qualitative effort within trusted relationships. Thus, *ReUnion* aims to model an alternative social welfare system with long-term, interpersonal care relations. Both (or all) participants in a trusted care relation—be it elder care, childcare, or digital nomads moving to a new city—can enter long-term, qualitative caring relations through *ReUnion*. Over time, the persons in a caring relation can take their relation to a new level by combining their individual coins awarded by the system into Composite Coins. They could endorse their jointly minted Composite Coins by depositing fiat money into it, which is then logged on decentralized ledger technology or blockchain. The Composite Coin functions as a complementary currency that can be exchanged for goods and services in places such as the local co-op, which studies have shown boost community economies.[18] Over time, what grows out of the interpersonal relations can develop into a "family of choice." The long-term ambition of *ReUnion* is to get the government to endorse long-term interpersonal care relationships as a valid complementary form of welfare, and to subsidize Composite Coins.

As of this writing the work is at the proof-of-concept stage. As the curator, I felt it would be insufficient to display the project as a speculative design project with diagrams and illustrative videos. Rather, I wanted to overcome the daunting gap between an artistic vison of a future society and a fully-fledged, implementable social program, and to render the vision experienceable. This is where I stepped in to help set up a residency for *ReUnion* at the Dinghaiqiao Mutual Aid Society, a self-organized space run by a group of artists, architects, social researchers, and activists in a working-class neighborhood in Shanghai. During the residency, the artist and collaborators designed a Live Action Role-Playing game to playtest the social and economic mechanisms in *ReUnion*. The play starts with players being assigned characters from different social backgrounds, whose biographies they imagine and enact. As the game progresses, players follow personal pursuits and establish friendships and care relationships with each other. Events such as illness, relocation, changes in social, political, and economic conditions change the course of one's life. Thus, the players try to weather uncertainties with the help of one another or the collective, discover themselves, and find meanings in their avatars' biographies.

The role-playing method performatively suspends the dominant market logic of individualized needs and solutions for

19 John Law, "Collateral realities," *The Politics of Knowledge*, ed. Fernando Dominguez Rubio and Patrick Baert, pp. 156–78 (London and New York: Routledge, 2011).
20 The tour included Leipzig, Amsterdam, Zurich, and Kassel. See published reports: Yin Aiwen, Mengyang Zhao, "Playing 'liquid dependencies': what does a decentralised caring society look like (2021–present)," https://artsoftheworkingclass.org/text/playing-liquid-dependencies-what-does-a-decentralised-caring-society-look-like-2021-present; Yin Aiwen, "Liquid dependencies," *Damn magazine* 82 (Summer 2022), https://www.damnmagazine.net/liquid-dependencies.

individualized risks, and instead allows for an activation of interpersonal relations based on trust and reciprocity to become the foundation of a social network. This care-based society in the game enacted a "collateral reality," which reveals that realities are culturally constructed and malleable.[19] The care relations are prefigurative in that they are not yet real but many players find them fully plausible. Until now, hundreds of players have participated and shaped the game before and during the Biennale, several dedicated players became NPCs (non-player characters) to help onboard new players and an amateur theater group grew out of the game. For many, this game is a site of civic education for imagining a society that one can build together. In this sense, though different in nature, it shares basic social aspirations with tech companies in some of their programs. They are grounded steps that can become building blocks for a more humanist, liberal social order.

The game was met with great enthusiasm when it toured various cities in Europe.[20] Crises of loneliness and aging are unevenly experienced in different societies, but the social demands are unprecedented everywhere, even in less "hyperindividualist" societies as East Asia. *ReUnion* believes that an interlinked reorganization of civic resources and social contracts and a new approach to intimate relationships can acutely respond to these conditions. And these uneven experiences may help each context formulate better approaches for themselves.

In line with the postcritical thinking of this book, *ReUnion* embodies both a tech critique and an active transformation

21 Tirdad Zolghadr, *Traction* (Berlin: Sternberg Press, 2016).

of the platform economy. What is demanded of a curator to contextualize this work is perhaps less how to display such a project in cultural institutions than it is how to link it to social institutions and the wider society. For a long time, art curating operated with a kind of "indeterminacy," allowing open-ended encounters between the artworks and the audience, not assuming positions—sometimes to the point of escapism.[21] Ambiguity can be powerful, but it must be founded on an understanding of the variably post-globalization, post-liberal contexts we find ourselves in.

This section has presented cultural trends in the tech sector and how art can meaningfully engage with tech stacks—some part of which may be considered hemispheric or multipolar. These "experiments" can be considered within this frame not only because they happened in the context of China, although they do build on the analysis of Chapter 3.2 and come out pragmatic and "light" on tech ideology. Indeed, in any cultural, political, economic context we should look for creative engagements with tech practices that articulate post-critique and strive to stake a claim in the real. The reason I focused on these two experiments is that they are exemplary for developing various concrete pathways toward the social functions of tech with other players (horizontal and vertical crisis management network, social programs, or app that allows new social ties to forge), building towards a basic civil education in the absence of active civil society. These experiments do not, by their own doing, transcend the conditions of multipolarity in art and cultural production—that's why revealing the creative possibilities at the backend of Kuaishou demands a lot of captioning, and is not evident for those who have set views on Big Tech or China, but they are nonetheless useful in recalibrating critique against the background of shifts to how neoliberalism functions. Their nonpartisan approach allows pedagogical possibilities across perceived lines of division in a multipolar world and as such, prepare us for thinking what art might mean after multipolarity.

1 Quinn Slobodian and Dieter Plehwe, "Introduction," *Nine Lives of Neoliberalism,* eds. Dieter Plehwe, Quinn Slobodian, and Philip Mirowski, (London and New York: Verso, 2020), p. 2.

2 Alan S. Blinder, *A Monetary and Fiscal History of the United States, 1961–2021* (Princeton, NJ: Princeton University Press, 2022).

4.2

Designing Institutions: Art After a Multipolar World

What is a post-globalization, multipolar world? This is not primarily an epistemological question, but an institutional one. As Quinn Slobodian and Dieter Plehwe write: "It would be ironic ... if leftist critics became fixated on the realm of ideas while the right adopted materialist explanations of the present."[1] In light of this historical sea change, how can we return to thinking about redesigning state, legal, social, and economic institutions in a fracturing world? What is the art of navigating a multipolar world?

It is worth remembering the tremendous efforts invested in pushing through the neoliberal globalization agenda, such as the global division of labor. Well into the 1970s, Western protectionism and economic nationalism were reigning forces. The Carter and Reagan administrations exercised neoliberalism at home, but not free trade aboard.[2] Furthermore, both neoliberal and non-neoliberal market actors did not hang around without any oversight. On the contrary, they always needed states or superstate mechanisms to secure them. As Slobodian documents carefully, neoliberals repeatedly sought solutions to the problem of order in a vertical move—shifting to higher scales of governance in the League of Nations, international investment law, blueprints for supranational federation, systems of

3 Quinn Slobodian, *Globalists: The End of Empire and the Birth of Neoliberalism* (Cambridge, MA: Harvard University Press, 2018).

weighted franchise, European competition law, and ultimately the World Trade Organization (WTO) itself.[3]

In the artworld, the counter-movements that emerged during these years are often invoked superficially. When the artworld revisits the Non-Aligned Movement (NAM), for example, it can hardly hide the regret that it failed to change the world order in the long run. Yes, Bandung and similar cases are significant for recalling "actually existing" efforts at decolonization and associated emancipatory claims. But can we assume that showing artworks created back in the 1960s and 1970s in the name of solidarity automatically grants them political efficacy today? In such a way, Bandung becomes the canvas onto which today's social movements based in identification can project their politics and desires. But identification does not equal participation in concrete social movements—even less so through art and culture. This type of sociological approach must be refreshed in the critique of social media activism or socially engaged art as well. On top of this, we discern the anti-imperialist struggle of a bygone era as formal (based on a structural understanding of the world back then), and emotions from social injustices today as empirical. Further research could work to locate where proponents for these movements from the decolonial-minded Western context and their non-Western counterparts align today, and how identifications are refracted in this process.

If the cultural production around Bandung in recent years is a curatorial attempt to renew the lease of anti-imperialist and solidarity struggles, could it propose any idea as to *how* it could have succeeded? In the absence of a viable counterfactual history, speculation becomes warranted.[4] Beyond fanciful fabulations, we would be well-advised to produce multiple Bandungs, or in other words, multiple interpretations of the movement just as any other anti-hegemonic movement. For in each movement, there are multiple variables that cannot be neatly unified under artistic representation. In terms of a movement's relation to capitalism, we can discern competitive, reformist, or revolutionary approaches. In terms of its sphere of action, we have the economic and political spheres. At different intersections we could locate different aspects of anti-imperialist movements—some ideological, some realist. Why not study the economic and developmental agenda of NAM, and its engagement with existing international institutions? Why not reassess its economic policy proposals such as actively seeking foreign direct investment for the "right to development" and not dependency? What is the legacy of the New International Economic Order (NIEO), the revolt of the Global South against global rules in economic, legal, and political terms in the 1970s? The NIEO Declaration put forward that neo-colonialism continued to reproduce inequality after formal independence and called for the global redistribution of wealth, resources, and technology from developed to underdeveloped countries.[5] The South rightly recognized that trade liberalization was not embedded globally; the Global North did not allow actual free trade in key sectors such as agriculture in the Global South, for example. While the NIEO ground to a halt, internal

4 Admittedly, I also participated in the project *From Bandung to Berlin* in 2016, http://frombandungtoberlin.com.

5 See Nils Gilman, "The New International Economic Order: A Reintroduction," *Humanity: An International Journal of Human Rights, Humanitarianism, and Development* 6, no. 1 (March 2015): pp. 1–16. Associated movements include the 1967 Arusha Declaration by Julius Nyerere "The Arusha Declaration by Julius Nyerere 1967" (website), https://www.marxists.org/subject/africa/nyerere/1967/arusha-declaration.htm which proposed to re-politicize, rather than de-politicize money. On the latter points, see Stefan Eich, "Crypto Won't Solve Our Problems—We Need to Democratize Money," interview by Daniel Denvir, *Jacobin*, November 2, 2022, https://jacobin.com/2022/02/cryptocurrency-democratize-monetary-policy-economics-banks-financial-system-bitcoin.

fissure and debt crisis triggered a wave of programs that structurally weakened states in the South. It was in reaction to the NIEO that Hayekian reformers sought to scale up the solutions in a vertical move and created World Trade Organization in 1995.[6] Such is the dialectic underneath the history that we should invest in to heed lessons for the present moment. If NAM drove a wedge between major powers during the Cold War (under which one can view the Sino-Soviet split), could NAM be credited with ending the Cold War and heralding the era of globalization? Or from another perspective, what could be today's Bandung?

Surely, one could identify the heirs of this historical solidarity in contemporary grassroots, anti-globalization social movements across the world. In retrospect, peak anti-globalization coincided exactly with peak globalization, and thus much of its momentum was lost when some of the core demands and causes were taken up by states themselves. If institutional design is anything to go by, seeing NIEO as an "unfailure"[7] that helps denaturalize the inegalitarian global political economy that has been taken as the only viable path,[8] then there is indeed a renewed engagement in the Global South with de-dollarization and a rethink of the IMF and World Bank. Zoltan Pozsar, head of the macroeconomic advisory firm Ex Uno Plures, believes that the current global economic system is at a tipping point. "The global east and south are renegotiating the world order."[9] There is, to update the NAM for the present, a "multi-aligned" world.[10]

Perhaps we should tease out the "practical reason" of Bandung in our reengagement with it, which is not

6 See Quinn Slobodian, *Globalists*, pp. 219–56.

7 Jennifer Wenzel, *Bulletproof: Afterlives of Anticolonial Prophecy in South Africa and Beyond* (Chicago: University of Chicago Press, 2010).

8 See Nils Gilman, "The New International Economic Order: A Reintroduction" and Nils Gilman, "The NIEO as Usable Past," *Progressive International* (January 4, 2023), https://progressive.international/blueprint/e7bc30e1-d565-47de-a19f-80ad1bce9969-gilman-the-nieo-as-usable-past/en.

9 See Alec Russell, "The à la carte world: our new geopolitical order," *Financial Times*, August 21, 2023, https://www.ft.com/content/7997f72d-f772-4b70-9613-9823f233d18a; Bai Gao, "Trade Wars, Hot Wars and the Rise of the Global South: The Future of the Dollar Standard," *Reading the China Dream*, January 20, 2024, https://www.readingthechinadream.com/gao-bai-on-challenges-to-the-dollar-standard.html.

10 Multi-alignment means actors other than Washington and Beijing should seek the chance to "develop more effective bilateral relationships with each of the big powers but also to develop deeper strategic relationships with each other." Nader Mousavizadeh, an adviser to Kofi Annan when he was UN secretary-general, as cited in Alec Russell, Russell, "The à la carte world: our new geopolitical order," *Financial Times*, August 21, 2023.

impervious to historical and present ideologies. Sometimes, multialignment might be necessary. For art and culture institutions, this exercise might urge them to align in a kind of solidarity that transcends the dichotomy of political and economic doctrines and institutional boundaries. But this cannot be another general assembly, organizational chart, or self-smart contract design. This latter form of solidarity might only resemble “Bandung” prima-facie or not at all, before it starts mediating the institutional ambitions of global art institutions, which are rooted in the diffused distribution of political, economic, and cultural power. While it will be vital for the artworld to observe the new formations of multi-alignment, it is equally imperative to credit the non-Western world for defending and building Western art institutions where they stand for critical and daring art, as seen in Chapter 2.

Building art and political institutions are not the same thing, but both demand a great deal of imagination and skill in identifying and managing complex social imaginaries and needs. Both need to respond to the condition produced by deep pluralist post-globalization. This condition, however, should not work towards an endgame where people only work with one political and cultural context, within which one may or may not be accorded a particular version of multiculturalism dressed as universalism. Let us not be mired in this contested multipolarity.

As I discussed throughout the book, it is crucial to occupy multiple and multipolar political and cultural contexts at the same time, even or especially when it is uninvited. This multi-position may not be evident, and one must expect fastidious scrutiny from all sides: from the Western left for succumbing to authoritarian regimes and/or to capital, from the non-Western left for not being social enough, from the non-Western liberal left for not being liberal enough, from the domestic right for being too liberal, and so on. Often it demands more effort to keep to a liberal line when one is in one of the countries in the Global South, and a somewhat "statist" position outside of it. Within each society, this is also in the long-term interests of those wanting a healthy society: civil society needs the dialectic partner of the state, so when the state is performing antipolitics (poor anti-establishment, as by the current German government for example), civil society is also rendered redundant. Thus, it would make sense to focus on building political power and state capacity in places like the traditional West, and on building civil society where state power is oversized. The convenient choice is to revert the positions and succumb to the dominant discourses in a given social context. But that would be to allow multipolarity to rear its ugliest face. One can be self-critical, skeptical ("have we ruled out all alternatives"), tactical, but one should not be cynical or intellectually resigned. Not being afraid of critique, espousing the contradictions, and, crucially, not going for the low-hanging fruit, is a position the artworld needs to deeply invest in.

And now, finally, what is the art as a horizon of thinking *after* a multipolar world?

It is exactly in this multipolar and deeply pluralist world that art can take on the role of mediation (rather than

11 Danilo Scholz, "Koloniale Nahmen, Koloniale Gaben: Alexandre Kojève, Carl Schmitt Und Die Europäische Nachkriegsordnung," *Archiv DesVölkerrechts (AVR)* 61, nos. 2–3 (2023), pp. 287–326.

12 As in the call made by Lorenzo Marsili in "From The Age Of Empires To The Age Of Humanity," *Noēma Mag*, July 27, 2023, https://www.noemamag.com/from-the-age-of-empires-to-the-age-of-humanity/.

reproduction or representation), if not even an ambassador role. In a fractured, but not yet fully segregated world, art could fill the gap of communication where such communication lacks political incentives. Not reducing itself to the simple moral geography of good and bad, art can mediate perspectives and aspirations at individual, community, civil, and institutional levels that may appear divergent but still share rational common ground. Being acutely aware of the stakes in trafficking divergent viewpoints, art could resort to its claim to autonomy tactically, but not with condescending assertations that replace one truth with another, and not with self-heroism that undermines efforts at building institutions. The artful diplomatic skills of philosopher Alexander Kojève in creating para-institutions that pave the way for instantiating the political experiment of the European Union is a case in point, pace critique of his notion of colonialism.[11] This requires a self-understanding of the inconsistency of means and ends that go into institution building. Art and culture could start with what binds a common humanity at all political levels, from the institutional with processes like Conference of the Parties (COP) and the Intergovernmental Panel on Climate Change (IPCC), and new institutions on issues like artificial intelligence or global finance, to the grassroots where the place left vacant by the demise of the World Social Forum.[12] Artistic strategies undoubtedly can take on the role of creative advocacy, the most notable example being artworks commissioned for the UN Climate Conferences, although they can be met with public enthusiasm or incomprehension.

13 Compare, for example, the cases of Olafur Eliasson's iceberg that sends a brisk message to the public at COP Paris, Mary Ellen Carol's conceptual work at COP Glasgow, and Liam Gillick's cryptic piece that left many non-art professionals perplexed. See "A Climate (Art) Disaster in Paris Gare Du Nord," *Independent Scientists*, January 25, 2022, http://independent-scientists.com/a-public-art-disaster-in-gare-du-nord/.

Here the benchmark seems to be whether art can have popular appeal and still be conceptually rigorous?[13]

Advancing these agenda requires setting aside value differences, but it would be too exacting to define a teleological happy ending, i.e. a common denominator that holds everything together, a moral sentiment of (post)humanity that is at once too abstract and concrete. Perhaps we should not be talking about aligning values at all but about an instrumental relationship of different systems. We need a clear-headed picture of the planetary not as a naïve escapism from multipolarity, but as arising from the frictions caused by post-globalization multipolarity. Beyond the institutional edifice of the UN, there is perhaps more room for artistic thinking to serve as a force of reason amidst multiple moving targets, be they value systems, geopolitical contexts, or hitherto unthought of technologies and techniques of social ordering.

For example, as much as the tech space is splitting into hemispheric stacks in the image of contested multipolarity, it is thinkable, and historically demonstratable, that top scientists from different blocks can talk to and agree with one another on fundamental questions. Given value pluralism, how can art propose alternatives to AI Super Alignment, the proposal that superintelligent AI systems should act in ways that align with human values and intentions? Can art contribute to a discussion of data that shifts the focus away from the obsessions with personal preference data, which is in any case valueless when unaggregated? Or, when the talk of the town is about AI regulations and redlines, can

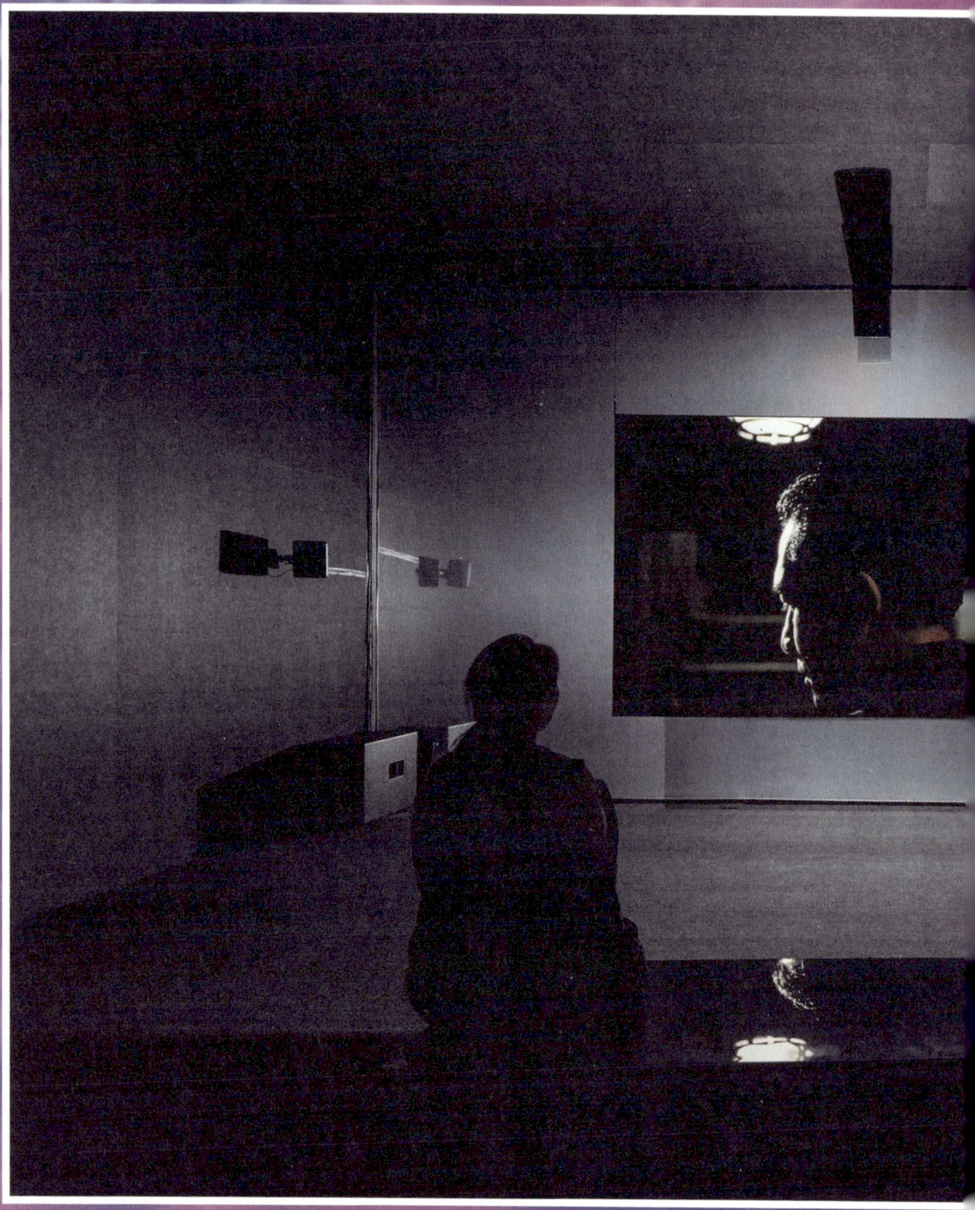

Ho Tzu Nyen
The Nameless, 2015
Synchronized double channel HD projection on two sides of a screen, with scrim wall separation, installation view

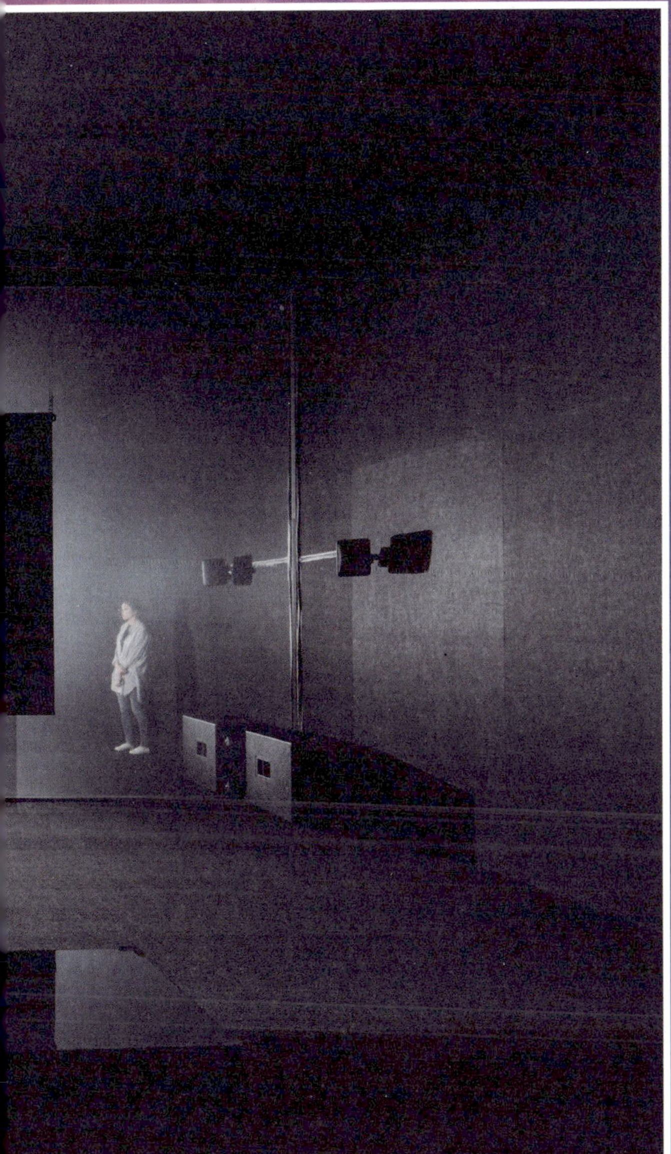

14 See the ongoing project of Antikythera led by Benjamin Bratton, in particular, the hemispherical stacks track: https://antikythera.org/hemispherical-stacks.
15 Aslak Aamot Helm, and Mandus Ridefelt, "The Black Hole Industry: Underdetermination in contemporary biomedicine and possible roles of art/science collaboration" (forthcoming).
16 Benjamin Bratton and Blaise Agüera y Arcas, "The Model is the Message," *Noēma*, July 12, 2022, https://www.noemamag.com/the-model-is-the-message/.

art invigorate a discussion on AI greenlines, or what work AI *should* be doing?[14]

Natural sciences are reaching a "wall of complexity" due to the accessibility of ever granular data through sensing and sequencing technologies. The multidimensionality of data makes it increasingly difficult to answer questions such as what causes cancer.[15] Not only that there are things in life and earth sciences that are fundamentally unknowable, but there are connections previously unthought of that come to the surface—e.g. large language models (LLM) have been used in predicting patterns in DNA fragmentation or the bio semiotics of animal language.[16] The wall of complexity is not only a challenge in scientific research, but concerns the public as they are increasingly presented with multi-dimensional science that confuses their understanding of life and shakes up their belief in objectivity. This deep operation of LLM that renders linguistics as structures of difference in a multidimensional space are not all that different from other structures that have underlying clusters of difference and probability: "you've been telling me all along that 2+2=4, now you tell me 2+2=purple?!" Compounded with the rise of populisms in the political sphere, the communication of the latest scientific and technological developments to a broader public must consider how not to undermine scientific rationality and objectivity. Cultural institutions can step in as a crucial mediator in this process of public reasoning.

As seen with the examples discussed in Chapter 4.1, through games and sci-fi we can model future societies,

17 Delton B. Chen, Joel van der Beek, and Jonathan Cloud, "Hypothesis for a risk cost of carbon: revising the externalities and ethics of climate change," *Understanding Risks and Uncertainties in Energy and Climate Policy*, eds. Haris Doukas, Alexandros Flamos, Jenny Lieu (New York: Springer, 2018), referenced in Chris Taylor, "Fight Carbon. With Coin," *Mashable*, 2021, https://in.mashable.com/science/20274/fight-carbon-with-coin.

but the question is how this can then gain a life in the public imagination and crucially, in policy making at the civic and state level. One instance of cultural production being popularly referred to in government circles is the *Ministry of the Future*, a sci-fi novel by US writer Kim Stanley Robinson. The "carbon coin" proposed in the novel that aims to achieve a genuine wealth transfer from affluent countries to poorer ones has a scientific foundation.[17] It elegantly points out the obvious, though inconvenient solution, for addressing global income inequality. In my engagement in numerous think tank dialogues, it has become evident that good sci-fi works are essentially deductive mental experiments, whereas in reality nothing is controllable. Like analytical philosophy, designing these imaginative speculations about the future requires establishing a starting point from which subsequent reasoning, scenarios, and consequences are developed as realistically and profoundly as possible. In this regard, not only George Orwell's *Animal Farm*, but also nineteenth century realist novels by Émile Zola, Honoré de Balzac, and Leo Tolstoy, and even Marxism can be read as good sci-fi works, as demonstrations of radical speculation. Through this kind of sci-fi exercise, we can consider challenging questions pertaining to a multipolar world, such as how to move beyond democratic nations, design new state alliances, reconfigure citizenship as a package of unbundled rights (but ensuring the stateless gain rights in the first place), and how to overcome the current right-wing resurgence. In this regard, I am inspired by one my acquaintances, a performer-turned-game-designer, who works

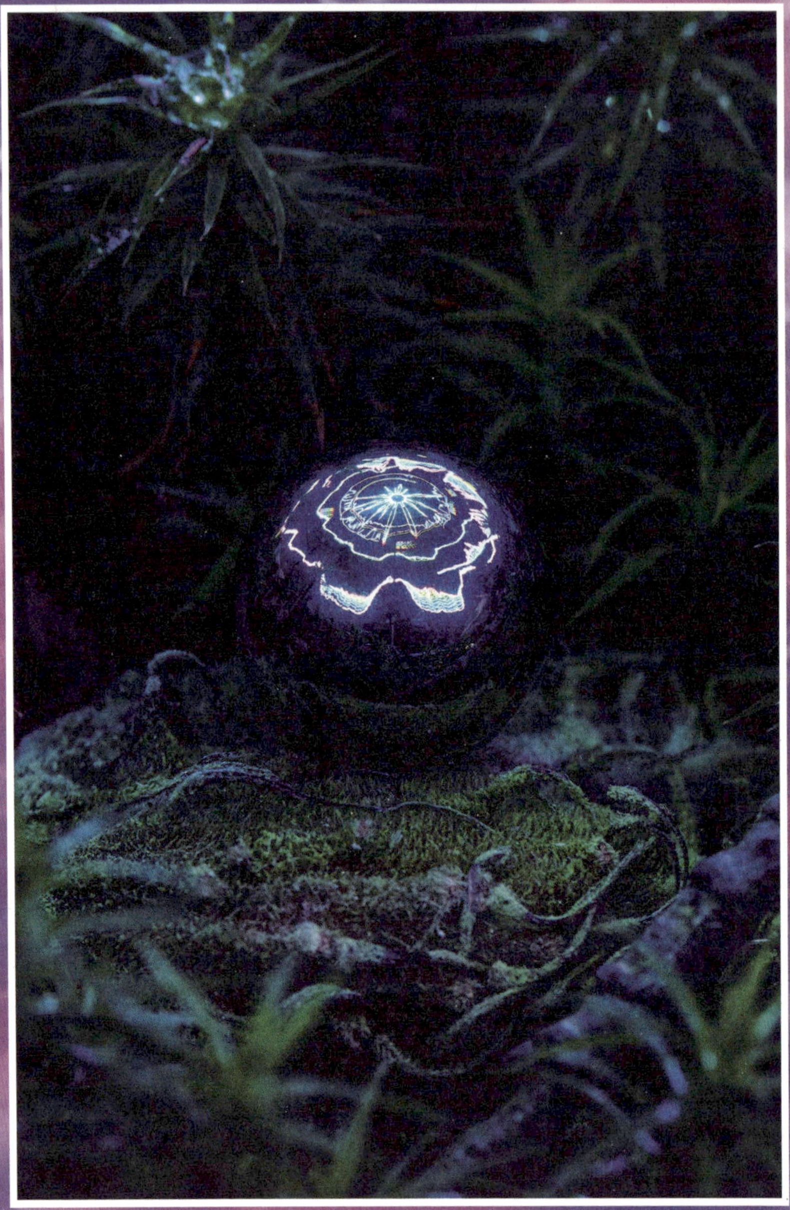

Diakron and Emil Rønn Andersen
Scries, 2021
Video stills

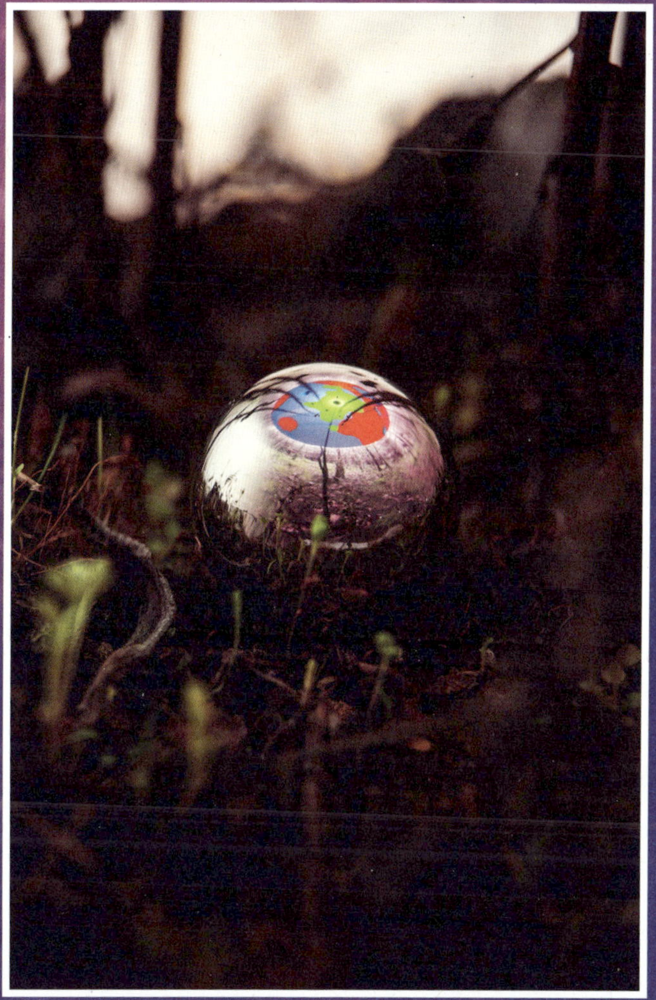

18 Žižek called for the left to grab state power, and qualified some military intervention as progressive. See Slavoj Žižek, *Freedom: A Disease without Cure* (New York: Bloomsbury Academic, 2023).

from the strategy unit of a national government where they design future scenarios and encourage public officers to performatively explore out-of-the-box thinking.

Where experiments are underway, my analysis can only be telegraphic. These are the spaces where art in a post-globalization world could thrive. Common among all the examples is an agency premised on and harnessed by experiences of the multipolar world. This horizon of art and culture to come may not look like the work we see in biennales, centers of contemporary art, and university programs today. Indeed, art and culture will not be the end product but can move up the scale of complexity, and—let it be said—power.[18] There is something deeply empowering about being an agent in setting agendas for a world after multipolarity. This is an era in which we need to update our compass for states, institutions, civic spaces, and value.

Notes on Artwork Inserts
Notes on Memes
Bibliography
Acknowledgments

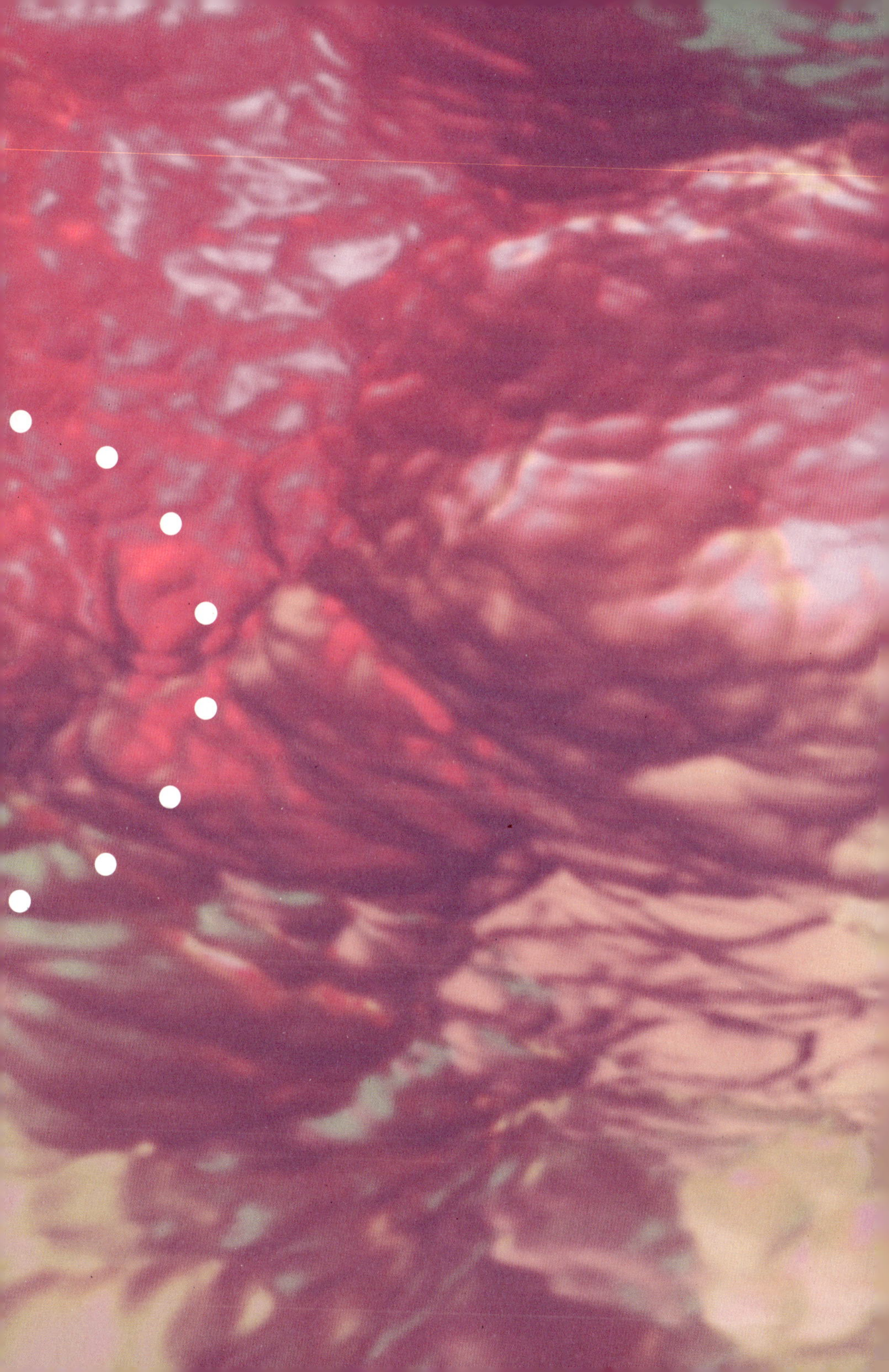

Notes on Artwork Inserts

The artworks inserted in the book are not intended as illustrations. Rather, they suggest answers to the question: “what if the book were an exhibition?” If this book is analysis, the art inserts are poetry. The works sampled here carve out a realm for affective intellectual interlocution that engages with complexitiy. Variably, they provide a contrapuntal perspective, a distilled symbol, an ambiguous emotional tableau, a deep dive into historical uncertainties, and a steadfast companion for journeying into future unknowns. In some cases, I chose two works from the same artist to highlight the intrinsic tensions dramatized by the works or different takes on the same topic, be it how to overcome modernity, or to negotiate political and ideological positions at odds with each other.

Notes on Memes

This book is accompanied by a series of commissioned memes from Cem A., a.k.a. *Freeze Magazine*, who has been producing memes on the artworld since 2021. The concepts nod to Mike Watson, who provocatively titled his book *Can the Left Learn to Meme?* (Winchester, WA: Zero Books, 2012). Part parody, part call to action, Watson directs our attention to a cultural phenomenon, the intuitions of which might contradict our own. It is not that the social space of memes necessarily reacts more positively to right-wing content but rather that within this space a "successful" discursive gesture must be a meme first, and a political text second. Some parts of the right, and a smaller part of the left, are able to leverage their fluency in this language exactly because they understand that memes are not simply political propaganda or didactics in a digital form but an intensified and abstracted social forum where jokes, observations, and political opinions are fused together. To "authentically" participate in this forum might mean that one cannot always be too precious about one's political principles and must allow for speech to mutate in the process. The far-right, by appealing to contradictory, unconscious grievances and ressentiments, does not suffer the loss of coherence, as their aim is not truth but resonance. Therefore, its base political tenets, albeit modified, can be easily propagated and proliferated in this system. The intellectual progressive (left, humanist, left-liberal, etc.) forms of speech are not as easily adaptable to this system as they are too concerned with producing coherence and dispelling ideologies and "false consciousness." Watson remarks, "Within online image culture there is an extreme level of apathy admixed with sarcasm that laughs in the face of the dire social realm we live in, yet equally in the face of any attempt at redemption or transcendence."[1] *Freeze Magazine* has captured the sarcasm and rubs salt into the wounds of the self-righteous egos of the artworld. Not unlike Theodor W. Adorno, one of the rare leftist thinkers to make it to meme culture, there is a belief in exaggeration as a means of telling the truth. Hence, part of the book employs memes as a form of critique, while hinting at a broader vision beyond.

1 Mike Watson, *The Memeing of Mark Fisher: How the Frankfurt School Foresaw Capitalist Realism and What To Do About It* (Winchester, UK: Zero Books, 2020)

Bibliography

"Accelerate Manifesto for an Accelerationist Politics." *Critical Legal Thinking*. http://criticallegalthinking.com/2013/05/14/accelerate-manifesto-for-an-accelerationist-politics6.

Acharya, Amitav, and Barry Buzan. *The Making of Global International Relations*. Cambridge, UK: Cambridge University Press, 2019.

"A Climate (Art) Disaster in Paris Gare Du Nord." *Independent Scientists*, January 25, 2022, http://independent-scientists.com/a-public-art-disaster-in-gare-du-nord/.

Adorno, Theodor W. *Aesthetic Theory*, eds. Gretel Adorno and Rolf Tiedeman. New York: Continuum, 2002.

Aima, Rahel, and Catherine G. Wagley. "Reviewing the Reviews: Documenta 15." *Momus*, December 10, 2022, https://momus.ca/reviewing-the-reviews-documenta-15/.

Anderson, Perry. *American Foreign Policy and Its Thinkers*. New York and London: Verso, 2015.

Antariksa. "Cross-Cultural Counterparts: The Role of Keimin Bunka Shidosho in Indonesian Art, 1942–1945." *Tsuyoshi Ozawa: The Return of Painter F*, eds. Keiko Toyoda and Fumi Toyoda. Tokyo: Shiseido, 2015. English translation available from Nusantara archive, https://www.heath.tw/nml-article/cross-cultural-counterparts-the-role-of-keimin-bunka-shidosho-in-indonesian-art-1942-1945/?lang=en.

Antikythera. "Hemispherical Stacks." https://antikythera.org/hemispherical-stacks.

Appadurai, Arjun. "The Wealth of Dividuals." *Banking on Words: The Failure of Language in the Age of Derivative Finance*. Chicago: The University of Chicago Press, 2016, pp. 101–24.

Bailey, Stephanie. "Diriyah Biennale, between the lines." *Spike Art Magazine*, March 22, 2022, https://www.spikeartmagazine.com/articles/diriyah-biennale-between-the-lines.

Bar-On, Tamir. "Understanding Political Conversion and Mimetic Rivalry." *Totalitarian Movements and Political Religions* 10, no. 3–4 (September 1, 2009), pp. 241–64.

Bar-On, Tamir. *Where Have All the Fascists Gone?* New York and London: Routledge, 2007.

Beech, Dave. *Art and Value: Art's Economic Exceptionalism in Classical, Neoclassical and Marxist Economics*. Leiden, The Netherlands: Brill, 2015.

Beer, Stafford. *Designing Freedom*. Toronto: CBC Publications, 1974.

Beery, Tal. "Instituent Practices: Art After (Public) Institutions." *Temporary Art Review*, January 2, 2018, https://temporaryartreview.com/instituent-practices-art-after-public-institutions/.

Bekmurzaev, Nurbek, Philipp Lottholz, and Joshua Meyer. "Navigating the safety implications of doing research and being researched in Kyrgyzstan: cooperation, networks and framing." *Central Asian Survey* 37, no. 1 (2018), pp. 100–18.

Belting, Hans. "From World Art to Global Art. View on a New Panorama." *What's next?*, 2013, http://whtsnxt.net/011.

Belting, Hans. "Contemporary Art as Global Art: A Critical Estimate." *The Global Art World: Audiences, Markets, and Museums*, eds. Hans Belting, Andrea Buddensieg. Ostfildern: Hatje Cantz, 2009, pp. 38–73.

Ben-Ami, Daniel. "Identity Politics Is Breathing New Life into Anti-Semitism." *Spiked*, July 3, 2022, https://www.spiked-online.com/2022/07/03/identity-politics-is-breathing-new-life-into-anti-semitism/.

Benjamin, Walter. "The Work of Art in the Age of Mechanical Reproduction." *Illuminations*, ed. by Hannah Arendt, trans. Harry Zohn. New York: Schocken Books, 1969.

Berlin, Isaiah. "Two Concepts of Liberty." *Four Essays on Liberty*. Oxford: Oxford University Press, 1969.

Beyes, Timon, and Ditte Vilstrup Holm. "How Art Becomes Organization: Reimagining Aesthetics, Sites and Politics of Entrepreneurship." *Organization Studies* 43, no. 2 (February 2022), pp. 227–45.

Bissenova, Alima, ed., *Kasakhstan: Labirinty sovremennogo postcolonialnogo discursa* (Kazakhstan: The labyrinths of the contemporary postcolonial discourse). Almaty: Tselinny publishing, 2023.

Blinder, Alan S. *A Monetary and Fiscal History of the United States, 1961–2021*. Princeton, NJ: Princeton University Press, 2022.

Bogdanov, Alexander. *Tektology: Universal Organizational Science*, 1989, https://monoskop.org/images/e/e9/Bogdanov_Alexander_Tektology_Book_1.pdf.

Bourdieu, Pierre. *Distinction: A Social Critique of the Judgement of Taste*, trans. Richard Nice. Cambridge, MA: Harvard University Press, 1984.

Bovino, Emily Verla. "Nation Branding by Evasive Curation: The Case of Q Art Group—A Hong Kong-made Image of China through Central and Eastern European Art." Presented on December 1, 2022 at the conference "China's Cultural Diplomacy and Nation Branding," Birmingham City University.

Bratton, Benjamin. "The Stack At The Edge Of Planetarity: Convergence, Divergence And War." *Vertical Atlas*. Arnhem: ArtEZ Press, 2022, https://verticalatlas.net/#benjamin-h.-bratton.

Bratton, Benjamin, and Blaise Agüera y Arcas. "The Model is the Message." *Noēma*, July 12, 2022, https://www.noemamag.com/the-model-is-the-message/.

Bratton, Benjamin. *The Stack: On Software and Sovereignity*. Cambridge, MA and London: The MIT press, 2015.

Bräutigam, Deborah. "A critical look at Chinese 'debt-trap diplomacy': The rise of a meme." *Area Development and Policy* 5.1 (2020), pp. 1–14.

Bröckling, Ulrich. *The Entrepreneurial Self: Fabricating a New Type of Subject*. London: SAGE Publications Ltd, 2016.

Buchanan, James M. *The Limits of Liberty: Between Anarchy and Leviathan*. Chicago: University of Chicago Press, 1975.

Bude, Heinz. *Peter Ludwig. Im Glanz der Bilder.* Cologne: Bastei Lübbe, 1996.

Budianta, Melani. "Discourse of cultural identity in Indonesia during the 1997–1998 monetary crisis." *Inter-Asia Cultural Studies* 1, no. 1 (April 2000), pp. 109–28.

Budianta, Melani. "Decentralizing Engagements: Women and the Democratization Process in Indonesia." *Signs* 31, no. 4 (Summer 2006), pp. 915–23.
Buhr, Elke. "Antisemitismus-Polemik gegen die Documenta geht nach hinten los." *Monopol*, January 13, 2022, https://www.monopol-magazin.de/antisemitismus-polemik-gegen-die-documenta-geht-nach-hinten-los.
Bündnis gegen Antisemitismus Kassel. "Documenta fifteen: Antizionismus und Antisemitismus im lumbung." *bga-kassel* (blog), January 7, 2022, https://bgakasselblog.wordpress.com/2022/01/07/documenta-fifteen-antizionismus-und-antisemitismus-im-lumbung/.
Butler, Judith. *What World Is This? A Pandemic Phenomenology.* New York: Columbia University Press, 2022.
Carmody, Pádraig. "Dependence not debt-trap diplomacy." *Area Development and Policy* 5, no. 1 (2020), pp. 23–31.
Chan, Hera and Alvin Li. "Becoming Ethnic in China: A 'Good Story' Told in Painting and Dialect." *Afterall* 53, September 13, 2022, https://www.afterall.org/articles/logic-of-the-written-word-and-oral-logic-conflict-at-the-heart-of-the-archive/.
Chatterjee, Partha. *The Nation and Its Fragments: Colonial and Postcolonial Histories*. Princeton, NJ: Princeton University Press, 2020.
Chen, Delton B., et al. "Hypothesis for a risk cost of carbon: revising the externalities and ethics of climate change." *Understanding Risks and Uncertainties in Energy and Climate Policy*, eds. Haris Doukas, Alexandros Flamos, Jenny Lieu. New York: Springer, 2018.
Chen, Kuan-Hsing. *Asia as Method: Toward Deimperialization*. Durham, NC: Duke University Press, 2010.
Chen, Kuan-Hsing, and C.B. Huat. "An Introduction," *Inter-Asia Cultural Studies* 1, no. 1 (2000), pp. 9–12.
Chibber, Vivek. *Postcolonial Theory and the Specter of Capital*. London and New York: Verso, 2013.
Choi, Binna, and Marion von Osten. "Trans-Local, Post-Disciplinary Organizational Practice: A Conversation between Binna Choi and Marion von Osten." *Cluster: Dialectionary,* eds. Binna Choi et al. London: Sternberg Press, 2014.
Chukhrov, Keti. "The Postdramatic Theater's Misadventures in the Age of Contemporary Art." *e-flux Journal*, no. 120 (September 2021), https://www.e-flux.com/journal/120/415768/the-postdramatic-theater-s-misadventures-in-the-age-of-contemporary-art/.
"Clouds, Power and Ornament—Roving Central Asia," *CHAT* (blog), https://www.mill6chat.org/event/clouds-power-and-ornament-roving-central-asia/.
Collective letter. "We Are Angry, We Are Sad, We Are Tired, We Are United: Letter from lumbung Community—Notes—e-Flux." *e-flux Notes*, September 10, 2022, https://www.e-flux.com/notes/489580/we-are-angry-we-are-sad-we-are-tired-we-are-united-letter-from-lumbung-community.

"疫情下的社区互助经验| 社区团购、互助就医、握手平台、行动转化 (Community Mutual Aid Experiences under the Epidemic | Community Group Purchase, Mutual Aid for Medical Care, Handshake Platform, Action Transformation)." https://c.m.163.com/news/a/HMASQ16V0525D88B.html.

Conn, Virginia L. "Sinofuturism and Chinese Science Fiction: An Introduction to the Alternative Sinofuturisms (中华未来主义) Special Issue." *SFRA Review* 50, no. 2–3 (2020), pp. 66–70.

"2018–2019 COOP Study Group: Unmapping Eurasia. Tutor Team: Binna Choi, Mi You. Partner: Casco Art Institute: Working for the Commons." http://dutchartinstitute.eu/page/11986/2018-2019-coop-study-group-unmapping-eurasia.-tutor-team-binna-choi.

Cui, Zhiyuan. "从重庆领悟'社会主义市场经济': 国资增值与藏富于民携手并进" (Coming to an understanding of "market socialism" from Chongqing: appreciation in value of state assets and wealth stored among the people go forward hand-in-hand), 文化纵横 *Beijing Culture Review* (2009). www.cui-zy.cn.

Cui, Zhiyuan: "Introduction". In *Politics: The Central Texts*. Ed. Zhiyuan Cui. London and New York: Verso, 1997.

Dai, Ruwei. "从工程控制论到综合集成研讨厅体系——纪念钱学森归国50周年from Engineering to Hall for Workshop of Metasynthetic Engineering: Commemorating 50th Anniversary of Qian's Return to China," 复杂系统与复杂性科学 *Complex Systems and Complexity Science* 3, no. 2 (2006).

Daum, Jeremy. "China through a Glass, Darkly." *China Law Translate* (blog), December 24, 2017, https://www.chinalawtranslate.com/china-social-credit-score/.

Davidson, Miri. "Sea and Earth." *New Left Review Sidecar*, April 4, 2024, https://newleftreview.org/sidecar/posts/sea-and-earth.

Davies, William. "The Politics of Recognition in the Age of Social Media." *New Left Review* 128, March/April 2021, https://newleftreview.org/issues/ii128/articles/william-davies-the-politics-of-recognition-in-the-age-of-social-media.

De Baere, Bart. "Whatever the Future Will Be, It Is Made Now." *Afterall*, March 14, 2023, https://www.afterall.org/articles/whatever-the-future-will-be-it-is-made-now-2/.

Degot, Ekaterina, and David Riff, eds. *steirischer herbst '22: A War in the Distance. Ukraine and the Return of History*. Berlin: Hatje Cantz, 2023.

Deleuze, Gilles, and Félix Guattari. *A Thousand Plateaus: Capitalism and Schizophrenia*, trans. Brian Massumi. Minneapolis: University of Minnesota Press, 2007.

Deng, Jun, and Craig A. Smith. "The Rise of New Confucianism and the Return of Spirituality to Politics in Mainland China." *China Information* 32, no. 2 (July 2018), pp. 294–314.

de Seta, Gabriele. "Sinofuturism as Inverse Orientalism: China's Future and the Denial of Coevalness." *SFRA Review* 50, no. 2–3 (2020), pp. 86–94.

Dirlik, Arif. "The Bandung Legacy and the People's Republic of China in the Perspective of Global Modernity." *Inter-Asia Cultural Studies* 16, no. 4 (2015), pp. 615–30.

Dirlik, Arif. "Chinese History and the Question of Orientalism." *History and Theory* 35, no. 4 (December 1996), pp. 96–118.

Djagalov, Rossen. *From Internationalism to Postcolonialism: Literature and Cinema between the Second and the Third Worlds*. Montreal: McGill-Queen's University Press, 2020.

documenta Institut. *Workshop report: The Future that Will Have Been*. https://www.documenta-institut.de/artikel/workshop-bericht-the-future-that-will-have-been.

dpa (Deutsche Presse-Agentur), "Zentralrat der Juden: Bei Documenta nicht berücksichtigt—Kritik an Roth." *Monopol*, April 28, 2022, https://www.monopol-magazin.de/zentralrat-der-juden-bei-documenta-nicht-beruecksichtigt-kritik-roth.

Dreyer, Jacob. "China Dreams of a Palace in the Sky." *Noēma*, February 1, 2022, https://www.noemamag.com/china-dreams-of-a-palace-in-the-sky/.

Eich, Stefan. "Crypto Won't Solve Our Problems—We Need to Democratize Money." Interview by Daniel Denvir, *Jacobin*, November 2, 2022, https://jacobin.com/2022/02/cryptocurrency-democratize-monetary-policy-economics-banks-financial-system-bitcoin.

Elkins, James. *Is Art History Global?* New York and London: Routledge, 2007.

Elkins, James, Zhivka Valiavicharska, and Alice Kim. *Art and Globalization*. Philadelphia: Penn State University Press, 2015.

Ekeman, Karl. "On Gramscianism of the Right." *Praxis* 13, no. 13 (November 11, 2018), https://blogs.law.columbia.edu/praxis1313/karl-ekeman-on-gramscianism-of-the-right/.

England, Andrew. "'Bridges with everyone': how Saudi Arabia and UAE are positioning themselves for power." *Financial Times*, August 23, 2023, https://www.ft.com/content/3889c33d-4830-407c-a3f6-f9e3cfaaa35f.

Fare, Marie, and Pepita Ould Ahmed. "Complementary Currency Systems and Their Ability to Support Economic and Social Changes." *Development and Change* 48, no. 5 (September 2017), pp. 847–72.

Flyvbjerg, Bent, Todd Landman, and Sanford Schram, eds. *Real Social Science: Applied Phronesis*. Cambridge, UK: Cambridge University Press, 2012.

Fourcade, Marion, and Daniel N. Kluttz. "A Maussian bargain: Accumulation by gift in the digital economy." *Big Data & Society* 7, no. 1 (2020), pp. 1–16.

Framer Framed. "Symposium: (un)Common Grounds." *framerframed.nl*, September 2022, https://framerframed.nl/en/projecten/uncommon-grounds-reflecting-on-documenta-fifteen/.

Frank, Simon. "Does Liu Chuang's new film challenge the colonial gaze or merely reproduce it?" *Frieze*, June 1, 2019, https://www.frieze.com/article/does-liu-chuangs-new-film-challenge-colonial-gaze-or-merely-reproduce-it.

"From Bandung to Berlin: If all of the moons aligned." http://frombandungtoberlin.com.

Gan, Yang, 通三统 *(Unifying the three traditions)*. Beijing: Sanlian Shudian, 2007.

Gao, Bai. "Trade Wars, Hot Wars and the Rise of the Global South: The Future of the Dollar Standard." *Reading the China Dream* (blog), January 20, 2024, https://www.readingthechinadream.com/gao-bai-on-challenges-to-the-dollar-standard.html.

Gao, Shiming. 后万隆 *(Post Bandung)*. Shanghai: Shanghai Arts Publishing House, 2022.

Gao, Shiming. "The Dismantling and Re-Construction of Bentu ('This Land' or 'Native Land'): Contemporary Chinese Art in the Post-Colonial Context." *A New Thoughtfulness in Contemporary China,* eds. Jörg Huber and Chuan Zhao. Bielefeld: transcript Verlag, 2011, pp. 103–20.

Gao, Shiming. "Observations and Premonitions of 'After Post-Colonialism.'" *Farewell to Post-Colonialism: 3rd Guangzhou Trienniale*, eds. Shiming Gao, Sarat Maharaj, Johnson Chang. Hangzhou: China Academy of Art Press, 2008, pp. 44–51.

Gardels, Nathan. "What comes after liberalism." *Noēma*, October 6, 2023, https://www.noemamag.com/what-comes-after-liberalism/.

Gardels, Nathan. "Planetary Politics When the Nation-State Falters." *Noēma*, September 3, 2021, https://www.noemamag.com/planetary-politics-when-the-nation-state-falters/.

Geertz, Clifford. "Culture and Social Change: The Indonesia Case." *Man* 19, no. 4 (December 1984), pp. 511–32.

Geertz, Clifford. *Agricultural Involution: The Processes of Ecological Change in Indonesia.* Oakland, CA: University of California Press, 1963.

Gilman, Nils. "The NIEO as Usable Past." *Progressive International*, January 4, 2023, https://progressive.international/blueprint/e7bc30e1-d565-47de-a19f-80ad1bce9969-gilman-the-nieo-as-usable-past/en.

Gilman, Nils. "The New International Economic Order: A Reintroduction." *Humanity: An International Journal of Human Rights, Humanitarianism, and Development* 6, no. 1 (March 2015), pp. 1–16.

Gladston, Paul. "International Curatorial Practice and the Problematic De-Territorialization of the Identity Show: Deconstructing the Third Guangzhou Triennial, Farewell to Post-Colonialism." *Journal of Curatorial Studies* 4, no. 1 (February 1, 2015), pp. 6–32.

Goldenweiser, Alexander. "Loose Ends of Theory on the Individual, Pattern, and Involution in Primitive Society." *Journal of American Folklore* 43, no. 170 (1930), pp. 228–41.

Goriunova, Olga. *Art Platforms and Cultural Production on the Internet*. London: Routledge, 2012.

Graeber, David. *Fragments of an Anarchist Anthropology*. Chicago: Prickly Paradigm Press, 2004.

Gray, John. *Post-Liberalism: Studies in Political Thought*, 1st ed.. London: Routledge, 1996.

Groys, Boris. *The Total Art of Stalinism*. Princeton, NJ: Princeton University Press, 1992.

Guha, Ranajit. *Elementary Aspects of Peasant Insurgency in Colonial India*. New York: Oxford University Press USA, 1983.

Halpern, Orit. *Beautiful Data: A History of Vision and Reason Since 1945*. Durham, NC: Duke University Press, 2014.

Hammond, Kenneth J. "The Return of the Repressed: The New Left and 'Left' Confucianism in Contemporary China." *The Sage Returns: Confucian Revival in Contemporary China*, eds. Kenneth J. Hammond and Jeffrey L. Richey. Albany: State University of New York Press, 2015.

Haq, Nav. "Preface." In *Eurasia. An Atlas*, eds. Nav Haq and Joanna Zielińska. Antwerp: M HKA Museum of Contemporary Art Antwerp and Jap Sam Books, 2023.

Harvey, David. "Rate and Mass: Perspectives from the Grundrisse." *New Left Review*, no. 130 (2021), pp. 73–98. https://newleftreview.org/issues/ii130/articles/david-harvey-rates-and-mass.

Harvey, David. "Globalization and the 'Spatial Fix.'" *Geographische Revue* 2 (2001), pp. 23–30.

Havel, Václav, quoted in Welton, Michael. "Václav Havel and the Power of the Powerless." *Counterpunch*, February 26, 2016, https://www.counterpunch.org/2016/02/26/vaclav-havel-and-the-power-of-the-powerless/.

Hayek, Friedrich. *Studies in Philosophy, Politics and Economics.* Chicago: University of Chicago Press, 1967.

Hayek, Friedrich. *The Sensory Order: An Inquiry into the Foundations of Theoretical Psychology*. Chicago: University of Chicago Press, 1952.

Heiser, Jörg. "'Contested Histories': On Documenta 15." *e-flux Criticism*, June 29, 2022, https://www.e-flux.com/criticism/477463/contested-histories-on-documenta-15.

Helm, Aslak Aamot, and Mandus Ridefelt. "The Black Hole Industry: Underdetermination in contemporary biomedicine and possible roles of art/science collaboration." (forthcoming).

Hendrikse, Reijer. "The Rise of Neo-Illiberalism." *Krisis* 41, no. 1 (June 15, 2021), pp. 65–93.

Holert, Tom. *Knowledge Beside Itself: Contemporary Art's Epistemic Politics*. London: Sternberg Press, 2020.

Holmes, Brian. *Escape the Overcode: Activist Art in the Control Society.* Eindhoven: Van Abbemuseum, 2009.

Holslag, Jonathan. "The EU's 'global gateway'—an answer to China, or a dead-end?" *EU Observer*, December 1, 2021, https://euobserver.com/opinion/153678.

Holt, Claire. *Art in Indonesia: Continuities and Change*. Ithaca, NY: Cornell University Press, 1967.

Hoskoté, Ranjit. "Documenta Resignation Letter." *e-flux Notes*, November 13, 2023, https://www.e-flux.com/notes/575318/documenta-resignation-letter.

Hou, Hanru. "Entropy, Chinese Artists, Western Art Institutions: A New Internationalism (1994)." *Contemporary Chinese Art: Primary Documents*, ed. Wu Hung. New York: The Museum of Modern Art, 2010.

Huang, Philip C.C. "Chongqing: equitable development driven by a 'Third Hand'?" *Modern China* 37, no. 6 (November 1, 2011), pp. 569–622.

Hui, Yew-Foong. "The (Un)Changing World of Peasants: Two Perspectives." *Journal of Social Issues in Southeast Asia* 24, no. 1 (April 2009), pp. 18–31.

Hui, Yuk. *The Question Concerning Technology in China: An Essay in Cosmotechnics*, 3rd corrected edition. Falmouth: Urbanomic, 2022.

Hui, Yuk. "For a Planetary Thinking." *e-flux Journal*, no. 114 (December 2020), https://www.e-flux.com/journal/114/366703/for-a-planetary-thinking/.

Hui, Yuk. "Cosmotechnics as Cosmopolitics." *e-flux Journal*, no. 86 (November 2017), https://www.e-flux.com/journal/86/161887/cosmotechnics-as-cosmopolitics/.

Hujatnika, Agung, and Almira Belinda Zainsjah. "Artist Collectives in Post-1998 Indonesia: Resurgence, or a Turn (?)" International Conference on Aesthetics and the Sciences of Art (AESCIART), published in *Art Creation, Mediation, and Reception in the 21st Century Indonesia*. Bandung: Bandung Institute of Technology, 2020, pp. 256–63.

Ivanova, Victoria. "Two Lives, One Order." *The Draft* (blog), June 2014, https://barddraft.wordpress.com/wp-content/uploads/2015/01/ivanova.pdf.

Ivanova, Victoria, and Gerald Nestler. "Art, Markets, and Finance." *The Routledge Handbook of Critical Finance Studies*, eds. Christian Borch and Robert Wosnitzer, London: Routledge, 2020.

Jatiwangi art Factory. "Introducing the lumbung members: Jatiwangi art Factory." YouTube video, 33:43 min. *documenta fifteen*, April 23, 2021, https://www.youtube.com/watch?v=S9SRLhyYmzs.

Jessop, Bob. *State Power: A Strategic-Relational Approach*. Cambridge, UK: Polity Press, 2010.

Jhala, Kabir. "'Germany Has Cancelled Us': As Embattled Documenta 15 Closes, Its Curators Ruangrupa Reflect on the Exhibition—and What They Would Have Done Differently." *The Art Newspaper*, September 22, 2022, https://www.theartnewspaper.com/2022/09/22documenta-15-closes-curators-ruangrupa-exhibition-kassel.

Jiang, Qing. *A Confucian Constitutional Order: How China's Ancient Past Can Shape Its Political Future*. Princeton, NJ: Princeton University Press, 2012.

Jin, Keyu. *The New China Playbook: Beyond Socialism and Capitalism*. New York: Viking, 2023.

Johnson, Matthew D. "The Science Education Film: Cinematizing Technocracy and Internationalizing Development." *Journal of Chinese Cinemas* 5, no. 1 (2011), pp. 31–53.

Juliastuti, Nuraini. "Ruangrupa: A Conversation on Horizontal Organisation." *Afterall*, no. 30 (Summer 2012), https://www.afterall.org/articles/ruangrupa-a-conversation-on-horizontal-organisation/.

Junaedi, Deni. "Benturan Estetis antara Liberalisme, Sosialisme, dan Islam" (Aesthetic Clash between Liberalism, Socialism and Islam). *Proceeding of JICM (Jakarta International Conference of Muslim Intellectuals)*. Jakarta, 2013, pp. 26–40.

Kent, Elly. "The History of Conscious Collectivity Behind Ruangrupa." *ArtReview Asia*, July 6, 2022, https://artreview.com/the-history-of-conscious-collectivity-behind-ruangrupa/.

Khalil, Nadine. “The DIY Chaos of Documenta 15.” *Frieze*, July 7, 2022, https://www.frieze.com/article/diy-chaos-documenta-15-2022-review.

“Khudozhnik Iz Uzbekistana Gotovit Ogromnuiu Kartinu, Posviashchionnuiu Velikomu Shelkovomu Puti” (An Artist from Uzbekistan Is Preparing a Huge Painting Dedicated to the Great Silk Road), Podrobno.Uz, August 26, 2019, https://podrobno.uz/cat/uzbekistan-i-kitay-klyuchi-ot-budushchego/khudozhnik-iz-uzbekistana-gotovit-ogromnuyu/.

King, Dylan Levi. “The Genealogy of Chinese Cybernetics.” *Palladium Mag*, October 17, 2022, https://www.palladiummag.com/2022/10/17/the-genealogy-of-chinese-cybernetics/.

Koch, Franziska. “‘Chineseness’ in Contemporary Art Discourse and Practice: Negotiating Multiple Agencies, Localities and Vocalities.” *Journal of Contemporary Chinese Art* 3, no. 1 (June 2016), pp. 3–11.

Kuo, Kaiser. “China’s draft regulations on generative AI, with Kendra Schaefer and Jeremy Daum.” *The China Project podcast*, May 11, 2023, https://thechinaproject.com/podcast/chinas-draft-regulations-on-generative-ai-with-kendra-schaefer-and-jeremy-daum/.

Lan, Xiaohuan. *How China Works: An Introduction to China’s State-Led Economic Development.* Singapore: Palgrave Macmillan, 2024.

Laruelle, François. *Principles of Non-Philosophy*, trans. Anthony Paul Smith. New York: Bloomsbury Academic, 2013.

Lasminingrat, Lula, and Efriza Efriza. “The Development of National Food Estate: The Indonesian Food Crisis Anticipation Strategy.” *Jurnal Pertahanan & Bela Negara* 10, no. 3 (2020), pp. 229–48.

Law, John. “Collateral realities.” *The Politics of Knowledge,* eds. Fernando Dominguez Rubio and Patrick Baert. London and New York: Routledge, 2011, pp. 156–78.

Lefebvre, Henri. *The Production of Space*, vol. 1. Oxford, UK: Wiley-Blackwell, 1992.

Lefkowitz, Melissa. “Revolutionary Friendship: Representing Africa during the Mao Era.” *China-Africa Relations*, eds. Kathryn Batchelor and Xiaoling Zhang. New York and London: Routledge, 2017.

Léger, Marc James. “Art and Art History after Globalisation.” *Third Text* 26, no. 5 (2012), pp. 515–27.

Lewis, David G. “Grossraum Thinking in Russian Foreign Policy.” *Russia’s New Authoritarianism: Putin and the Politics of Order Edinburgh Scholarship Online*, September 17, 2020.

Li, Alvin. “West Side Stories.” *The Contest of the Fruits*, eds. Guangtian Ha and Slavs and Tatars. Cambridge: The MIT Press, 2021.

Li, Eric Shimo. “Eric X. Li: A tale of two political systems.” *TED talk*, July 1, 2013, TED, YouTube video, 20:37, https://www.youtube.com/watch?v=s0YjL9rZyR0.

Li, Miao, et al. “Shehui Ren: Cultural Production and Rural Youths’ Use of the Kuaishou Video-Sharing App in Eastern China.” *Information, Communication & Society* 23, no. 10 (August 23, 2020), pp. 1499–1514.

Li, Tania Murray. “Commons, co-ops, and corporations: assembling Indonesia’s twenty-first century land reform.” *The Journal of Peasant Studies* 48, no. 3 (April 2021), pp. 613–39.

Lin, Yao. “Beaconism and the Trumpian Metamorphosis of Chinese Liberal Intellectuals.” *Journal of Contemporary China* 30, no. 127 (2020), pp. 85–101.

Liu, Cixin. *The Three-Body Problem.* New York: Tor Books, 2016.

Lobo, Sascha. “Willkommen auf der Antisemita 15.” *Der Spiegel*, June 22, 2022, https://www.spiegel.de/netzwelt/netzpolitik/sascha-lobo-ueber-den-documenta-skandal-willkommen-bei-der-antisemita-a-424a0c6f-ec04-4158-92be-9ab8f03f17ad.

Lottholz, Philipp. *Post-Liberal Statebuilding in Central Asia: Imaginaries, Discourses and Practices of Social Ordering*. Bristol: Policy Press, 2022.

Lottholz, Philipp. “Political Change in Post-socialist Eurasia: Towards a Post-Liberal Research Agenda.” *openDemocracy*, February 27, 2019, https://www.opendemocracy.net/en/odr/political-change-in-post-socialist-eurasia/.

Lu, Mingjun. 美术变革与现代中国:中国当代艺术的激进根源, (*Revolution of Art and Modern China: Radical Origins of Chinese Contemporary Art*). Beijing: Commercial Press, 2020.

Lugo, Maria Ana, Martin Raiser, and Ruslan Yemtsov. “What’s next for poverty reduction policies in China?” *Brookings*, September 24, 2021, https://www.brookings.edu/articles/whats-next-for-poverty-reduction-policies-in-china/?b=1.

Lütticken, Sven. “The Coming Exception: Art and the Crisis of Value.” *New Left Review*, no. 99 (May–June 2016), pp. 111–36.

Lütticken, Sven. “Social Media: Practices of (In)Visibility in Contemporary Art.” *Afterall* 40 (Autumn/Winter 2015), pp. 4–19.

MacGregor, Neil. “An ambitious Mumbai museum project sets Indian history in a world context.” *Financial Times*, December 30, 2023, https://www.ft.com/content/e14aea71-f668-46c8-aad5-4860ca17cdb0.

MacRae, Graeme, and Thomas Reuter. “Lumbung Nation.” *Indonesia and the Malay World* 48, no. 142 (December 2020), pp. 338–58.

Magnin, Eric, and Nikolay Nenovsky. “Calculating without Money. Theories of in-Kind Accounting of Alexander Chayanov, Otto Neurath and the Early Soviet Experiences.” *The European Journal of the History of Economic Though*t 28, no. 3 (2021), pp. 456–77.

Malachowski, Justin. “Staging Arts in the Historic City: Development Funding, Social Media Images, and Tunisia’s Contemporary Public Art Scene.” *Journal of City and Society* (2022), Volume 34, Issue 2–3, pp. 147–225.

Mallapaty, Smriti. “China’s Five-Year Plan Focuses on Scientific Self-Reliance.” *Nature* 591, no. 7850 (March 18, 2021), pp. 353–54.

Malzacher, Florian, conversation with Claire Bishop, et al. “XIV: Audience as Allies, Witnesses, and Enemies (Claire Bishop, Tania Bruguera, Ann Liv Young & Florian Malzacher).” *Art of Assembly* (podcast), March 28, 2022, https://art-of-assembly.net/podcast/xiv-audience-as-allies-witnesses-and-enemies-claire-bishop-tania-bruguera-ann-liv-young-florian-malzacher/.

Mandler, Peter. *Return from the Natives: How Margaret Mead Won the Second World War and Lost the Cold War*. New Haven: Yale University Press, 2013.

Marchart, Oliver. *Conflictual Aesthetics: Artistic Activism and the Public Sphere*. London: Sternberg Press, 2019.

Marsili, Lorenzo. "From The Age Of Empires To The Age Of Humanity." *Noēma*, July 27, 2023, https://www.noemamag.com/from-the-age-of-empires-to-the-age-of-humanity/.

Marsili, Lorenzo, and Fabrizio Tassinari. "Are we heading towards a far-right European Union?" *Al Jazeera Opinions*, July 19, 2023.

Marsili, Lorenzo. *Planetary Politics: A Manifesto*. Cambridge, UK: Polity, 2021.

Marsili, Lorenzo, and Mi You. "China and the West Can Build a Better World, Together." *Al Jazeera*, October 30, 2021, https://www.aljazeera.com/opinions/2021/10/30/china-and-the-west-can-build-a-better-world-together.

Martin, Randy. *Knowledge LTD: Toward a Social Logic of the Derivative*. Philadelphia: Temple University Press, 2015.

Marx, Karl. "The British Rule in India." *Marx & Engels Collected Works*, vol. 12. London: Lawrence & Wishart, 2010, pp. 131–32.

Marx, Karl, and Friedrich Engels. "Manifesto of the Communist Party." *Marx & Engels Collected Works*, vol. 6. London: Lawrence & Wishart, 2010, pp. 486–87.

Massey, Doreen, et al. *Human Geography Today*. Cambridge, UK: Polity Press, 2007.

Mayer, Maximilian, and Karolina Pawlik. "Politics of Memory, Heritage, and Diversity in Modern China." *Journal of Current Chinese Affairs* 52.2 (2023), pp. 139–62.

McAndrew, Clare. *The Art Market 2018: An Art Basel and UBS Report.* Basel: Art Basel, 2018.

McAndrew, Clare, et al. "Plotting the Art Market: An Interview with Clare McAndrew." *Finance and Society* 2, no. 2 (2016), pp. 151–67.

McRobbie, Angela. *Be Creative: Making a Living in the New Culture Industries*. Cambridge, UK: Polity Press, 2016.

Meaney, Thomas. "The Swaddling Thesis." *London Review of Books* 36, no. 5 (March 6, 2014), https://www.lrb.co.uk/the-paper/v36/n05/thomas-meaney/the-swaddling-thesis.

Mearsheimer, John J. "America Unhinged," *The National Interest* 129 (2014), pp. 9–30.

Mearsheimer, John J. "Why the Ukraine Crisis Is the West's Fault. The Liberal Delusions that Provoked Putin," *Foreign Affairs* 93, no. 5 (2014), pp. 77–89.

Meinhof, Marius. "Colonial Temporality and Chinese National Modernization Discourses." *InterDisciplines. Journal of History and Sociology* 8 (October 19, 2017), pp. 51–80.

"Meituan to change delivery algorithm rules as China urges labour protection." *Reuters*, September 13, 2021, https://www.reuters.com/world/china/meituan-change-delivery-algorithm-rules-china-urges-labour-protection-2021-09-13/.

METRUM Managementberatung. "Consulting and Support for the further development of documenta und Museum Fridericianum gGmbH." December 15, 2023. https://www.documenta.de/files/231215_Summarizing_Final_Report_ENGLISH.pdf.

Mignolo, Walter D. "The Global South and the World Dis/Order." *Journal of Anthropological Research* 67, no. 2 (July 2011), pp. 165–88.

Mignolo, Walter D. "Local Histories/Global Designs: Coloniality, Subaltern Knowledges, and Border Thinking." *Princeton Studies in Culture/Power/History.* Princeton, NJ: Princeton University Press, 2000.

Miller, Jacob C., and Sharon Wilson. "Museum as Geopolitical Entity: Toward Soft Combat." *Geography Compass* 16, no. 6 (May 6, 2022), pp. 1–13.

Mirowski, Philip. *Never let a serious crisis go to waste: how neoliberalism survived the financial meltdown*. London: Verso, 2013.

Mitter, Siddhartha. "Documenta Was a Whole Vibe. Then a Scandal Killed the Buzz." *The New York Times*, June 24, 2022, https://www.nytimes.com/2022/06/24/arts/design/documenta-review.html.

Morozov, Evgeny. "Digital Socialism? The Calculation Debate in the Age of Big Data." *New Left Review* 116/117 (2019), pp. 33–67.

Moss, Ian David. "An Ecosystem-Based Approach to Arts Research." *Fractured Atlas* (blog), October 17, 2011, https://blog.fracturedatlas.org/an-ecosystem-based-approach-to-arts-research-e95cbc0946fe.

Mouffe, Chantal. *The Return of the Political*. London and New York: Verso, 1993.

Mullaney, Thomas S. *Coming to Terms with the Nation: Ethnic Classification in Modern China*. Oakland, CA: University of California Press, 2011.

Neiman, Susan. Interview by Sebastian Frenzel. "Das Kulturleben nimmt Schaden." *Monopol* (online), November 28, 2023, https://www.monopol-magazin.de/interview-susan-neiman-bds-antisemitismus-kultur.

Niermann, Ingo. "Documenta 9/11?" Quoted in Rahel Aima and Catherine G. Wagley. "Reviewing the Reviews: Documenta 15." *Momus*, December 10, 2022, https://momus.ca/reviewing-the-reviews-documenta-15/.

Njami, Simon, Gong Yan, Kathrin Rhomberg, and María Inés Rodríguez. "Documenta Resignation Letter." *e-flux Notes*, November 16, 2023, https://www.e-flux.com/notes/575919/documenta-resignation-letter.

Noys, Benjamin. *Malign Velocities: Accelerationism and Capitalism.* Winchester: Zero Books, 2014.

Oakeshott, Michael. *Rationalism in Politics and Other Essays*. Indianapolis: Liberty Press, 1991.

Okonjo-Iweala, Ngozi. "Why the World Still Needs Trade: The Case for Reimagining—Not Abandoning—Globalization." *Foreign Affairs* 102, no. 4 (2023), pp. 94–103.

Oltermann, Philip. "'Free speech is a facade': how Gaza war has deepened divisions in German arts world." *The Guardian*, March 25, 2024, https://www.theguardian.com/world/2024/mar/25/free-speech-is-a-facade-how-gaza-war-has-deepened-divisions-in-german-arts-world.

Osborne, Peter. *Anywhere or Not at All: Philosophy of Contemporary Art.* London and New York: Verso, 2013.

Palmer, David A. *Qigong Fever: Body, Science, and Utopia in China*. New York: Columbia University Press, 2007.

Peters, Benjamin. *How Not to Network a Nation: The Uneasy History of the Soviet Internet*. Cambridge, MA: The MIT Press, 2016.

Pistor, Katharina. "Rule by Data: The End of Markets?" *Law and Contemporary Problems*, 83 (2020), pp. 101–24.

Plehwe, Dieter. "Dieter Plehwe in the Past, Present, and Future of Neoliberalism," *The Syllabus*, https://www.the-syllabus.com/ts-spotlight/post-neoliberal-moment/conversation/dieter-plehwe.

Presiden Republik Indonesia. *Undang-Undang Nomor 5 tahun 2017 tentang pemajuan kebudayaan*, (Law of the Republic of Indonesia Number 5 of 2017, Regarding Advancement of Culture), http://kebudayaan.kemdikbud.go.id/wp-content/uploads/2017/12/Undang-Undang-No-5-Tahun-2017-tentang-Pemajuan-Kebudayaan.pdf.

Qian, Xuesen, et al. "A New Discipline of Science—The Study of Open Complex Giant System and its Methodology." *Journal of Systems Engineering and Electronics* 4, no. 2 (June 1993), pp. 2–12.

Qin, Hui. "Dilemmas of Twenty-First Century Globalization: Explanations and Solutions, with a Critique of Thomas Piketty's Twenty-First Century Capitalism." *Reading the China Dream*, November 15, 2018, https://www.readingthechinadream.com/qin-hui-dilemmas.html.

Qin, Hui. *Chuantong Shilu* (Ten Treatises on Tradition). Shanghai: Fudan University Press, 2004.

Qin, Hui and Jin Yan. *Tianyuanshi yu kuangxiangqu: guanzhong moshi yu qianjindai shehui de zairenshi* (Idyllic and rhapsody: The Guanzhong model and the re-understanding of the pre-modern society). Beijing: Central Compilation & Translation Press, 1996.

Qiu, Jack Linchuan, and Hongzhe Wang. "Radical Praxis of Computing in the PRC: Forgotten Stories from the Maoist to Post-Mao Era." *Internet Histories* 5, no. 3–4 (October 2021), pp. 214–29.

Rachman, Gideon. "America breaks global rules as it defends the free world." *Financial Times*, May 27, 2024, https://www.ft.com/content/8249cd96-bda3-48c9-bf91-005df4125f9d.

Rancière, Jacques. "Aesthetic Separation, Aesthetic Community: Scenes from the Aesthetic Regime of Art." *Art and Research. A Journal of Ideas, Contexts and Methods* 2, no. 1 (Summer 2008), pp. 1–15.

Rath, Christian. "Risiken bei Bekenntnispflicht." *Taz*, March 25, 2024, https://taz.de/Kulturfoerderung-und-Antisemitismus/!5999871/.

Raunig, Gerald. "Flatness Rules: Instituent Practices and Institutions of the Common." *Institutional Attitudes: Instituting Art in a Flat World*, ed. Pascal Gielen. Amsterdam: Valiz, 2013.

Rebentisch, Juliane. "Autonomie? Autonomie! Ästhetische Erfahrung heute." *Ästhetische Erfahrung: Gegenstände, Konzepte, Geschichtlichkeit*, ed. Sonderforschungsbereich 626. Berlin, 2006, https://www.geschkult.fu-berlin.de/e/sfb626/veroeffentlichungen/online/aesth_erfahrung/aufsaetze/rebentisch.pdf.

ReUnion Network. https://www.reunionnetwork.org/.

Rodrik, Dani. “Dani Rodrik on choosing the right policy priorities.” *The Syllabus*, https://www.the-syllabus.com/ts-spotlight/post-neoliberal-moment/conversation/dani-rodrik.

Rosamond, Emily. “Shared Stakes, Distributed Investment: Socially Engaged Art and the Financialization of Social Impact.” *Finance and Society* 2, no. 2 (2016), pp. 111–26.

Rostow, Walt Whitman. *The Stages of Economic Growth: A Non-Communist Manifesto.* Cambridge, UK: Cambridge University Press, 1990.

Rueda, Daniel. “Alain De Benoist, Ethnopluralism and the Cultural Turn in Racism.” *Patterns of Prejudice* 55, no. 3 (May 27, 2021), pp. 213–35.

Russell, Alec. “The à la carte world: our new geopolitical order.” *Financial Times*, August 21, 2023, https://www.ft.com/content/7997f72d-f772-4b70-9613-9823f233d18a.

Saadawi, Ghalya. “Vapid Virtues, Real Stakes.” *Between the Material and the Possible: Infrastructural Re-examination and Speculation in Art*, ed. Bassam El Baroni. London: Sternberg Press, 2022.

Sakai, Naoki, and Sun Ge. *Universality and Particularity: What is Asianness?* Berlin: Archive Books, 2020.

Salazkina, Masha. *World Socialist Cinema: Alliances, Affinities, and Solidarities in the Global Cold War*. Oakland, CA: University of California Press, 2023.

Salemy, Mohammad. “Antisemitism Is the Least of Documenta Fifteen’s Problems: Let’s Be Fucking Honest.” *Arts of the Working Class*. June 24, 2022, https://artsoftheworkingclass.org/text/antisemitism-is-the-least-of-documenta-fifteens-problems.

Santayana, George. *Dominations and Powers: Reflections on Liberty, Society, and Government*. New York: Charles Scribner’s Sons, 1951.

Saros, Daniel. *Information Technology and Socialist Construction: The End of Capital and the Transition to Socialism*. New York: Routledge, 2014.

Scholz, Danilo. “Koloniale Nahmen, koloniale Gaben: Alexandre Kojève, Carl Schmitt und die Europäische Nachkriegsordnung,” *Archiv Des Völkerrechts* (AVR) 61, nos. 2–3 (2023), pp. 287–326.

Scholz, Trebor, and Nathan Schneider. *Ours to Hack and to Own: The Rise of Platform Cooperativism, a New Vision for the Future of Work and a Fairer Internet.* London: OR Books, 2016.

Schormann, Sabine. “Statement by Dr. Sabine Schormann on the deinstallment of the banner ‘People’s Justice’ by Taring Padi.” *documenta fifteen*, June 21, 2022, https://documenta-fifteen.de/en/news/statement-by-dr-sabine-schormann-on-the-deinstallment-of-the-banner-peoples-justice-by-taring-padi/.

Scott, James C. *The Moral Economy of the Peasant: Rebellion and Subsistence Southeast Asia.* New Haven: Yale University Press, 1976.

Shen, Xin. TRANSMISSIONS TV, Episode 3, 2021, https://www.transmissions.tv/season-three/.

Shi, Qing. “Qian Xuesen and the Yangtze River Computer.” Exh. cat. Shanghai: 13th Shanghai Biennale, 2021.

Slobodian, Quinn. *Globalists: The End of Empire and the Birth of Neoliberalism*. Cambridge, MA: Harvard University Press, 2018.

Slobodian, Quinn, and Dieter Plehwe. "Introduction." *Nine Lives of Neoliberalism,* eds. Dieter Plehwe, Quinn Slobodian, and Philip Mirowski. London and New York: Verso, 2020.

Smirnov, Nikolay. "The Island Imagination of Tamagne." Golubitskoe Art Foundation, 2020, https://golubitskoefoundation.com/imagination-of-taman.

Smirnov, Nikolay. "Left-Wing Eurasianism and Postcolonial Theory." *e-flux Journal*, no. 97 (2019), https://www.e-flux.com/journal/97/252238/left-wing-eurasianism-and-postcolonial-theory/.

Smith, Terry. "DOCUMENTA 15, 2022: Collectivism and Controversy." *Artlink*, April 11, 2022, https://www.artlink.com.au/articles/4983/documenta-15-2022-collectivism-and controversy/.

Smith, Terry, Okwui Enwezor, and Nancy Condee. *Antinomies of Art and Culture: Modernity, Postmodernity, Contemporaneity*. Durham, NC: Duke University Press, 2009.

Solod, Darina. "A Guide to the Violent Unrest in Uzbekistan's Karakalpakstan Region." *Open Democracy*, August 4, 2022, https://www.opendemocracy.net/en/odr/protests-karakalpakstan-zbekistan-former-soviet/.

"Speech by Ade Darmawan (ruangrupa) in the Committee on Culture and Media, German Bundestag, July 6, 2022." *documenta fifteen*, July 9, 2022, https://documenta-fifteen.de/en/news/speech-by-ade-darmawan-ruangrupa-in-the-committee-on-culture-and-media-german-bundestag-july-6-2022/.

Srnicek, Nick. *Platform Capitalism*. Cambridge, UK: Polity Press, 2017.

Stakemeier, Kerstin, and Marina Vishmidt. *Reproducing Autonomy: Work, Money, Crisis and Contemporary Art*. Berlin: Mute, 2016.

Steyerl, Hito. "Context Is Everything, Except When It Comes to Germany." &&&, June 4, 2022. https://tripleampersand.org/context-everything-except-comes-germany/.

Strike MoMA. "Strike MoMA: Framework and Terms for Struggle." *Decolonial Hacker*, April 8, 2021, https://decolonialhacker.org/article/framework-and-terms-for-struggle-strike-moma.

Suitner, Johannes. *Imagineering Cultural Vienna: On the Semiotic Regulation of Vienna's Culture-Led Urban Transformation*. Bielefeld, Germany: transcript Verlag, 2015.

Sun, Ge. "How Does Asia Mean? (Part I)." *Inter-Asia Cultural Studies* 1, no. 1 (2000), pp. 13–47.

Sun, Ge. "How Does Asia Mean? (Part II)," *Inter-Asia Cultural Studies* 1, no. 2 (2000), pp. 319–41.

Taipei Fine Arts Museum. "Post-Nature: A Museum as an Ecosystem." Taipei Biennial, website, https://www.taipeibiennial.org/2018/?lang=en.

Taylor, Chris. "Fight Carbon. With Coin." *Mashable*, 2021, https://mashable.com/feature/carbon-coin-climate-change-crypto.

"Technical Issues with Yuk Hui and Aleksandr Dugin." *Sreda podcast*, 2020, https://www.youtube.com/watch?v=-ZZFxM50w7Q.

Teh, David. "Who Cares a Lot? Ruangrupa as Curatorship." *Afterall*, no. 30 (Summer 2012), https://www.afterall.org/articles/who-cares-a-lot-ruangrupa-as-curatorship/.

"The Arusha Declaration by Julius Nyerere 1967." https://www.marxists.org/subject/africa/nyerere/1967/arusha-declaration.htm.

The New Silk Roads initiative. The University of Leiden. Accessed July 17, 2024, https://newsilkroads.info/books-and-projects/.

Tlostanova, Madina. "Id'et sorevnovaniye travm. A nuzhno nauchit'sya slushat' drug druga" (There is a competition of injuries. But we need to learn to listen to each other), *Teatr Soprotivleniya* (Theater of Resistance), August 13, 2023, https://syg.ma/@resistancetheatre/madina-tlostanova-idiet-sorievnovaniie-travm-a-nuzhno-nauchitsia-slushat-drugh-drugha.

Tooze, Adam. "Putin's Challenge to Western Hegemony—the 2022 Edition." *Chartbook* (blog), January 12, 2022, https://adamtooze.substack.com/p/chartbook-68-putins-challenge-to.

Tooze, Adam. *Shutdown: How Covid Shook the World's Economy*. London: Penguin UK, 2021.

Toto, Abhijan. "Abhijan Toto and Pujita Guha for the Forest Curriculum on documenta 15." *Artforum* 61, no. 1 (September 2022), https://www.artforum.com/events/abhijan-toto-and-pujita-guha-for-the-forest-curriculum-on-documenta-15-250197/.

Toukan, Hanan. "On Being 'The Other' in Post-Civil War Lebanon: Aid and the Politics of Art in Processes of Contemporary Cultural Production." *Arab Studies Journal* 18, no. 1 (Spring 2010), pp. 118–61.

Trotsky, Leon, John Dewey, and George Novack. *Their Morals and Ours: Marxist Versus Liberal Views on Morality*. New York: Merit Publishers, 1966.

Trubetskoi, Nikolai. "On the Turanian Element in Russian Culture." *Anthropology & Archeology of Eurasia* 37, no. 1 (July 1998), pp. 8–29.

Valjakka, Minna. "Arts and Ecosystems: Building Towards Regeneration of 'Cultural Resilience' in Indonesia." *Forces of Art: Perspectives from a Changing World*. Eds. Carin Kuoni, Jordi Baltà Portolés, Nora N. Khan, and Serubiri Moses. Amsterdam: Valiz, 2021.

Vallverdú, Jordi. "Matter, Spirit, AI." *Vertical Atlas*. Arnhem: ArtEZ Press, March 2022.

Velthuis, Olav, and Erica Coslor. "The Financialization of Art." *Handbook of the Sociology of Finance*, eds. Karin Knorr Cetina and Alex Preda. Oxford: Oxford University Press, 2012.

Vishmidt, Marina. "Only as Self-Relating Negativity: Infrastructure and Critique." *Journal of Science and Technology of the Arts* 13, no. 3 (March 2022), pp. 13–24.

Vishmidt, Marina. "Between Not Everything and Not Nothing: Cuts Towards Infrastructural Critique." *Former West: Art and the Contemporary After 1989*, eds. Maria Hlavajova and Simon Sheikh. Cambridge, MA: MIT Press, 2017.

Vishmidt, Marina. *Speculation as a Mode of Production*. Leiden, The Netherlands: Brill, 2018.

von Busse, Mark-Christian, Bettina Fraschke, and Florian Hagemann. "documenta-Geschäftsführer: Wir sollten keine Notlösung erwägen." *Die Hessische/Niedersächsische Allgemeine* (HNA), November 21, 2023, https://www.hna.de/kultur/documenta/wir-sollten-keine-notloesung-erwaegen-92694107.html
Vukovich, Daniel F. *China and Orientalism: Western Knowledge Production and the P.R.C.* London: Routledge, 2012.
Wang, Hongzhe, and Jiang Yuan. "Seeking a Cybernetic Socialism: Qian Xuesen and the Transformation of Information Politics in Socialist China." *Resurrecting Cybernetics*. Shanghai: CAC publication, 2019.
Wang, Hui. *The Rise of Modern Chinese Thought*, ed. Michael Gibbs Hill. Cambridge, MA: Harvard University Press, 2023.
Wang, Hui. *China's Twentieth Century: Revolution, Retreat and the Road to Equality*, ed. Saul Thomas. London and New York: Verso, 2016.
Wang, Hui. *China from Empire to Nation State*, trans. Michael Gibbs Hill. Cambridge, MA: Harvard University Press, 2014.
Wang, Hui. "The Economy of Rising China." *Reading the China Dream* (blog), originally published in *Beijing Cultural Review*, no. 2 (2010), pp. 24–35, https://www.readingthechinadream.com/wang-hui-the-economy-of-rising-china.html.
Wang, Hui. *The Rise of Modern Chinese Thought*. Beijing: Sanlian Shudian, 2004.
Wang, Hui and Matthew A. Hale. "The Politics of Imagining Asia: A Genealogical Analysis." *Inter-Asia Cultural Studies* 8, no. 1 (2007), pp. 1–33.
Wang, Peggy. *The Future History of Contemporary Chinese Art.* Minneapolis: University of Minnesota Press, 2020.
Wang, Shaoguang and An'gang Hu. *The Chinese Economy in Crisis: State Capacity and Tax Reform*. Armonk, NY: M.E. Sharpe, 2001.
Weber, Isabella. "Origins of China's Contested Relation with Neoliberalism: Economics, the World Bank, and Milton Friedman at the Dawn of Reform." *Global Perspectives* 1, no. 1 (April 9, 2020), pp. 1–14.
Weizman, Eyal. "In Kassel." *London Review of Books* 44, no. 15, August 4, 2022, https://www.lrb.co.uk/the-paper/v44/n15/eyal-weizman/in-kassel.
Wenzel, Jennifer. *Bulletproof: Afterlives of Anticolonial Prophecy in South Africa and Beyond*. Chicago: University of Chicago Press, 2010.
White, Benjamin. "'Agricultural Involution' and its Critics: Twenty Years After." *Bulletin of Concerned Asian Scholars* 15, no. 2 (1983), pp. 18–31.
Wilcox, Emily. *Revolutionary Bodies Chinese Dance and the Socialist Legacy*. Oakland, CA: University of California Press, 2019.
Williams, Raymond. "Base and Superstructure in Marxist Cultural Theory." *New Left Review*, no. 82 (November/December 1973), https://newleftreview.org/issues/i82/articles/raymond-williams-base-and-superstructure-in-marxist-cultural-theory.

Woeller, Marcus. “Jetzt steht da schwarz auf weiss, was Claudia Roths Verantwortung ist.” *Welt*, March 22, 2024, https://www.welt.de/kultur/plus250665025/Antisemitismus-Gutachten-Jetzt-steht-da-schwarz-auf-weiss-was-Claudia-Roths-Verantwortung-ist.html?icid=search.product.onsitesearch.

Yang, Guoqiang. “论新文化运动中的个人主义 (On Individualisms in the New Culture Movement)”. 探索与争鸣 *Exploration and Free Views*. vol. 1, issue 8 (2016), pp. 12–22, https://www.tsyzm.com/CN/Y2016/V1/I8/12.

Yin, Aiwen and Mengyang Zhao. “Playing ‘liquid dependencies’: what does a decentralised caring society look like (2021–present).” https://artsoftheworkingclass.org/text/playing-liquid-dependencies-what-does-a-decentralised-caring-society-look-like-2021-present.

Yin, Aiwen. “Liquid dependencies.” *Damn magazine* 82 (Summer 2022), https://www.damnmagazine.net/liquid-dependencies.

Yoon, Duncan M. “Bandung Nostalgia and the Global South.” *The Global South and Literature,* ed. Russell West-Pavlov. Cambridge, UK: Cambridge University Press, 2018, pp. 23–33.

You, Mi. “China-Africa: Performing the Image of Migration and Migration of Image.” *Entangled Histories of Art and Migration: Theories, Sites and Research Methods*, eds. Bublatzky, Catherine, Burcu Dogramaci, Kerstin Pinther, and Mona Schieren. London: Intellect, 2024.

You, Mi. “Another Currency, Another Speculation: Reflections on Art and Economies Projects at Documenta Fifteen.” *On-Curating* 58 (2023), https://www.on-curating.org/issue-58-reader/another-currency-another-speculation-reflections-on-art-and-economies-projects-at-documenta-fifteen.html.

You, Mi. “Confucianism and Technology: Conceptual borders between tradition and modernity, Chinese and Euro-American modernity.” *Visualizing Chinese Borders*, eds. Paul Gladston, Beccy Kennedy and Ming Turner. London: Palgrave, 2021.

You, Mi. “Future Art Ecosystems: Focus on China.” Serpentine Galleries, August 18, 2020, https://www.serpentinegalleries.org/art-and-ideas/future-art-ecosystems-focus-on-china/.

You, Mi. “Silk Roads, Tributary Networks and Belt and Road Initiative.” *Tidal Thinking: What comes after nations?*, eds. Katrin Klingan, Nanna Heidenreich, Rana Dasgupta. Berlin: Berlin Haus der Kulturen der Welt and Matthes & Seitz Berlin, 2020.

You, Mi. “Manchukuo, Capitalism and the East Asian Modern: Transhistorical Desire in Kishi the Vampire.” *Southeast of Now: Directions in Contemporary and Modern Art in Asia* 2, no. 2 (2018), pp. 93–117.

You, Mi, and Royce Ng. “News from Nowhere.” *Hybrid Transactions*, 2019, https://www.adkdw.org/en/article/1844_hybrid_transactions.

You, Mi, and Federico Ruberto. “Sg_Dao.Inc.” *Lonely Vectors,* eds. Mi You, Joella Kiu, Kenneth Tay. Singapore: Singapore Art Museum, 2022.

Zaretsky, Eli. “Injured Egos.” *New Left Review* (blog), November 29, 2022, https://newleftreview.org/sidecar/posts/injured-egos.

Zhao, Dingxin, "路径不依赖、政策不相干——什么才是中国经济成功的关键 (Path Independence, Policy Irrelevance—What Holds the Key to China's Economic Success), 2017.
Zhao, Dingxin. *Politics of Legitimacy: The State-Society Relations in Contemporary China*. Taiwan: National Taiwan University Press, 2017.
Zhao, Dingxin. "State Legitimacy, State Policy, and the Development of the 1989 Beijing Student Movement." *Asian Perspective* 23, no. 2 (1999), pp. 245–84.
Zhang, Feng, and Barry Buzan. "The Relevance of Deep Pluralism for China's Foreign Policy." *The Chinese Journal of International Politics* 15, no. 3 (2022), pp. 246–71.
Zhang, Gary Zhexi. "The Artist of the Future." *ArtReview* (April 2020), https://artreview.com/back-to-the-drawing-board/.
Zhang, Lin. *The Labor of Reinvention: Entrepreneurship in the New Chinese Digital Economy*. New York: Columbia University Press, 2023.
Zhang, Xiaoxing, Yu Xiang, and Lei Hao. "Virtual gifting on China's live streaming platforms: hijacking the online gift economy." *Chinese Journal of Communication* 12, no. 3 (2019), pp. 1–16.
Zhang, Xudong. *Cultural Identity in the Age of Globalization: Historical Reflections on Western Discourses of the Universal*. Shanghai: Shanghai Renmin Press, 2021.
Zhang, Yongle. *The Rivalry of Nations: Kang Youwei and the Decay of the Vienna System*. Beijing: Commercial Press, 2017.
Zhang, Yongle. *Remaking An Old Country: 1911–1917*. Beijing: Peking University Press, 2011.
Zhang, Yukun, Xia Yining, and Ding Feng. "In Depth: China's Trillion-Dollar Local Government 'Hidden Debt' Dilemma." *Caixin Global*, September 19, 2023.
Zhao, Tingyang. "A Political World Philosophy in Terms of All-under-Heaven (Tian-Xia)." *Diogenes* 56, no. 1 (2009), pp. 5–18.
Žižek, Slavoj. *Freedom: A Disease without Cure*. New York: Bloomsbury Academic, 2023.
Zolghadr, Tirdad. *Traction*. Berlin: Sternberg Press, 2016.
Zuboff, Shoshana. *The Age of Surveillance Capitalism: The Fight for a Human Future at the New Frontier of Power*. New York: Public Affairs, 2019.

Acknowledgments

This book is the crystallization of my thinking over the last few years. I am deeply indebted to friends and colleagues who provided intellectual interlocution, critique and inspiration. For reasons of space, I shall mention some of them and in no particular order. Nikolay Smirnov, Andreas Niegl, Suhail Malik, Brian Kuan Wood, Andreas Petrossiants, Max Grünberg, Binna Choi, and Aiwen Yin nurtured this book by providing a constantly affectionate and critical community. Over the years, I've had stimulating exchanges about topics in this book with Marina Vishmidt, Anselm Franke, Bernd Scherer, Aslak Aamot Helm, Bjarke Hvass Kure, Elvia Wilk, Xinyi Cheng, Wang Tuo, Su Wei, Irwan Ahmett, Mona Schieren, Eugene Tan, June Yap, Stephanie Bailey, Ala Younis, Royce Ng, David Teh, David Morris, Ho Tzu Nyen, Payam Sharifi, Gary Zhexi Zhang, and Jamilya Nurkaliyeva. I have benefited tremendously from open-minded conversations beyond art theory proper with Lorenzo Marsili, Dingxin Zhao, Wang Hui, Benjamin Bratton, Danilo Scholz, Maximilian Mayer, Terance Renaud, Chor Pharn Lee, Jia Rong, Jacob Dreyer and Philipp Reichmuth. In the book, I wish to honor a kind of practice that is both rooted in the arts and aspires to be more than art. In this, I'm inspired, and often feel challenged in a positive way, by Madhusree Dutta, Seonghee Kim, Josien Pieterse,

Katleen Ditzig, Victoria Ivanova, Arthur Steiner, Vienne Chan, Fernando Garcia Dory, Shawn Chua Ming Ren, and Huang Sun Quan.

For engaging conversations and continued support, my sincere thanks to colleagues at the documenta Institut and University of Kassel, Heinz Bude, Andreas Hoffmann, Michael Flörchinger, Felix Vogel, Maria Neumann, Yulia Gromova, Philipp Oswalt, Kai-Uwe Hemken, Martin Schmidl, Alexis Joachimides, Elisabeth Tuider, Kerstin Jürgens, Alla Vronskaya and Gabu Heindl. Special thanks to Sofia Asvestopoulos and Franziska Rozicki for their editorial assistance.

Finally, I am always grateful to my family for their loving encouragement, and for having taught me to ask the question: why?

Some chapters were previously published as essays and have been recontextualized for the book. The earliest text was published at the beginning of the pandemic as "The social support networks stepping up in coronavirus-stricken China," in *openDemocracy*, March 2020. I have published two essays on documenta fifteen, "What Politics? What Aesthetics? Reflections on documenta fifteen," in *e-flux Journal*, no. 131, 2022, and "What Community?," in Martin Köttering and Sabine Boshamer (eds.) *The Controversy over documenta fifteen: Background, Interpretation, and Analysis*, Hamburg: Materialverlag, 2023. Parts of Chapter 3 appeared as "Silk Road as Geo-Imagination of China," in Nav Haq and Joanna Zielińska (eds.) *Eurasia—An Atlas*, Antwerp: M HKA Museum of Contemporary Art Antwerp,

2024, and "Speculation against Speculation: science-fiction and science-non-fiction in China," in Marina Vishmidt (ed.) *Speculation* (Whitechapel: Documents of Contemporary Art), Cambridge: MIT Press, 2023.

Image Credits

P. 16: Courtesy Kraupa-Tuskany Zeidler, Berlin
P. 48: Courtesy of the artist and Kiang Malingue, Hong Kong
P. 70: Courtesy of the artist
P. 92: Courtesy of the artist
P. 118: Courtesy of the artist
P. 134: Courtesy Kraupa-Tuskany Zeidler, Berlin
P. 154: Courtesy of the artist
P. 187: Courtesy of the artist
P. 205: Courtesy of the artist
P. 239: Courtesy of the artist and MMCA Seoul
P. 243: Courtesy of the artists

Colophon

Author: Mi You
Managing editor: Sofia Asvestopoulos
Project management: Adam Jackman
Copy-editing: Tom Melick
Graphic design: Rutger Fuchs Amsterdam
Cover, chapter opener and background visuals: Royce Ng
Typeface: Akkurat, Arnhem
Production: Kati Klaeske
Reproductions: DLG Graphic, Paris
Paper: Enviro Polar, 135 g/m^2
Printed by: Westermann Druck Zwickau GmbH
Crimmitschauer Str. 43, 08058 Zwickau, Germany

documenta Institut

Founding Director: Prof. Dr. Heinz Bude
www.documenta-institut.de
The responsible body for the documenta Institut is the documenta und Museum Fridericianum gGmbH
Managing Director: Prof. Dr. Andreas Hoffmann
Friedrichsplatz 18
34117 Kassel
www.documenta.de

Its shareholders are the City of Kassel and the State of Hesse. The Chairman of the Supervisory Board is the Lord Mayor of the City of Kassel, Dr. Sven Schoeller.

Published by
Hatje Cantz Verlag GmbH
Mommsenstraße 27
10629 Berlin
Germany
www.hatjecantz.com
A Ganske Publishing Group Company

ISBN 978-3-7757-5824-6
EPUB: ISBN 978-3-7757-5825-3
PDF: ISBN 978-3-7757-5826-0

Printed in Germany

www.blauer-engel.de/uz195
- ressourcenschonend und umweltfreundlich hergestellt
- emissionsarm gedruckt
- überwiegend aus Altpapier

MI6

Dieses Druckprodukt ist mit dem Blauen Engel ausgezeichnet

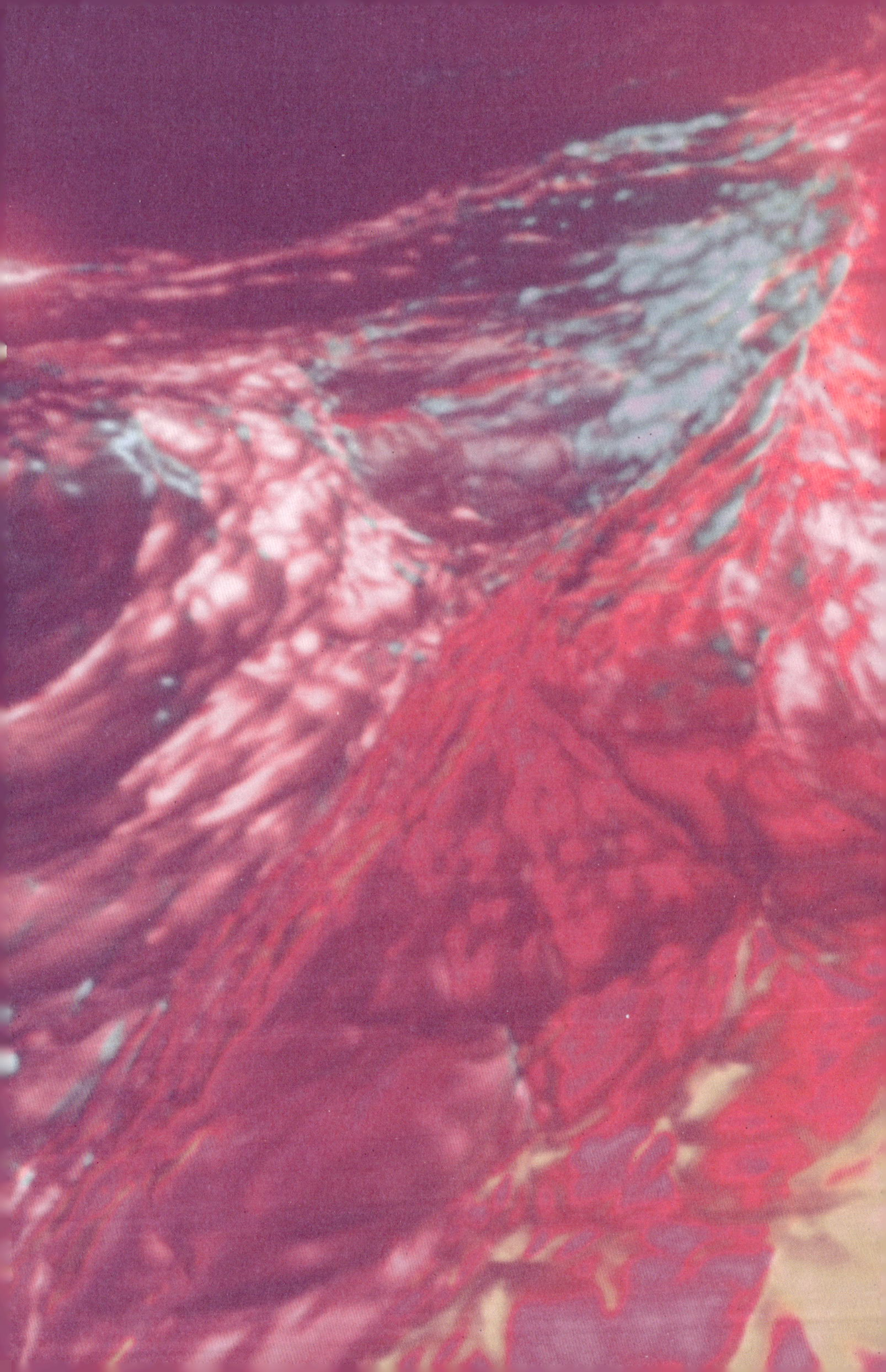